– REVISED & ENLARGED 3RD EDITION –

LOLA T70

THE RACING HISTORY & INDIVIDUAL CHASSIS RECORD

Also from Veloce Publishing -

Colour Family Album Series

Alfa Romeo by Andrea & David Sparrow
Bubblecars & Microcars by Andrea & David Sparrow
Bubblecars & Microcars, More by Andrea & David Sparrow
Citroen 2CV by Andrea & David Sparrow
Citroen DS by Andrea & David Sparrow
Custom VWs by Andrea & David Sparrow
Fiat & Abarth 500 & 600 by Andrea & David Sparrow
Lambretta by Andrea & David Sparrow
Mini & Mini Cooper by Andrea & David Sparrow
Motor Scooters by Andrea & David Sparrow
Porsche by Andrea & David Sparrow
Triumph Sportscars by Andrea & David Sparrow
Vespa by Andrea & David Sparrow
VW Beetle by Andrea & David Sparrow
VW Bus, Camper, Van & Pick-up by Andrea & David Sparrow
VW Custom Beetle by Andrea & David Sparrow

SpeedPro Series

How to Blueprint & Build a 4-Cylinder Engine Short Block for High Performance by Des Hammill
How to Build a V8 Engine Short Block for High Performance by Des Hammill
How to Plan and Build a Fast Road Car by Daniel Stapleton
How to Build & Modify Sportscar/Kitcar Suspension & Brakes by Des Hammill
How to Build & Modify SU Carburettors for High Performance by Des Hammill
How to Build & Power Tune Weber DCOE & Dellorto DHLA Carburetors Second Edition by Des Hammill
How to Build & Power Tune Harley-Davidson Evolution Engines by Des Hammill
How to Build & Power Tune Distributor-type Ignition Systems by Des Hammill
How to Build, Modify & Power Tune Cylinder Heads Second Edition by Peter Burgess
How to Choose Camshafts & Time them for Maximum Power by Des Hammill
How to Give your MGB V8 Power Updated & Revised Edition by Roger Williams
How to Improve the MGB, MGC & MGB V8 by Roger Williams
How to Modify Volkswagen Beetle Chassis, Suspension & Brakes for High Performance by James Hale
How to Power Tune Mini Engines on a Small Budget by Des Hammill
How to Power Tune the BMC 998cc A-Series Engine by Des Hammill
How to Power Tune BMC/Rover 1275cc A-Series Engines by Des Hammill
How to Power Tune the MGB 4-Cylinder Engine by Peter Burgess
How to Power Tune the MG Midget & Austin-Healey Sprite Updated Edition by Daniel Stapleton
How to Power Tune Alfa Romeo Twin Cam Engines by Jim Kartalamakis
How to Power Tune Ford SOHC 'Pinto' & Sierra Cosworth DOHC Engines Updated & Revised Edition by Des Hammill
How to Power Tune Rover V8 Engines for Road & Track by Des Hammill
How to Power Tune Jaguar XK Engines by Des Hammill

General

Alfa Romeo Berlinas (Saloons/Sedans) by John Tipler
Alfa Romeo Giulia Coupe GT & GTA by John Tipler
Anatomy of the Works Minis by Brian Moylan
Automotive A - Z - Lane's Complete Dictionary of Automotive Terms by Keith Lane
Automotive Mascots by David Kay & Lynda Springate
Bentley Continental, Corniche and Azure, by Martin Bennett
BMW Z-Cars by James Taylor
British Cars, The Complete Catalogue of, 1895-1975 by Culshaw & Horrobin
British Police Cars by Nick Walker
British Trailer Caravans 1919-1959 by Andrew Jenkinson
British Trailer Caravans from 1960 by Andrew Jenkinson
Bugatti Type 40 by Barrie Price
Bugatti 46/50 Updated Edition by Barrie Price
Bugatti 57 - by Barrie Price
Chrysler 300 - America's Most Powerful Car by Robert Ackerson
Cobra - The Real Thing! by Trevor Legate
Cortina - Ford's Bestseller by Graham Robson
Daimler SP250 'Dart' by Brian Long
Datsun/Nissan 280ZX & 300ZX by Brian Long
Datsun Z - From Fairlady to 280Z by Brian Long
Dune Buggy Handbook by James Hale
Essential Handbook of Caravanning & Trailer Tenting by Len Archer
Fiat & Abarth 124 Spider & Coupe by John Tipler
Fiat & Abarth 500 & 600 by Malcolm Bobbitt
Ford F100/F150 Pick-up by Robert Ackerson
Ford GT40 by Trevor Legate
Ford Model Y by Sam Roberts
Half-Ton Military Land Rover, The by Mark Cook
Jaguar XJ-S, by Brian Long
Jim Redman - Six Times World Motorcycle Champion by Jim Redman
Karmann-Ghia Coupe & Convertible by Malcolm Bobbitt
Lea-Francis Story, The by Barrie Price
Lexus Story, The by Brian Long
Lola - The Illustrated History (1957-1977) by John Starkey
Lola - All The Sports Racing & Single-Seater Racing Cars 1978 - 1997 by John Starkey
Lola T70 - The Racing History & Individual Chassis Record, 3rd Edition by John Starkey
Lotus 49 by Michael Oliver
Mazda MX-5/Miata 1.6 Enthusiast's Workshop Manual by Rod Grainger & Pete Shoemark
Mazda MX-5/Miata 1.8 Enthusiast's Workshop Manual by Rod Grainger & Pete Shoemark
Mazda MX-5 Renaissance Sportscar by Brian Long
MGA by John Price Williams
Mini Cooper - The Real Thing! by John Tipler
MR2 - Toyota's Mid-engined Sports Car by Brian Long
Porsche 356 by Brian Long
Porsche 911R, RS & RSR, 4th Ed. by John Starkey
Porsche 914 & 914-6 by Brian Long
Porsche 924 by Brian Long
Porsche 944 by Brian Long
Rolls-Royce Silver Shadow/Bentley T Series Corniche & Camargue Updated Edition by Malcolm Bobbitt
Rolls-Royce Silver Spirit, Silver Spur & Bentley Mulsanne by Malcolm Bobbitt
Rolls-Royce Silver Wraith, Dawn & Cloud/Bentley MkVI, R & S Series by Martyn Nutland
RX-7 - Mazda's Rotary Engine Sportscar by Brian Long
Singer Story: Cars, Commercial Vehicles, Bicycles & Motorcycles by Kevin Atkinson
Taxi! The Story of the 'London' Taxicab by Malcolm Bobbitt
Triumph Motorcycles & the Meriden Factory by Hughie Hancox
Triumph Tiger Cub Bible by Mike Estall
Triumph Trophy & Tiger Bible by Harry Woolridge
Triumph TR2/3/3A, How to Restore, by Roger Williams
Triumph TR4/4A, How to Restore, by Roger Williams
Triumph TR5/250 & 6, How to Restore, by Roger Williams
Triumph TR6 by William Kimberley
Turner's Triumphs, Edward Turner & his Triumph Motorcycles by Jeff Clew
Velocette Motorcycles - MSS to Thruxton by Rod Burris
Volkswagens of the World by Simon Glen
VW Beetle - The Car of the 20th Century by Richard Copping
VW Beetle Cabriolet by Malcolm Bobbitt
VW Bus, Camper, Van, Pickup by Malcolm Bobbitt
Works Rally Mechanic by Brian Moylan

This third edition published in 2002 (first published in 1993; updated and revised second edition published in 1997) by Veloce Publishing Ltd., 33 Trinity Street, Dorchester, DT1 1TT, England. Fax: 01305 268864/e-mail: info@veloce.co.uk/website: www.veloce.co.uk
ISBN: 1-903706-04-1/UPC: 36847-00204-6

British Library Cataloguing in Publication Data - A catalogue record for this book is available from the British Library.
Typesetting design and page make-up all by Veloce on AppleMac.
Printed and bound in the EC.

– REVISED & ENLARGED 3RD EDITION –

LOLA

T70

THE RACING HISTORY & INDIVIDUAL CHASSIS RECORD

JOHN STARKEY

VELOCE PUBLISHING
THE PUBLISHER OF FINE AUTOMOTIVE BOOKS

T70

DEDICATION

I dedicate this book to Denny Hulme, a rare kind of driver and man. Although I only met Denny twice before his death from a heart attack in, of all things a racing car, he impressed me greatly with his sheer enthusiasm for racing. Here he was, enjoying the animal grunt of eight and a half litres of racing Chevrolet in a McLaren M8F at a guest appearance at Silverstone in 1992 and he was lyrical in his praises and reminiscences of the Lola T70.

"You could take her round Druids with just one finger on the steering wheel" he remarked about driving Sid Taylor's Mark 3B. "Those were the days."

Denny was World Champion in Formula one in 1967. But not only did he scale the heights of the single seater world, he was also Can-Am Champion twice for McLaren. He also drove at Indianapolis and, in his spare time(!), he drove Lola T70s, one spyder and three coupés for entrant Sid Taylor. His chief mechanic, Ron Bennet, remembered Denny thus: "If Denny made a mistake, he admitted it, he was always straight, Denny was. If it was his fault, he'd say so. Usually, he'd just say 'She'll be right' and it was. He'd just climb in and go! Amazing; he was amongst the best drivers I've worked with and he was the one I liked the most. Very genuine, Denny was, very genuine."

Denny was a superlative driver, usually winning the national races the team entered, and leading the Lola brigade in the international events. He was one of the few men who could conquer these very powerful and fast cars. He will be very much missed ...

Sid Taylor at the wheel with a garlanded Denny Hulme alongside after yet another victory in 1966 in SL71/31.

ACKNOWLEDGEMENTS

Thanks are due, first of all, for the help afforded by my wife, Sandra, who has suffered my obsession with Lola T70s, in all their forms, over the last few years and helped with the preparation of the manuscript. Secondly, to Laurie Bray of Lola Cars Limited who very kindly helped me to sort out some of the individual histories. Doug Nye, that noted automotive historian, was good enough to contribute some of the individual histories, and Brian Redman, who drove T70s in their heyday in both open and closed bodywork, helped by sharing his memories.

Clive Robinson, who worked at Lola cars and today tends to most of the T70s left racing in Britain, gets a big vote of thanks for explaining the technical aspects of the cars. Nigel Hulme, who has been racing T70s for ten years, helped at the beginning with a lot of the knowledge he had gained. Ron Bennett, who worked with Sid Taylor when he was entering T70s for Denny Hulme, Brian Redman and Frank Gardner among others kindly shared his reminiscenses.

From America, Gerry Weichers in Northern California filled several gaps in the subsequent history of the cars, whilst individual owners of the cars today filled in important holes in a lot of histories and George Follmer, who raced the T70 in USRRC and Can-Am events, kindly gave his impressions of the car when it was current.

Thanks are due, particularly where the T160 line is concerned, to RM Motorsport, consisting of Bud Bennett and his sons, Craig and Kurt. Where Lolas in America are concerned, they are the kings of race preparation and assistance.

For most of the photographs, particularly of the cars racing in their heyday, I have to thank *Autosport*, the premier British racing magazine. Richard, its picture librarian, was a great help. *Autosport*'s race reports from the 1960s also proved invaluable in tracing which car did what at the races. Thanks also to Kathy at LAT for photographs.

David Piper, who raced many cars during this glorious period gets a big "thank you" for his memories of the period, particularly of racing his IIIb coupé, SL76/150. His frequent co-driver, Richard Attwood, was very helpful in his reminiscenses. Thanks, too, to owner and racer, Robin Darlington, who supplied some excellent period photographs of his Mark II spyder. Also, thanks to all the owners who supplied photographs and reminiscences.

A big "Thank you" to Paul Mackley who, through all adversity, always succeeded in getting me to the startline of numerous historic races to enjoy my own Lola T70 Mark 111b coupé in Europe. Here in America, I must also thank Mike Ogren for performing the same service in my present T70 coupé.

CONTENTS

T70

INTRODUCTION

I stood on the bank at Copse Corner at Silverstone, in pouring rain, one day in August 1969 and watched a beautiful white sports racing coupé with a central blue stripe spin once again in its dogged pursuit of a similar, but orange, car. It appeared madness for these big, powerful cars to even attempt to race in such conditions but, true professionals as most of the drivers were, they gritted it out to the finish. At the end "my" car, driven by Brian Redman, finished second. All I knew in those days was that it was one of Sid Taylor's stable of Lola T70s. Since 1966 I had seen the cars, usually white with a green racing stripe and in both open and coupé versions, romping home to win, usually with Denny Hulme at the wheel.

As I stood there that day at Silverstone, I little realised that twenty years later I would be sitting in that seat myself and facing the daunting sweeps of Spa Francorchamps in a race for Can-Am and Endurance sportscars. Such was the impression made on me by those cars in the late sixties that, when one became available, I knew I simply had to have it. The actuality of racing the Lola far exceeds the expectation; the car has no hidden vices and obeys the driver's commands to order, particularly through the very fastest corners where, undoubtedly, the superb body shape adds downforce felt through the steering as it stiffens up.

Surely there have been few 'big-banger' sports prototypes which have so captured the imagination of race fans? Even today, most admiring spectators and commentators at historic race meetings refer to them as "the most beautiful sports racing car ever made" and I, although biased, cannot disagree.

The Lola T70 has achieved the recognition it deserves. In its day, although powered by what was basically a "road car" engine, it could usually be counted upon to give a hard time to the opposition in short distance events, be they Ford or Ferrari mounted. That it could not survive most of the endurance races it was entered in was due either to the low octane fuel allowed in Europe or lack of development by a small factory that, in order to survive financially, had any number of projects running at the same time.

Over the last twelve years I found myself mixing with the drivers and mechanics who were involved with the cars in their heyday in historic racing and realised that a book concerning their racing career was sadly lacking. I hope this will fill the gap. The gathering of the necessary information has provided me with as much enjoyment, as has meeting the people who make writing a book like this such a pleasure.

John Starkey
St. Petersburg, Florida

1

NEW BEGINNING

Like many developments in modern motor racing, the story of the Lola T70 began with Enzo Ferrari.

In March 1963 the Ford Motor Company decided to expand racing operations from its USA homeland to Europe. More specifically, Ford wanted to win Le Mans. Rightly, Ford reasoned that *Le 24 heures du Mans* was THE race to win in order to establish its new performance-orientated image with the car-buying public in Europe. Realising that it lacked the racing knowledge its European counterparts possessed of long distance sports cars, Ford set out to buy it.

Specifically, Ford approached Enzo Ferrari with a view to purchasing his company. Ferrari was not averse to this offer: he was no longer a young man, and had been financing his racing for several years by building expensive road cars to sell to a small but well-heeled sector of the public. Naturally, this involved extra effort from him. An effort which he begrudged, having a passion only for 'true' racing cars, *i.e.* those cars which would bring him and his factory glory on the race tracks around the world. Making road-going cars, no matter how glamorous, was simply a means of financing his racing passion.

Initially, his asking price for his company was $18 million, but, as Ford accountants scoured the details of his books, this became lower and lower until, realising just how little autonomy he would have left after the deal, Ferrari broke off negotiations on the 21st May 1963.

Lee Iacocca, the man put in charge of the 'Total performance' project by Henry Ford, was not disillusioned. He simply decided to buy other European expertise and create a totally Ford controlled project. To do this, he knew that he would have to hire one of the pre-eminent English racing chassis builders and his choice, after sending Roy Lunn, Ray Geddes and Carroll Shelby to England to consider Cooper, Lotus and Lola, fell on Lola. These three engineers

1963. Bob Olthoff and Tony Maggs at the Nürburgring.

1963. It's June and the Mark VI Lola is the focus of attention in the Le Mans pits. The car was to be driven by Dickie Attwood and David Hobbs.

felt that Cooper, whilst having been successful, were falling back in the technology stakes and Ford was wary of Colin Chapman whom it considered would demand total control of the whole project.

Their attention then turned to one Eric Broadley. He was the founder and chief designer of Lola Cars Ltd. A quantity surveyor turned racecar builder, he had been successful from the start with his exquisite Mark I sports racing car. This was essentially a club racer which proved so successful that it continued in production for four years. Mark III-V Lolas were single-seater Formula Junior and Formula One cars employing spaceframe construction. What probably clinched Ford's decision to buy Lola's expertise was the fact that Lola had introduced, in January that year at the Racing Car Show in London, its Mark VI coupé, a car which Ford considered close to the

1963. Tony Maggs driving the Mk VI in the Silverstone International Trophy race of May: he finished a creditable 9th.

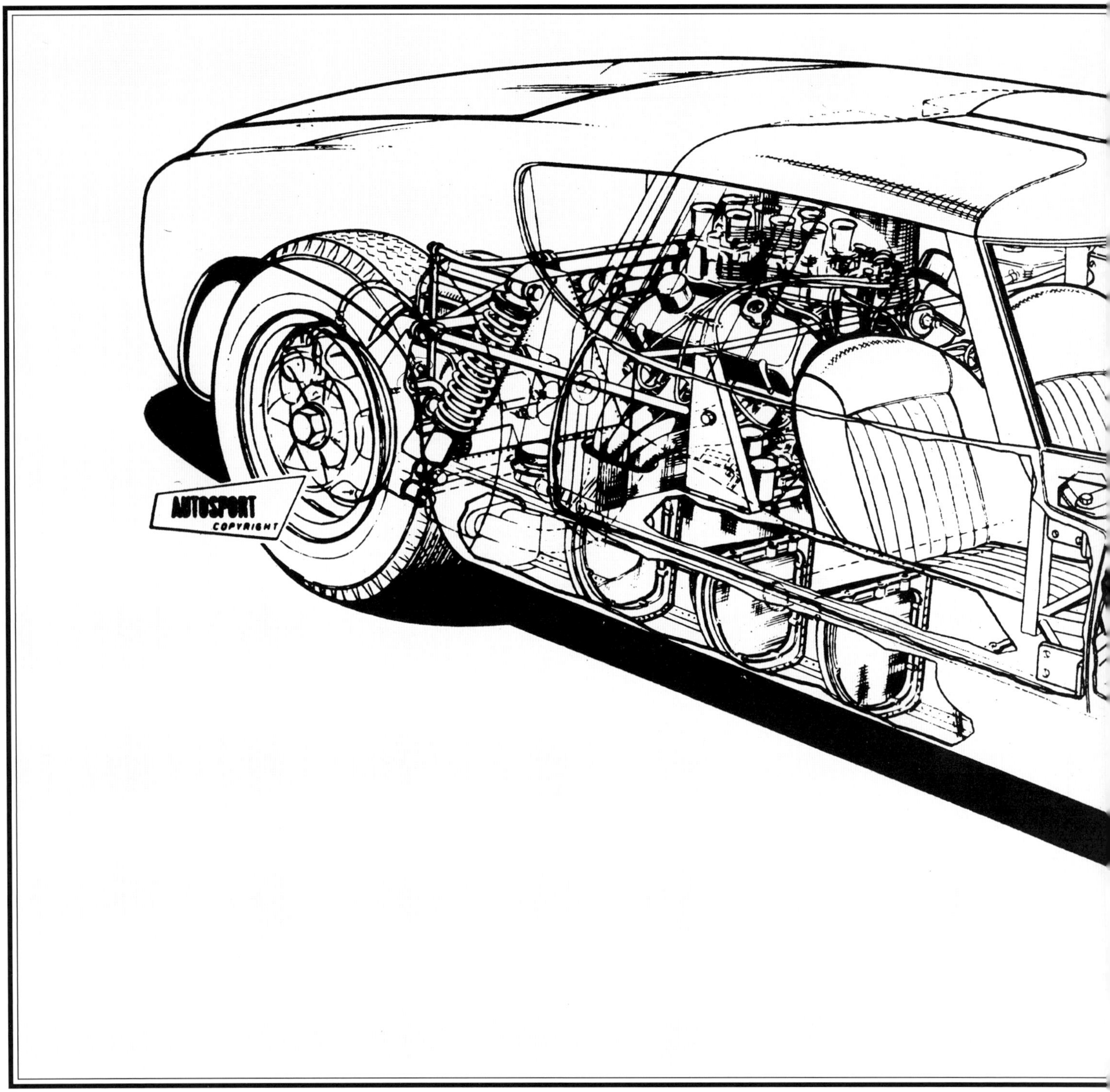

one it wished to produce.

The Lola Mark VI coupé was a mid-engined car with a Ford 4.2 litre (256 cu. in.) V8 engine, giving a quoted 350bhp at 7000rpm, and driving the rear wheels through a Colotti transaxle. Gear selection was via bowden-type cables instead of the more usual long rod which turned and slid back and forth. Oddly, for a racing car, the gearlever was centrally mounted instead of being to the driver's right. The sleek bodywork, designed by John Frayling, was in glass reinforced plastic (GRP) and made by Specialised Mouldings, a company based in Upper Norwood and headed

by Peter Jackson which was to have a long relationship with Lola cars.

The new coupé was based on a monocoque tub which consisted of two 'D'-shaped fuel tanks at each side of the cockpit, joined by a stressed skin aluminium floor. In front of this structure was a sub-frame built up of tubes to support the radiator and front suspension, which used upper and lower wishbones, dampers and coil springs in conjunction with an adjustable anti-roll bar. The steering was by rack and pinion mounted ahead of the front suspension. Behind the rear bulkhead (which marked the end of the driver's

The Lola GT Mark VI on display at the Racing Car Show in January 1964.

compartment) was the engine bay, culminating in a crossmember which carried the rear suspension. This consisted of wishbones at the base of the uprights, top links and paired radius arms with an anti-roll bar. Once again coil springs and dampers were employed, coupled with outboard disc brakes. Light alloy wheels of 15 inch front and 16 inch rear width were fitted.

A tail spoiler was tried on the car but, so good was the body's shape, that it merely served to slow the car down! The little coupé (only 92 inches in wheelbase and with a track of 51.5 inches) weighed a mere 675 kilograms and had to carry ballast to bring it up to the minimum allowed weight of 875 kilograms.

The Mark VI coupé, although arriving late for the 1963 Racing Car show at Olympia that January, was the undisputed star of the show. It was reported that Eric Broadley had gone 52 hours without sleep in order that the car could be displayed at the Lola stand.

It was at this time that the configuration of racing cars was undergoing a transformation. With a new generation of racing tyres produced by Dunlop, suspension systems needed good suspension control to keep the tyre as nearly vertical as possible, thus maximising the usefulness of the ever-increasing width of the tread. On top of this, designers were having to investigate the shape of the bodywork as cars became faster and aerodynamics began to play an increasing role in design. Specifically, as racing cars (particularly sports and GT cars with their all-enveloping bodywork) began to reach speeds in excess of 150-160mph, they began to suffer a phenomenon known as front end lift, which resulted in the driver losing steering effect. This was caused by air passing underneath the car which, with its upturned aerofoil shape, meant the car's front developed lift.

Rear end lift was the opposite. In this case the car became light and twitchy as the back of the car unloaded itself at high speed. A spoiler, a thin strip of aluminium added at the upper rear across the bodywork, was found to cure this and therefore designers reasoned that tabs added at the nose would reduce front end lift also.

However, we are a little ahead of ourselves. The new Lola had been designed bodywise to comply with the then appropriate 'GT' class and, in May of 1963, the prototype Mark VI, driven by Tony Maggs, took part in its first race at the Silverstone International Trophy race.

Poor Maggs did not even have

End of the race for the Lola GT Mark VI at the Sebring twelve hour race in Florida in March 1964.

the chance to practice in the car. John Surtees had originally agreed to drive it but the Ferrari team manager withdrew his consent at the last moment and Cooper works driver Maggs was forced to start from the back of the grid as he had no chance to even practice in the car before the start of the race! Despite this impediment, he finished a creditable 9th, still on the same lap as the leader. On one lap he overtook nine other cars. The next outing was in May at the Nürburgring 1000 kilometres where Maggs was paired with Bob Olthoff. There they retired after (officially) the distributor drive failed. Unofficially, the wheel nuts kept loosening ...

Third, and last, international outing was in June at Le Mans, and here the drivers were Dickie Attwood (later to win the 1972 race in a Porsche 917) and David Hobbs, another English driver on the upward path). To get the car to the Sarthe circuit in time for scrutineering, Eric Broadley drove it from Dunkirk himself, thus arriving well before the transporter containing the second car. The latter was never used, though, as the arrangement for Roger Penske and Augie Pabst to drive the car fell apart, and the small Lola équipe found itself in trouble with its own car due to the air trunking to the carburettors being deemed to block the rear view. Also, the scrutineers informed Eric Broadley that the rear bodywork was not wide enough to cover the rear tyres. Fortuitous planning meant that Peter Jackson was present with sufficient fibreglass resin and matt to remodel the rear bodywork with the trunking taking its air from intakes now

The interior of the Mark VI coupé.

One of the three Lola GT Mark VIs today. Note the wider wheels and wheelarch extensions.

mounted behind the rear side windows, and the rear wheelarches widened sufficiently to accommodate the rear wheels. In addition, the fuel tank capacity was reduced to the specific size by inserting fourteen plastic bottles!

After delays occasioned by a slipping fan belt the Mark VI reached 12th place by midnight. After that it slipped back again with gear selector problems until the early hours of the morning when Hobbs couldn't find third gear going into the esses and crashed the car. Thankfully, he was unhurt.

Ford purchased two of the three Mark VIs made as part of its twelve month agreement with Eric Broadley (later extended by six months), and shipped one to Dearborn for testing and evaluation. The other was taken to the Goodwood circuit in England for the same purpose. Bruce McLaren tested it there and at Monza in November where he prepared a very enthusiastic report for the Ford management. In his *Autosport* column, McLaren reported that the car would spin its wheels in the rain in top gear whilst the power available made the throttle work "just like a tap".

The third car had been purchased by John Mecom, a wealthy Texan with multiple interests in the oil industry (and later to become Lola's agent in the USA). It was fitted with a small block Chevrolet V8 and, driven by Augie Pabst, won a race at Nassau speed week in 1965 after appearing at the 1963 Guards Trophy in England, where it retired with no oil pressure. In 1964, Augie Pabst drove it in the June sprints at Road America and the '500' event. It then went to Mosport Park and to Riverside where it crashed due to the throttle jamming open.

During August 1963 Ford also took on John Wyer. He had a formidable reputation as the team manager of Aston Martin, culminating in the victory at Le Mans in 1959 when Carroll Shelby shared the winning Aston Martin DBR1/300 with Roy Salvadori. Second place had gone to another team car driven by Paul Frere and Maurice Trintignant. Wyer took over as manager of the project in Slough in October 1963 and, by early 1964, a new company called Ford Advanced Vehicles Limited (FAV for short), had been set up in spacious factory buildings after the original Lola works had been found to be too cramped.

Wyer and Broadley shared the responsiblity of design and

production of the Ford GT (as the new car was to be called) with the ex-patriate British engineer Roy Lunn. Lunn, whilst manager of Vehicle Concepts Department at Ford in the USA, had been heavily involved in a show-car project called 'Mustang 1'. This car bore no resemblance to the later production Mustang but was an attempt to investigate future trends. To this end, it was mid-engined with the Ford Fairlane 265cu. in. engine mated to the Colotti type 37 transaxle mounted in a tubular frame, with independent suspension all round, side-mounted radiators and alloy body. The seats were fixed, whilst the pedal box was adjustable to suit the different heights of the drivers. The oil tank, spare wheel and battery were in the nose.

The design of the new Ford GT caused problems. Roy Lunn, with a marketing division behind him which envisaged a productionised version of the racer sometime in the future, insisted on a steel chassis which was anathema to Eric Broadley who wanted the car's tub fabricated in aluminium with steel bracing for light weight. Broadley even envisaged a glassfibre roof for the coupé which did not please Lunn at all. Soon events reached such an impasse that, although the two men occupied adjoining offices, they would only communicate through John Wyer. Shortly thereafter, Eric Broadley decided that he wanted his works to produce cars bearing his name again and requested that his contract with Ford be renegotiated to enable this.

John Wyer and the Ford management acquiesced with regret. The parties came to a mutually satisfactory parting of the ways in the summer of 1964, and Lola Cars Limited set up new premises almost adjacent to FAV in Slough during the latter half of that year.

The Ford GT40 turned out with a steel (and therefore heavy) monocoque chassis with deep 'D'-shaped sills, in which were housed two 140 litre bag tanks, with front and rear bulkheads and with the roof forming the main structure. The front and rear sub-frames carrying the independent suspension front and rear were also fabricated from sheet steel and the doors cut well into the roof to improve access. Like the Mustang concept car, the pedals and not the driver's seat were adjustable.

The engine was an aluminium version of the Fairlane unit fitted with four Weber carburettors and delivered 350bhp at 7200rpm. A Colotti type 37 transaxle was employed for the transmission.

The car's competition debut itself was, to say the least, unremarkable. At the Le Mans test days in April 1964, both the cars used were crashed, one by Jo Schlesser after he lost control at some 170mph on the Mulsanne Straight, and one by Roy Salvadori as a result of late braking in the wet at the end of that same straight. Luckily, both drivers were unhurt.

After the addition of a four and a half inch high spoiler across the rear deck, the stability of the car was vastly improved but the Colotti gearboxes let it down at subsequent Le Mans and Rheims races, despite the car having shown great promise.

It would take serious development, both by John Wyer's team in England and Carroll Shelby's team in Venice, California, to turn the car into the world-conquering endurance racer it became. In the meantime, Eric Broadley had reconstituted Lola Cars and had spotted a gap in the racing car market which he was quick to exploit.

T70

2

T70 MARKS I & II

Across the Atlantic in North America, the early 1960s saw a series of races held under the auspices of the Sports Car Club of America (SCCA), which mainly consisted of wealthy amateurs driving cast-off European sports-racers, such as Ferrari Testa Rossas and Maserati 300s and 450Ss, mixed together with some home-built V8 specials. Such was the popularity of these races that the SCCA started the United States Road Racing Championship (USRRC) in 1963 in order to award big prize money and, therefore, bring top drivers and cars from all over the world to compete with one another.

In 1962, a very bright young racer called Roger Penske had seen a way to beat the established opposition when he purchased a crashed F1 Cooper T53 from Briggs Cunningham's racing team. His mechanic, Roy Gaine, modified the car with all-enveloping bodywork and, with Penske driving, it promptly showed a clean set of heels to his opponents at Riverside and Laguna Seca.

Naturally the car was banned by the American racing authorities and the 'Zerex Special', as it was named, was sold to John Mecom who had it reworked to a more normal side-by-side seating configuration to conform to the rules concerning passenger space. The resulting car was then driven by Penske to further success in America, before coming to England and winning the Guards Trophy at Brands Hatch in 1963. Bruce McLaren saw the potential, bought the car and replaced the Climax 2.7-litre engine with a 3.5-litre aluminium Oldsmobile V8.

Now with more power and with Bruce driving, the car achieved many wins, repeating its Guards Trophy win of the year before, ahead of the Lotus 30 which Colin Chapman had designed and put into limited production to accommodate the Ford 289 cu. in. V8 engine.

Around this time, the FIA, realising the ground swell of change which these Anglo-American hybrids were bringing to sportscar racing, reorganized the categories of cars which could compete in international races. Groups 1-4 were allocated to production cars, whilst Groups 5 and 6 were for small production runs. Groups 7-9 were for, respectively, Formula racing cars and Formula Libre racing cars, and the FIA, under pressure from the American federation and the RAC, added Group 9, (under Category 'C' for racing cars) specifically for '2-seater racers'. It was obvious that these big, American-engined sports-racers were 'the next big thing', both in the UK and the US, and Eric Broadley introduced the T70 to sell to this market.

In January 1965, the result of his small company's labours was

Data sheet for a typical Mark I Lola T70 spyder.

LOLA

DATA SHEET

Type 70 MKI

Chassis No. SL 70/14

Delivered

Delivered to

Engine Installation Components Ford

Engine Manufacturer Ford — No. 4F108B

Type/Modification

Transmission Standard

Gearbox Hewland LG 500

Crown Wheel & Pinion Ratio Std, 4-Speed

Clutch Borg & Beck - Triple Disk

Wheel Base 95"

Front Track 57"

Rear Track 57½"

Steering

Gear Teeth	
1	23/52
2	31/44
3	34/41
4	36/38
5	
6	

Front Suspension

Spring — Shock Absorbers Armstrongs

Roll Bar 3/4" — Hubs Standard

Rear Suspension

Spring — Shock Absorbers Armstrongs

Roll Bar 5/8" — Hubs Standard

Drive Shafts Standard

	Front	Rear
Discs	Solid 12½"	Solid 12½"
Caliper	Girling	Girling
Pad Material	DS 11	DS 11
Master Cylinder		
Wheels	Lola 15"x 8"	Lola 15" x 10"
Tyres	Goodyear	Goodyear

Petrol Tank Capacity 50 gals. — Oil Capacity 12 qts.

Modifications from Standard

seen when the new Lola T70 was displayed at the Racing Car Show in London, where it was the star of the exhibition. Beneath the beautifully shaped glass reinforced plastic (GRP) body, built by Peter

The monocoque of the first Mark I at the factory in 1965 during the car's build-up.

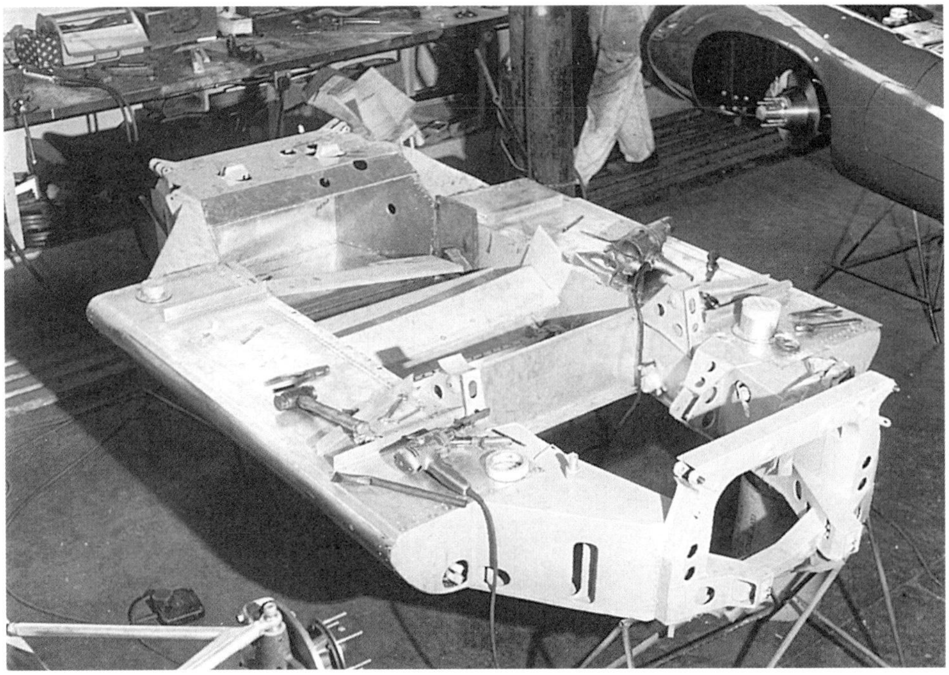

Below - The rear of a Mark I spyder with the cylinder heads removed at the factory.

Jackson's Specialised Mouldings, the chassis was all that Roy Lunn had NOT allowed Eric Broadley to produce.

The central structure was a sheet steel floor extending sideways to encompass 'D'-shaped sills on either side which did not use bag tanks. Instead, to save weight, aluminium fuel tanks - which could carry 32 gallons of fuel - were hung from the steel sides and fastened top and bottom with flanges. The slope of the rear bulkhead formed the back to which the driver's seat was fitted, and the rear tub sides embraced the engine which was a semi-stressed member. The new Hewland LG (Large Gearbox) 500 (the amount of horsepower the box could handle) 4-speed gearbox was used, connected to the engine via Lola's own design of bellhousing. This gearbox featured a detachable rear cover which enabled all the dog-clutch engaged gear ratios to be changed in as little as thirty minutes and, with a magnesium casing, weighed only 125 pounds. This was surrounded by two rear castings, top and bottom, attached to the chassis from which the suspension took its pick-up points.

At the front, the pedal box was enclosed, whilst two radiators, and the mandatory spare wheel, were supported in the GRP nose, although from chassis SL70/7 the nose was made detachable and a box-shaped aluminium fabrication now supported the radiators. The airflow for these was ducted out through the top of the nose in front of the windscreen, thus giving some useful downforce, and the rear of the bodywork was quickly detachable via pip pins.

The glassfibre nose, therefore, became a semi-stressed part of the car which took some time to remove, much to the mechanics' disgust. On the Mark III, all this was alleviated with the introduction of a nose made to be quickly detachable via four pip pins.

Probably the most unusual feature of the design was the brakes. These were mounted inboard of the

Looking down on the nose of the first Mark I spyder with the centre panel removed showing the chassis plate, fluid reservoirs and twin radiators bonded into the nose. Note the line of fasteners holding the nose section onto the monocoque.

fifteen inch diameter by eight inch wide front and the same diameter by ten inch wide rear wheels, providing better cooling for the solid iron discs which were retarded by single piston calipers.

The front suspension employed top and bottom wishbones connected to a magnesium upright by Armstrong coil and damper units and six-stud fixings for wheel location. BMC rack and pinion steering (from the Austin 1100) was used. At the rear, inverted wishbones were used at the bottom whilst, at the top, a single link sufficed - twin radius rods on each side - to locate the entire suspension. The rear anti-roll bar acted on the top links, whereas the front one acted on the lower wishbones.

Wheelbase was 95 inches and track 54 inches. Broadley had designed the T70 to take any American stock block engine up to 6 litres, and the show model sported a 4.5-litre Oldsmobile V8.

John Surtees had gone into partnership with Lola to form Team Surtees, and the first car (SL70/1) - painted bright red with green longitudinal stripes - went to him. In initial testing the car proved phenomenally fast, soon beating the Formula One lap record at most circuits. Witness 1min. 36.6 sec. at Oulton Park in May, 1.2 seconds less than the F1 lap record. Even so, Surtees requested more power still and progressed through the season via a 5-litre Chevrolet to a 5.9-litre version, (all tuned by the American Traco concern) which put out some 550bhp on high octane fuel.

Other noteworthy drivers of the T70 Mark I were Walt Hansgen (driving John Mecom's cars), Hugh Dibley (driving Stirling Moss's car, SL70/4, afterwards re-chassised with tub number SL70/7) and Carroll Shelby acting as a team

The front of the prototype Mark I showing the spare wheel, twin radiators and the bodywork fastened to the tub with screws.

The front brake disc, caliper and hub of a Mark I.

Below: The Lola T70 Mark I spyder at the Racing Car show in 1965. (Courtesy Autosport).

owner with SL70/10.

Although some fifteen cars were made, Broadley knew that, at 1375 pounds the car was too heavy and was already designing the Mark II as a lighter version.

The tub of the Mark II used 85% aluminium alloy with only 15%

sheet steel, compared to 60% steel for the earlier car. Riveted construction now took the place of the welding used on Mark Is and, according to the factory, this alone saved seventy pounds in weight.

Fuel bags giving an increase in capacity to fifty gallons were now inserted into the sponsons as the previous design led to leaks with the distortion of the sponsons in racing; now no less than three Bendix fuel pumps were used. The wheel widths were quoted at eight inches front and ten inches rear. Cooling was taken care of via a single radiator with an oil cooler incorporated. This was made possible as the Group 9 rules had been changed so that a spare wheel no longer needed to be carried, thus freeing-up space in the nose section.

A weight saving of 35lb was made by not colour impregnating the bodywork: the factory advised as little paint as possible be applied subsequently. The brake discs were radially ventilated to improve cooling, whilst the rear suspension radius arms were moved further

Proud owner Robin Darlington poses in the ex-Red Rose SL71/27 Mark II in his farmyard.

LOLA

DATA SHEET

Type ..... 70 Mk 2.

Chass. No. SL71/38

Delivered 26-8-66

Delivered to ..... J. Epstein Esq.

Benvenuto.

North Holmwood

Surrey.

No. .....

Engine Installation Components ..... Chevrolet

Engine Manufacturer ..... Chevrolet

Type/Modification ..... Alan Smith

Transmission ..... Standard

Gearbox ..... Hewland LG 500-82

Crown Wheel & Pinion Ratio 13/43

Clutch ..... Borg & Beck

Wheel Base ..... 95"

Front Track ..... 57"

Rear Track .....

Steering ..... tooth pinion

Gear Teeth

1. 24/50
2. 30/45
3. 34/41
4. 37/38
5. .....
6. .....

Front Suspension

Spring ..... 315 lbs/in. Shock Absorbers ..... Armstrong AT9

Roll Bar ..... 3/4" Hubs ..... Knock on.

Rear Suspension

Spring ..... 260 lbs/in. Shock Absorbers ..... Armstrong AT/0

Roll Bar ..... 3/4" Hubs ..... Knock on.

Drive Shafts ..... Rotoflex Inner Joints
B.R.D. Outer Joints.

	Front	Rear
Discs	.60"	7/16"
Caliper	Girling BR	Girling BR.
Pad Material	Ferodo DS11	Ferodo DS11
Master Cylinder	.70"	.70"
Wheels	Lola 15" x 8" Knock on	Lola 15" x 10" Knock on.
Tyres	Firestone Indy 9.20-15	Fireston Indy 12.[illegible]-15

Petrol Tank Capacity ..... 50 gallons. Oil Capacity .....

Modifications from Standard

Wheels, hubs, drive sha[illegible] discs (see above)
Front and [illegible] spoilers [illegible] roll-over bar strut.

Data sheet for a Mark II spyder, SL71/38, which was raced by Paul Hawkins in England in Group 7 races and in the 1966 Can-Am series.

A Mark II, chassis number SL71/27. This belonged to the Red Rose Team, and was originally driven by Brian Redman.

Cutaway drawing of the Lola T70 spyder. (Courtesy Autosport).

inboard to bring them directly in-line with the suspension mountings.

A typical example (SL71/38), was delivered to Jackie Epstein on 26th August 1966, and featured an Alan Smith (of Derby) tuned Chevrolet, knock off hubs, and Armstrong dampers. Tyres were Firestone Indy 9.20-15 front and 12.00-15 rear, and front and rear spoilers were fitted.

Driving the new Mark II, Surtees demonstrated it to be appreciably faster than the original car and won the Guards International Trophy at Brands Hatch in the new Team Surtees car, chassis number SL71/16. The gap to second place man Bruce McLaren was over ninety seconds but Bruce was to learn many lessons and eventually humble the Lola T70s in the Championship they were destined to compete in first of all: the Can-Am series.

Meanwhile, in England in June 1966, the RAC announced that Group 9 racing was to be cancelled from the end of the season through lack of interest. Could this have had something to do with the RAC favouring Formula Two at the time?

SL71/16 was, incidentally, written off in Surtees' huge accident at Mosport Park in practice for the Pepsi 100. Thanks to two marshalls on the spot, Surtees survived a series of horrendous end-over-end flips, although the accident put him out of racing until the middle of 1966. The remains of number 16 were buried at Mosport.

Lola T70

3

RACING IN 1965

With the FIA and CSI (FISA's forerunner) adopting the Sports Car Club of America's rules and calling them Group 9 in 1965, the way was now open for racing these new 'hairy monsters' for the first time on both sides of the Atlantic.

Bruce McLaren, after buying Roger Penske's 'Zerex Special' and modifying it still further, produced what was called a McLaren Elva Oldsmobile, whilst Colin Chapman introduced his Lotus 40, a development of the Lotus 30, to race in these events. This had a Ford V8 engine of 4.7-litres and, to handle the increased 'urge' of this engine, Lotus replaced the ZF gearbox of the type 30 with a Hewland 4-speed LG500. Girling, in conjunction with Lotus, came up wih a 3-pad caliper design in partnership with ventilated discs and stronger uprights, radius arms and wishbones were fitted.

Both these Lotus designs developed reputations as ill-handling monsters, even the great Jim Clark having trouble keeping them on the track. With the advent of the well mannered, good handling Lola T70, they were relegated to the also-rans. The McLaren designed line of Group 7 cars was, however, another matter, destined to provide Lola with hard opposition in the years to come.

Straight away the Lola started

First time out for SL70/4/7. Hugh Dibley storms away from the start at Silverstone in his first race in his new Lola in May 1965.

Jerry Grant at Continental Divide Raceway in 1965 in John Klug's 'Pacesetter Homes'-sponsored Mark I. Sometimes you just can't help telling the crew "what it was like out there". (Photo: kind permission of Pete Bird)

Bob Bondurant driving SL70/8 at Riverside in 1965. John Klug, the owner of this Mark I, remembered the car as being: "Very nice to drive. Predictable and good handling, with plenty of power. (Photo courtesy of John Klug)

John Surtees in 1965.

John Surtees leads Bruce McLaren in the Martini Trophy at Silverstone in July 1965.

embarrassing the current Formula One designs. At Silverstone the car was no less than one and a half seconds faster than the Grand Prix lap record at 1:31.0. By June, Surtees had taken his big red T70 around in 1:28.3 and the promoters were concerned about the Formula One fans turning out to watch Group 7/9 cars instead. Perhaps this was one of the reasons that races for Group 7 cars were dropped from the British calender at the end of 1966.

March 20th at Silverstone and

Bob Bondurant concentrating hard at Nassau, December 1965. Note the huge 'periscope' air intakes to the carburettors of SL70/8. (Photo courtesy of Bill Dunne)

John Surtees, the development driver for Lola, led his race easily until falling back just three laps from the end with mechanical problems. He finished second to Jim Clark in the works Lotus 30. Surtees then took the car to America for the Players 200 at Mosport Park and, with an easy victory, really showed the SCCA regulars what the new British design could do.

In England, David Hobbs had taken the second car, (so new that it raced unpainted) to a third place finish at Goodwood in April, ahead of BOAC Airline pilot Hugh Dibley in his new Lola but behind Jim Clark in the Lotus and Bruce McLaren in his McLaren Elva Oldsmobile. Hobbs then took a second place in the Tourist Trophy at Oulton Park in May behind Denny Hulme in a 2-litre Brabham BT8. At last, Hobbs drove to victory on June 7th in the Guards Trophy at Mallory Park, a race held over two heats, the winner having the best result on aggregate.

Back in England for the Martini Trophy race at Silverstone on July 24th, Surtees took pole but did not finish the race. Neither did Hugh Dibley, for his gearbox failed whilst lying second after twenty-four laps.

Probably the most notable victory yet for the new T70 was the Guards International Trophy at Silverstone on August 30th where John Surtees won in the first Mark II with a ninety second lead ahead of Bruce McLaren. Jackie Stewart came third in the very first T70 made, but Pierpoint, Hobbs and Dibley all retired their Lolas, whilst Walt Hansgen, in the second Mark II

March 20th 1965. Surtees in SL70/1 in the BARC Senior Service 200 at Silverstone where he came second to Jim Clark in a Lotus 30.

David Hobbs in characteristic setting at Oulton Park in SL70/2 in 1965.

May 1965, Oulton Park and David Hobbs takes part in the T.T. in SL70/2. Following him are Jim Clark in the Lotus 30 and Bruce McLaren in a McLaren Elva.

Hugh Dibley (in a somewhat slower machine than his usual mount!) taking part in the drivers' parade for the Los Angeles Times Grand Prix at Riverside in 1965.

Dibley again in SL70/7 "somewhere in England" in 1965.

John Surtees in SL71/16, the first Mark II spyder at Brands Hatch in August 1965 for the Guards Trophy.

The winner! Surtees waves to the crowds as he accompanies SL71/16 on a victory lap after the Guards Trophy 1965.

John Surtees adjusts the carburettor balance whilst a mechanic looks on at Brands Hatch in practice for the Guards Trophy. Jackie Stewart sits impassively waiting in SL71/16. He would finish 3rd in SL70/1.

built, finished ninth.

In September David Hobbs joined the money trail in America at Mont Tremblant-St. Jovite to come third overall, whilst Surtees took the victory. The following week, however, saw John Surtees suffer a huge accident at Mosport in

Riverside 1965 and Hugh Dibley takes SL70/7 through turn 7a. Note the duct on the door, mounted in an attempt to funnel some cool air to the driver.

Oh Dear ... The sad remains of SL70/8 after it burned during a test session. Roy Campbell. The Mark I's faithful mechanic, sits amongst the ruins. The Pacesetter Homes team purchased a new Mark II, chassis number unknown. (Photo: John Klug collection)

David Hobbs in SL70/2 racing in the USA.

practice. A hub carrier broke while he was exiting turn one and the T70 vaulted over the guardrail and shot down a nearby embankment. John Surtees was lucky to survive and it was not until 1966 that he was racing again.

John Mecom had become the Lola agent in North America and he used Walt Hansgen as his driver in SCCA races in SL70/6. Hansgen turned in some fine performances, winning the race at Laguna Seca and coming second at Las Vegas in the Stardust Grand Prix. Roy

A view from the front of Hugh Dibley in his Mark I at Riverside. Note that the car appears to have a an oil cooler mounted on the nose.

Pierpoint, after building his own V8 powered car, the Attila Chevrolet, took David Good's T70 to South Africa where it lasted six of the Kyalami nine hours when the engine failed. Paul Hawkins then drove this car in the Cape International three hours at Killarney. It was to be his first race of many in a Lola T70.

SL70/7 in 1987.

Lola T70

4

RACING IN 1966

SL71/31 was a special Lola T70 Mark II.

Special, because SL71/31 was put together and driven by a winning combination where Lola T70s were concerned.

The 'putting together' was accomplished by Sid Taylor and his

This and following two pages: Press release and specification sheets for the T70 Mark II.

LOLA CARS LTD 826 YEOVIL ROAD TRADING ESTATE SLOUGH BUCKS

LOLA - 1966

Production at the Lola factory at Slough is currently devoted to Lola Type 70 Mk. II Group 9 Unlimited sports racing cars and Type 60 Mk. II monocoque Formula II/III cars.

Specifications of these cars are attached.

These are latest in the line of high performance racing cars produced by Lola Cars Limited. During the past seven years the company has produced Formula I, Formula II, Formula III, Formula Junior, Sports and GT cars and was responsible for initial design and development of the Ford GT.

The current production rate for Lola Type 70 Mk. II cars is two every three weeks with 70% of production sold to American customers.

An addition to the 1966 range of cars will be the recently announced Type 90 Indianapolis Speedway cars to be raced by Mecom Racing Enterprises.

E. H. Broadley G. J. Broadley R. E. Rushbrook

SPORTS-RACING CAR TYPE 70 Mk II - SPECIFICATION

Track:	58 in.
Wheel-Base:	95 in.
Ground Clearance:	4 in. with no fuel or driver
Chassis:	Light alloy and sheet steel, monocoque construction.
Body:	Glass fibre.
Seats:	Formed in the structure and covered with lightweight quickly removable upholstery.
Rear Section:	Quickly removable for access to engine compartment and rear suspension.
Suspension: Front	Double wishbone on self-aligning roller bearings and ball joints. Telescopic shock absorbers and co-axial coil springs. Steering - rack and pinion.
Rear	Double wishbone and radius rod on self-aligning roller bearings and ball joints. Telescopic shock absorbers and co-axial coil springs.
Brakes:	Girling disc. Front: 12 1/2 in. dia. disc, BR light alloy caliper. Rear: 12 1/2 in. dia. disc, BR light alloy caliper.
Wheels and Tires:	15 in. rim diameter, cast magnesium bolt-on wheels. Front: 8 in. rim width for 1060 x 50 Firestone or 550 x 15 Dunlop or Goodyear Equivalent. Rear: 10 in. rim width 1200 x 15 Firestone or 650 x 15 Dunlop or Goodyear equivalent.
Electrical:	6 in. headlamps in Perspex fairings, tail and brake lights, horn, engine, electrical equipment, etc.
Engine:	Ford or Chevrolet V8 standard or other V8 engines to spec order.

team, led by chief engineer, Ron Bennett. Ron's racing career started in 1962 when he went to work for David Buxton in Team Elite, racing in many events, including Le Mans, where they won the Index of Thermal Efficiency for their class every year they entered. In 1964 Ron wanted to get into sportscars, so Team Elite tried Lotus Elans, but decided against them as they had problems with cooling the differentials, so, in 1965, he left the team.

Ron worked for Midland Racing Partnership for six weeks and then left to join Sid Taylor Racing. Sid was an Irishman with his own construction business and a night club in West Bromwich near Birmingham which went under the name of 'The Steering Wheel Club'. To drive the new Mark II, Ron enlisted one Dennis Clive Hulme, a New Zealand ex-patriot who, on occasion, drove for Bruce McLaren and who, ironically, was to be the nemesis of Lola in the Can-Am Championship in later years. He cut his 'big-banger' teeth on Sid's first T70 to such good effect that, in the first five races Denny drove it, the car scored five victories.

One other driver who was to go on to a long and brilliant career in motor racing was Brian Redman. He remembered his first race (at Oulton Park) in a T70: "At the end of 1965 we had been at a meeting at Croft and appearing in one of the races was none

LOLA TYPE 70 MARK II

The Lola Type 70 Mk. II has resulted from the continuous development of the 1965 Mk. I Group 9 racing sports car. New features for the 1966 version are: -

CHASSIS

Substantial weight saving has been achieved by greater use of aluminum alloy in the construction of the highly developed, yet simple monocoque chassis. The Mk. II chassis uses approximately 85% aluminum alloy with only 15% sheet steel compared with 60% steel for the Mk. I. Riveted construction is now chiefly adopted in place of spot welding used in the Mk. I.

These chassis modifications have resulted in a 70 lb. weight saving without loss of torsional strength or stiffness.

FUEL SYSTEM

The fuel system has been completely redesigned and now utilizes synthetic rubber fuel bags within the chassis structure - one in each cell. Total fuel capacity is 50 Imp. Gals. (60 U.S. Gals.)

These fuel bags feed into a pick-up sub-tank via a non-return valve. Three high pressure Bendix fuel pumps are installed adjacent to this tank. The sub-tank is kept full by cornering and acceleration surge within the main fuel tanks, with fuel level maintained by the non-return valve. A fuel pressure gauge is fitted in the cockpit.

other than a certain Mr. D. Hobbs Esquire, driving a Lola-Chevrolet T70. This car really fired my imagination and, without any expectations whatsoever, I said to Charles Bridges (team owner of Red Rose Racing and owner of the Jaguar E-Type which Redman had been campaigning), if I had the choice of anything I would have a Lola T70. I had no forward views on what driving this car might lead to; I simply thought they were the greatest things on four wheels. Charles never really said yes or no to my suggestion but, in March of 1966, he called me down to Oulton Park and, when I arrived, there sat this magnificent red beast!

"Well, a fine sight it may have been, but it didn't take me very long to discover that the Lola was a very different proposition from the E-type ... Suddenly the straights disappeared, the corners came up with incredible speed and I was wondering whether we had made the right decision. None of these feelings were helped by the year's first race meeting, at Oulton Park, which was wet. Lodge Corner, the tricky right-hander leading to Deer's Leap, was taken very carefully for a number of practice laps but then 'Lead foot,' making one of his frequent misjudgements, decided it must be alright to apply full throttle in a more or less straight line. Wrong!

"Poor Charles Bridges suddenly saw his bright new car appear backwards over Deer's Leap and

The two fuel tanks are normally filled separately via filler caps on either side of the car. For quick refueling, however, a large filler cap can be installed on the right-hand side, with a large-diameter, cross-over pipe fitted between the tanks. The small cap on the left-hand side is opened to act as a "breather" during filling. This modification is to special order only.

ENGINES

The chassis is designed specifically for the installation of either the 327 in. Chevrolet or 289 in. Ford basic units (or stroked versions of these engines).

To special order engine mounts, exhaust manifolds, etc., can be supplied to take other engines - such as the Oldsmobile.

GEARBOX

Following continued racing development during 1965, the Hewland LG 500 four-speed gearbox is now fitted as standard to the Mk. II.

This has proved an extremely reliable unit and has the advantage that individual ratios can be changed by unbolting the rear cover of the gearbox without distrubing the crown wheel and pinion. A large range of ratios is available.

SUSPENSION GEOMETRY

Suspension components and geometry have been modified as a result of deveopment during 1965.

COOLING SYSTEM

A single radiator (incorporating an oil cooler) is now used. This has been made possible with the change of regulations specifying that no spare wheel need now be carried.

Gearbox :	Hewland gearbox Type LG 500 various ratios.
Weight:	Approx. weight with Ford engine, less fuel and driver, = 1500 lbs. With Chevrolet = 1600 lbs.

A light alloy oil cooler is also installed above the transmission.

Oil and water pipes between engine and radiator are now installed beneath the car. They are in channels and can be swiftly removed for repair.

BODYWORK

The glass fibre reinforced plastic bodywork does not now have color impregnated into the material. This eliminates a comparatively thick layer of Jellcoat and results in a weight saving of 35 lbs. Bodies are finished in primer. When painting the bodies, however, only the thinnest paint surface should be applied, with little or no additional primer. This is to obtain a crack-free finish during normal use.

OTHER MODIFICATIONS

Several other detail modifications and refinements are incorporated into the Mk. II. For example the bulkhead behind the seat is now of one piece. It can be removed by undoing eight quick action DZUS fasteners. Also the rollover bar now spans the car and fits into sockets in the chassis.

LOLA TYPE 70 MK. II

PRICE............

DELIVERY........

Denny Hulme in relaxed pose, awaiting the start of yet another race in 1966 in Sid Taylor's Mark II, SL71/31. Note the 58DCOE Weber carburettors mounted on the crossover manifold.

come spinning past his unbelieving eyes ... Of course, it was completely under control and we didn't hit anything ..."

April 10th, Good Friday, saw SL71/31's first race and win at Snetterton in the Archie Scott-Brown memorial trophy. Archie Scott-Brown had raced such large engined machines as Lister Jaguars and had been killed in one in May 1958 at the very fast Spa-Francorchamps circuit in Belgium. He would surely have approved of the glorious T70. Denny was fastest in first practice, ahead of Chris Amon in a McLaren Oldsmobile, whilst Graham Hill was 2 seconds slower in the Team Surtees T70. Graham put the Team Surtees car on pole position in the second practice although Denny and Chris were alongside him. Bruce McLaren was fourth fastest, only point four of a second slower, and Brian Redman in the Red Rose team Mark

1st October 1966. Robin Darlington takes SL71/27,the ex-Red Rose Mark II which had been raced previously by Brian Redman, to a win at Silverstone.

April 1966 and Peter Sergeant chases Brian Redman at Silverstone, both Mark II mounted, in one of their many duels that year.

II (SL71/27) was less than a second slower than Bruce. Hugh Dibley had an off with the Jersey Racing Partnership car although it was repaired for the race. He had raced the car the month previously at Snetterton until the oil pressure had disappeared in the Formula Libre race.

In the first twenty-five lap heat Hill led initially, to be replaced by Hulme at the end of the first lap. Graham then had to fend off Chris Amon who got by on lap eleven. Dibley parked his Lola after seven laps with no oil pressure and Hill's T70 suffered a crownwheel and pinion failure after seventeen tours.

Denny Hulme and Brian Redman leave the grid in their Mark II spyders on April 30, 1966. The event was the Tourist Trophy and Denny won for the second year running.

Denny on his way to victory.

Brian Redman in the Red Rose team's Mark II at Oulton Park in the T.T. of 1966.

This is what a T70 spyder on steroids looks like! Phil Scragg hustles SL71/23 up a hillclimb course in 1967. The car is still racing today. (Courtesy Autosport)

Although Amon threw his McLaren around, he could not stay with Denny and the winner averaged over 100mph for the heat. Brian Redman came in fourth, behind Bruce McLaren, with a sick sounding engine.

Heat two saw a depleted field form up on the grid and, after Amon

led initially, with his boss, Bruce McLaren, in second place, Denny steamrollered by both of them after two laps and streaked away to win - he left the lap record at 104.01mph. It was to be the story of the season in British races for the big Group 7/9 cars.

The Lola was out again on Easter Monday at Mallory Park where this time it was owner, Sid Taylor, who drove it. In the 'Easter Trophy' race, Sid was handily ahead of Tony Sergeant driving the Jersey Racing Partnership Lola until he

Tony Lanfranchi in SL70/5 in the pits at Castle Combe.

spun. Despite fighting his way back up the field, Sid could do no better than second as the laps ran out. In the Formula Libre race later that same afternoon, Sid took pole position but lost the big Lola coming out of the devil's elbow and made expensive contact with the bank. Tony Sergeant won at a canter and nothing else came close.

Denny Hulme got back into his boss's repaired car early in May to take home £1000 in winnings at Oulton Park in the TT. Although he was faced with multiple big-banger opposition, from Redman and Dibley in T70s, and Coundley, Gardner and Prophet in McLarens, Hulme was on pole by no less than three full seconds. He dominated both seventy mile heats to score his second TT win by five laps from second place man Tony Dean in a Brabham BT8. As an aside, Hugh Dibley's car had 'Jack Pierce' written on the side of the cockpit as he was taking the part of Steve McQueen in a film called *Race of the Champion* . To the delight of the film crew, he had the lead at one point in the first heat when Hulme pitted for oil. He soon relinquished it when Denny drove back through the field to lead again. Redman, meanwhile, had spun once whilst on his way to third place making it an all T70 front row for the start of the second heat.

Hulme made it look all too easy as he cruised from flag fall to flag fall again in the white and green car. Dibley abandoned his car with low oil pressure and, although Brian Redman held second place for much of the heat, his transmission failed towards the finish. Denny Hulme was to go on to make the Tourist Trophy almost his own, winning no less than five times, three of these victories being in T70s.

A soaking wet Prescott hillclimb saw another T70 Mark II, seemingly much too large a car for the small English course, take a meritorious second place in the RAC championship event early in May. Phil Scragg liked lots of power in his racing cars, having previously owned such cars as a lightweight E-type Jaguar, and the Ford 4.7-litre engined Lola provided him with just that. Why, it was even registered to be used on the road!

Silverstone was the venue for Denny's next win, a thirty-five lap race supporting the Formula One International Trophy race which was won by Jack Brabham in his 3-litre Brabham-Repco. Brabham qualified in pole position for his

SL71/27 after race preparation.

Graham Hill spins a Team Surtees T70 at Brands Hatch during the August bank holiday meeting in 1966. (Courtesy Autosport)

race at 1:29.8. In contrast, Denny left the lap record at 1:28.2, 118.66mph. In practice Hulme had actually lapped at over 120mph. Denny led from start to finish again, whilst Redman and Dibley (this time in a Chevrolet-powered T70) fought tooth and nail with only a few yards between them at the finish. Brian Redman took fourth place behind Chris Amon and Bruce McLaren in McLaren's own cars.

From April to July, SL71/31 took part in seven races and won six of them. In unofficial practice at Oulton Park, whilst trying out some new Firestones, Denny broke the lap record there by over 2 seconds. It was the story of the season.

The winning streak of Sid Taylor's Lola was broken, however, at Brands Hatch at the August Bank Holiday meeting. There, at the Guards Trophy meeting, John Surtees beat Chris Amon, Bruce McLaren, Denny Hulme, Frank Gardner and Graham Hill to win both thirty lap heats, even though the second was red flagged after a cloudburst descended onto the circuit. Denny crashed his Lola in practice when a front brake burst and, even though the car was repaired in time for the race, it blew up its engine comprehensively to post a DNF. John Surtees was using his new Mark II, SL71/43 and *Autosport* reported: "The sight and sound of these brilliant drivers fighting tooth and nail in their huge powerful cars, in fair weather and foul, will live long in the memory. If this is really to be the last we see of Group 7 racing in this country, then surely we are going to be deprived of some of the finest spectacle available today?"

At the same meeting was another brand new Lola T70 Mark II (SL71/38), purchased by Jackie

Below: A Mark II in the 90s. This is SL71/24, ex-Parnelli Jones, at Silverstone in 1993.

The interior of SL71/24.

The rear view of SL71/24. Car uses a Chevrolet 5.7-litre engine.

Right, top: Denny Hulme at work. In 1966 this car and driver combination took lap records at six British circuits.

Right, bottom: Bob Bucher in SL70/10 crossing the finish line with Hugh Dibley in SL70/7 behind. Note the cooling ducts (for the drivers!) on the doors.

Epstein for Paul Hawkins to drive, and fitted with a 6-litre Alan Smith-tuned Chevrolet. Paul finished fifth in this, his first race in a T70.

One final example of the excitement that the races for Group 7/9 cars could provide was the sportscar race supporting the British Grand Prix at Brands Hatch. There, Richard Attwood drove Sid Taylor's car and qualified on pole with Chris Amon in a McLaren alongside him. They were joined by Jackie Ickx in Alan Brown's McLaren-Elva-Ford, the first time the talented Belgian had driven at Brands Hatch. Brian Redman and Hugh Dibley were not far behind when Attwood and Amon led away for the first of twenty laps. On the very first lap Attwood got too far out of shape and Ickx made contact with him. This put both of them to the back of the field and left Hugh Dibley with a lead he held to the finish. He had to fight all the way, however, as Amon fought his way back to second place but outbraked himself at Druids on the last but one lap. The earlier contact with Attwood had left him with only half the steering lock on one side! Poor Ickx missed a gear at the start and then spun when trying to outbrake Redman and Dibley. He motored back in earnest to finish fifth. Attwood, after a charge through the pack, was forced to retire with a puncture.

It can be seen from the foregoing that, in reality, there were only four Lola T70s competing in Britain in 1966. Although the spectators loved them, the RAC was to announce in July an end to races for these cars. They complained of too few entries, as Lolas and McLarens made up the bulk of the cars. Manufacturers such as Felday and Kincraft were improving their cars, but would be too late to affect the governing body's decision. The start, and prize money, now went to Formula Two cars. In retrospect this seems an amazing decision as, surely, the big-banger sports cars were far more spectacular, any one of them with, all the power and opposite lock on, bringing gasps of admiration from the spectators? The answer probably lies in the fact that the promoters had more interest in

Can-Am 1966 and a T70 spins in the desert.

single-seater formula cars, and the building ambitions of makes such as Lotus and Brabham having more influence with organisers than either Lola or McLaren. *Autosport*'s September 2nd issue leader commented at length on the demise of this form of racing, and pointed out that, whereas at the start of Group 7/9 racing there had only been a handful of cars whose reliability was suspect, that had now completely changed. The oil companies had claimed it was too expensive to sponsor these races and had withdrawn their support, which meant that race promoters, in turn, could not afford to stage them. *Autosport* then went on to point out that, in its opinion, Formula 2 racing would become just as expensive; whereas the 'big-bangers' would be able to take part in the emergent Can-Am series (an export market which had already earned this country some £250,000). The Formula 2 cars would not be accepted in the United States. *Autosport* went on to suggest that the Group 7 cars should be allowed to take part in Group 4 or 6 races in 1967, and concluded by saying: "Whatever happens, it will be very sad indeed if all the Group 7 cars leave the country and we never again witness the hairy bangers pounding down from Druids."

The T70 finished the season with outright lap records at seven British circuits, beating by far the then current Formula One lap records, and they demolished the sports car record at the two remaining circuits.

Across the Atlantic, the USRRC was running its championship and Chuck Parsons, in a McLaren, was the first series winner. Lola T70s, driven by Buck Fulp and Skip Hudson, were second and third. In September, the Can-Am series started and, with prize money of $160,000 beckoning, Dibley, Hulme and Surtees set their sights on the six races. A new Jackie Epstein Mark II for Paul Hawkins also took part.

For the first race of the 1966 Can-Am series, at Mont Tremblant-St. Jovite, five Lola T70s were arraigned against the same number of McLarens. Two T70s did not start, those driven by Paul Hawkins (Jackie Epstein's car) and Hugh Dibley (SMART-entered car). Both these cars had, quite literally, flown whilst cresting the brow of a hill. Hawkins' car was repairable, despite skidding down the road upside down, grinding down the rollbar and Hawkins' helmet, but Dibley's car lost the floor of its monocoque when tree stumps came through it when he finally landed! Whatever, he was ready to take the start one week later at the second round at Bridgehampton.

Surtees' car won the race, with McLaren second, although the star of the race was Chris Amon in a McLaren who, after a pit stop to remove a front spoiler damaged after an 'off', had the crowd on its feet as he carved his way through to third place. Fifth place went to George Follmer, T70 mounted with Ford power, whilst Jerry Grant came seventh in another example.

On, then, to Bridgehampton. Situated near New York, this circuit saw a record crowd of 27,000 attend to watch the ground-pounding cars fight it out. A T70 won again, but this one was driven by Dan Gurney who led all the way to the finish. This had a Gurney-Weslake-Ford engine of 5.3-litres. He was followed by Amon only half a second behind, with McLaren third, and then Phil Hill in the Chaparral. The next Lola was a Penske entry for Mark

Can-Am 1966. Denny Hulme takes John Surtees as his passenger in SL71/31.

Below: In 1985, SL70/7 restored and taking passengers for a ride, is driven by Cheryl Schmitt. The car is known as "Madame!"

Donohue. Jerry Grant was seventh again. John Surtees retired with gear selection bother and a broken oil pipe.

Can-Am went to Mosport in Canada next and Ron Bennett remembers the difference between the English and American approach: "These days it takes about six blokes [to run a racecar] but then it was just Sid, Denny and me. We went to the Can-Am with the Mark II. We arrived at Mosport and pulled alongside Penske's crew - he'd got eight men - I unloaded and started working and a guy came up and said 'where's your crew?' I said 'I'm here.' He said 'where's the rest of 'em?' I said, 'I'm here!' He said, 'Bloody Limeys' and walked away!"

Mosport was the circuit where Surtees had his huge accident the year before. Another accident this year removed eight cars on the first lap, including John Surtees' T70 at the same corner he had crashed the year before, though, this time, fortunately, without injury. After the restart, Gurney led until he was forced to retire only ten laps from the end with a one lap lead with, of all things, a flat battery. For forty laps he had followed Amon, McLaren and Hulme, New Zealanders all, until getting by first Hulme (who later retired with a broken half-shaft) and then Amon. McLaren clipped a back marker and was out with broken rear suspension. After Dan dropped out, the lead was inherited by Mark Donohue, ('Captain Nice' to his fans) in Roger Penske's T70 running a five and a half litre Chevrolet engine. Mark recounted, in his book *The Unfair Advantage*, how he was unable to keep up with the opposition that first year. He freely admitted that any top places achieved in the series were down to his Lola's reliability. In the paddock, badges abounded announcing: 'God is a Chevy dealer from Philadelphia', testifying to Roger Penske's organisational skill. Phil Hill, in Jim Hall's Chaparral, was second, with Chuck Parsons third.

Jim Hall was a tall West Texan noted for his taciturnity. He had money acquired from oil exploration

Mark Donohue.

Mark Donohue in Roger Penske's Mark II spyder, SL 71/32, in a Can-Am race.

and raced a Lotus in Grand Prix events in 1963. Utilising the knowledge thus gained, he contacted General Motors and, with its help, built his own racecar producing plant coupled to its own race circuit, appropriately named 'Rattlesnake Raceway' in Midland, Texas. Hall was highly inventive, utilising an aerofoil in an upside down position in order to generate downforce through the suspension uprights. When the downforce wasn't required, the 2E's wing adopted a no-drag configuration through linkage with the throttle pedal, although this was later changed to put the aerofoil into full drag configuration when the pedal was released.

The 327 cu. in. Chevy-engined car also had a 2-speed automatic transmission, but the project suffered due to Hall dividing his effort between Can-Am and European endurance racing.

Laguna Seca in California was the next venue for the Can-Am series and the Chaparrals finished first and second in the first heat. They looked set to repeat the trick in the second until Parnelli Jones hurtled by near the end in a T70 after Surtees' car had retired with deranged steering sustained when Jones and he had banged together. Result: Hill first, Hall second. Jones finished twenty-first overall as he had failed to finish the first heat due to a holed sump. Donohue was fourth whilst Dibley came in tenth and John Mecom was heard bemoaning the Ford engines his Lolas used. He had blown four in the first three races and two more in practice for this race: "I've still got four left in LA but I guess they'll make someone a darn good boat anchor at $10,000 each." Shortly after, he changed to Chevrolet motors.

John Surtees was back in style at the penultimate race held at Riverside raceway in California on October 30th. Bruce McLaren's car sported a cockpit-adjustable aerofoil like the Chaparral and took pole position. 81,000 people turned out in the ninety-two degree heat to watch Bruce McLaren lead for the first ten laps until ignition problems set in, eventually causing his retirement seven laps later. The Chaparrals were experiencing all kinds of fuel vaporisation problems, however, and Phil Hill retired his car on the seventh lap.

After that, it was Surtees and Hall fighting all the way to the finish with the lead changing seven times. Surtees managed to grab the lead with five laps left, even though Jim Hall had set a new lap record. Graham Hill was third in the other Team Surtees car, and Donohue came in fourth with team mate George Follmer sixth. This left the series tied between Phil Hill and John Surtees with Mark Donohue only one point behind. There was everything to play for in the last round at Las Vegas.

Optimistically called the 'Stardust Grand Prix', this final event on November 13th actually took place on the Las Vegas Raceway. Although Surtees was only fourth on the grid behind the two Chaparrals and Chris Amon, at flag fall he grabbed the inside line into the first corner and drove a relatively untroubled race to win. He set fastest lap on the way with a time of 1:35.7, compared with Jim Hall's qualifying lap of 1:34.5. Hall himself retired with a broken aerofoil after a collision with Parnelli Jones. Mark Donohue was third behind Bruce McLaren, and Paul Hawkins came in eighth with Parnelli Jones behind him, both in T70s. Denny Hulme and Hugh Dibley retired.

John Surtees won more than $50,000; more money than could have been won for the entire 1966 Formula One World Championship! The first series of Can-Am races had proved a huge success. There was so much money beckoning for this series that Lola and McLaren concentrated on it for years to come.

The last races in America for 1966 were held in Nassau in the Bahamas for the 'Speed week' in November, a week of races, parties and generally a fun time. Mark Donohue drove Penske's T70 to victory after the team had installed an extra fuel tank in the passenger compartment to save on refuelling at the mandatory pit stop. In the event, Donohue spun and lost half the nose against a tree and thought his race was through but Penske urged him on and the leader, Peter Revson, dropped out with brake

The 1966 Times Grand Prix, Riverside. This time SL70/7 is driven by Scooter Patrick. The car was retired after 36 laps.

Doug Serrurier in his Mark I, SL70/5, gives an errant Honda a wide berth during the Kyalami 9-hours in 1969. The car led at the start but was forced out after a fire in the pits. (Courtesy Autosport).

failure. This left only Skip Scott in front of Donohue who took the lead when Scott pitted for fuel. Donohue lost the lead when he made his pit stop, pausing only to leap out and back in the car, but Scott spun behind a backmarker on the very last lap leaving Donohue the jubilant victor.

Whilst these jollities had been taking place, another series of races which would heavily feature the T70 had been starting in South Africa. Called the 'Springbok' series, it was the ideal winter holiday for many European drivers and sportscar teams. This year, it kicked off with the nine-hour race at Kyalami in November, and David Piper, a driver who always excelled in long distance racing with various Ferraris, had to fight hard to beat a Mark I Lola T70 to victory. This was SL70/5, which had been bought originally by David Cunningham in England. He had raced it once and then sold it to David Good, a hillclimber who, because of a withered arm, was unable to take part in international races. He let Roy Pierpoint, of Attila Chevrolet fame, drive it for him and he, in turn, shared the drive with Doug Serrurier in the Springbok races.

At Kyalami, the Ford-powered Lola led for the first hour before breaking a rocker arm. This was repaired in half an hour and the Lola was flying again. Alas, after three hours the car was retired with no oil pressure, leaving Piper to win in his Ferrari 365 P2/3.

They were at it again in late November at the Cape International three hours. Although Piper won again, the Lola was second this time and had led the race to start with. Despite numerous 'offs' in the chase to catch David Piper who drove the whole event solo, the Lola had the satisfaction of closing to within ten seconds at the flag.

The last race of 1966 was the Dickie Dale three hours at the Roy Hesketh circuit, Pietermaritzburg. Here again, the T70 led the field before spinning off on the second lap. Fighting his way back, Pierpoint retook the lead on lap twenty-five, and proceeded to pull away from the opposition at one and a half seconds per lap. After setting the fastest lap of the race, Pierpoint then had the misfortune to have the rear suspension collapse just as he was about to hand over to Serrurier. The car could not be repaired in time and, sadly, was retired. Mike Hailwood and David Hobbs went on to win in the Lola's spiritual predecessor, a Ford GT40.

5

MARK III SPYDERS AND COUPÉS

By the end of 1966 Lola had produced forty-seven T70s, and Eric Broadley saw that he could produce a Group 6 coupé version for endurance events in Europe.

Group 6 was the category coined by the CSI (Commission Sportive International) to cover so-called 'Sports-prototypes'. This covered cars such as the Ferrari P-series and the Ford GT40, pure endurance racers, even though Ford management did attempt to adapt its product for road use. Furthermore, if the T70 spyder production was taken into account, Lola would be able to homologate its new coupé into Group 4 when the required 50 examples had been completed. Broadley's interpretation of the rules led him to believe that this would happen and he therefore designed the Mark III, which could be used as both spyder (Group 9) and coupé version (Group 4 and 6) simply by swapping bodywork.

Jackie Epstein found that, with the deletion of Group 7/9 racing, he could use a Group 4 coupé, based on his experience with a T70 in 1966 when Paul Hawkins was driving his car, in the first Can-Am events. Epstein had been racing a Ferrari 275LM in long distance sports car events until outclassed by Ford GT40s. He now approached Eric Broadley with the idea of assembling a coupé body on the T70 spyder. Ideally, he would also have liked a Ferrari V12 engine behind him but Lola could see a bigger market by retaining the American V8s they had used previously.

It was at this time that Lola and Aston Martin arrived at an agreement in which the second Team Surtees Mark II was used as a test bed for Aston Martin's new 5-litre V8, which was intended to replace the trusty twin camshaft six-cylinder engine in its road cars. They were pleased with the results, even though the engine put a connecting rod through the side of the block due to oil starvation whilst testing in the T70 spyder.

The differences between the Lola T70 Marks II and III were few. The front and rear bulkheads were narrowed by two inches per side at the pick-up points for the suspension links (which were lengthened from 5in to 7in to give revised geometry). The top of the front uprights were machined slightly differently to suit the new set-up, whilst wheel widths were now 8in front and 10in rear, although still 15 inches in diameter. The track remained the same as on a Mark II. The steering rack was from a BMC 1800 instead of a BMC 1100, and knock-off hubs could be specified with beautiful polished cast alloy three-eared spinners fitted.

12 inch ventilated disc brakes with light alloy four-pot calipers were fitted, together with Lola-designed bridge pieces, and the twin wishbone suspension had self-aligning roller bearings and ball

LOLA

DATA SHEET

Type 70 Mk 3 | Delivered to

Chassis No. SL 73/119

Delivered

Engine Installation Components: Chevrolet

Engine Manufacturer: None | No.

Type/Modification: -

Transmission: Standard

Gearbox: Hewland LG 600 - 17

Crown Wheel & Pinion Ratio: Std. 5 speed

Clutch: None

Wheel Base: 95"

Front Track: 57"

Rear Track: 57½"

Steering

Gear Teeth	
1	24/50
2	28/47
3	33/42
4	35/40
5	37/38
6	

Front Suspension

Spring: 340 lbs/in | Shock Absorbers: Koni 82X - 1541

Roll Bar: 3/4" Adjustable | Hubs: Standard

Rear Suspension

Spring: 380 lbs/in | Shock Absorbers: Koni 82X - 1541

Roll Bar: 13/16" | Hubs: Standard

Drive Shafts

	Front	Rear
Discs	Vented	Vented
Caliper	Lola	Lola
Pad Material	DS 11	DS 11
Master Cylinder	.75"	.70"
Wheels	Lola 15" x 8"	Lola 15" x 8"
Tyres	Scrap	Scrap

Petrol Tank Capacity: 60 U.S. Galls. | Oil Capacity: -

Modifications from Standard None

Build sheet for a Mark III spyder.

joints. The first Chevrolet engines used in the new coupés were 5.5-litre Ryan Falconer tuned units with crossover inlet manifolds for the sidedraught Weber 58DCOE carburettors fitted.

The racing tyres available were improving in leaps and bounds at this time, with Firestone pioneering the flat crown type for Formula One in 1966. The T70 Mark III was designed around these tyres, which called for the tread to be kept parallel to the surface of the road. Suspension design now became more critical than ever before, and allowed tread width to grow steadily year after year from this point.

The car also featured an easily changeable radiator and oil cooler, with an oil reservoir fitted at the front of the car - alongside the master cylinders in the case of the dry-sumped Aston Martin-engined cars. A quick-change dashboard assembly was fitted. It was not, however, a rapid job to convert the open car to its closed version and vice-versa. A conversion kit to give the LG500 gearbox five speeds instead of four was offered in the USA.

Jim Clark, a New Zealander, had designed the sensational new coupé for Specialised Mouldings to make, and it was the first racing car to feature carbon-fibre reinforced bodywork. Using a wind tunnel, the beautiful bodywork had been designed not only with low drag in mind, but also with a measure of downforce front and rear. A notable feature was the gullwing doors, fitted with a positive lock 'T' handle on the outside in an effort to overcome the problem from which the Ford GT40 had suffered, of doors lifting at speed. The side windows, which were made of Perspex, featured small diagonal flaps that could be fastened in the open position to provide some cooling air for the driver. The latches were parts from the Vauxhall Viva saloon.

From the front of the car, the quick release nose section had a wide grille opening to duct air into the front-mounted radiator, which then exhausted itself from a slot in front of the windscreen. Large brake cooling holes flanked the grille opening, with single headlights mounted behind perspex covers above them. Mirrors, which provided a vestige of rear view, were usually fitted on top of the front wings, and small angled spoilers to their own designs were sometimes

A view of the big sidedraught 58 DCOE Webers.

added by race teams. These were fitted between the brake cooling ducts and the front wheelarch.

The windscreen was bonded into the bodyshell, rather than being mounted in a rubber grommet (the more usual manner), in the central bodywork section which was attached to the monocoque via spire nuts. The front and rear body sections were quickly detachable via pip pins. The rear body section featured cooling ducts on each side of the cockpit bulkhead, plus two more small openings facing forward on the top of the rear deck which forced air into two aluminium periscope-type cooling ducts to the rear brakes. The mandatory spare wheel was mounted horizontally at the rear of the car, just inside the bodywork and above the gearbox. It was visible through the large cooling slot cut into the back. Some customer cars, however, had the spare wheel fitted vertically.

To match the front spoiler bibs, trim tabs of aluminium, which could be adjusted for height via four bolts, were fitted across the top of the rear bodywork (some teams simply riveted them on in a fixed position).

The prototype hall at Specialised Mouldings. The new Lola-Aston has just been finished.

LOLA TYPE 70 Mk. III G.T.

SPECIFICATION

TRACK		58 inches
WHEEL-BASE		95 inches
GROUND CLEARANCE		4 inches with fuel and driver.
CHASSIS		Light alloy and sheet steel, monocoque construction.
BODY		Glass fibre
SEATS		Formed in the structure and covered with lightweight quickly removable upholstery.
FRONT SECTION		Quickly removable for access to cooling system and front suspension.
REAR SECTION		Quickly removable for access to engine compartment and rear suspension.
SUSPENSION	Front	Double wishbone on self-alignin[illegible]er bearings and ball joints. Telesc[illegible] shock absorbers and co-axial coil springs.
	Rear	Double wishbone and radius rod on self-aligning roller bearings and ball joints. Telescopic shock absorbers and co-axial coil springs.
BRAKES		Girling disc. Front and Rear: 12½ in. dia. disc. B.R. light alloy caliper. Vented discs optional extra.
STEERING		Rack and pinion.
WHEELS & TYRES		15 inch rim diameter, cast magnesium knock-on wheels.
	Front	8 inch rim width for 10.60 x 15 Firestone, 550x15 Dunlop or Goodyear equivalent.
	Rear	10 inch rim width for 1200 x 15 Firestone, 650 x 15 Dunlop or Goodyear equivalent.
ENGINE		Chevrolet 333 cu. in. V8 standard. Ford or other V8 engines to special order.
WEIGHT		Less driver and fuel 1760 lbs. With Ford 289 cu. in. engine 1660 lbs.

The factory's specification details for the Mark IIIGT coupé.

The twin exhausts exited straight through the large slot in the centre of the rear bodywork, whilst a "luggage space" was mounted beneath the rear of the car. Full lighting equipment was carried in the coupé, with one large single wiper blade fitted to sweep the screen.

A full-length aluminium undertray was employed and ground clearance was set to four inches. In the monocoque itself, a stiffening rib was fitted between the driver and passenger compartments, whilst another ran in line with the lower mountings for the front wishbones. The new dashboard was supported by an alloy box section which strengthened the tub at the juncture between the big sill compartment and the nose section.

Ron Bennett, having previously prepared a GT40 (1001), commented on the reason a GT40 would ultimately go faster in top speed than a T70: "If you look at a GT40 in plan view, it's a coke bottle in shape. Ultimately, it passes through the air with less disturbance than a T70 coupé. We went around Silverstone with, I think, Laurie Bray driving the coupé with wool tufts all over it. It was doing around 60-80mph with cameras all around it and I asked Eric [Broadley] "What's it like ?" and he answered: 'I think we'll just race it as it is!' We cut away underneath the nose because we always reckoned that was a high pressure area, you could see all the oil from other cars collecting there."

Production of the spyder as a Group 7/9 sports racing car continued alongside that of the coupé and, in all, a total of nineteen

The Racing Car show, London, January 1967, and the Lola - Aston shows off its stunning lines. (Courtesy Autosport).

The engine bay of SL73/112 exposed at Spa-Francorchamps. This was the car's first race appearance where it finished fourth in the 1000 kilometre race, driven by Paul Hawkins and Jackie Epstein. Note the sidedraught Weber carburettors and the long neck for the oil filler. (Courtesy Autosport).

spyders and twelve coupés were built at Slough. The last Mark III, in the shape of a rolling chassis, was sent to Franco Sbarro in Switzerland. He fitted it out as a road-going car with air-conditioning, electric windows, leather trim and silencing. Lola says that it did make one coupé as a road-going car, painted it silver and sent it to America to be displayed in a dealer's showroom. This car featured a ZF gearbox. Factory records have this down as SL73/117, a car later raced by James Garner's AIR team.

The first coupé, fitted with a Chevrolet engine, was displayed at the 1967 Racing Car Show. Decked out in British Racing Green with a white stripe painted longitudinally it was the star of the show, like the 1965 roadster and the Mark VI before it. This car had already been earmarked for Team Surtees with another one on order. Both were destined to use the Aston Martin V8 engine. This was the new Tadek Marek-designed engine with a project number of DP218. With wet cast iron liners in its aluminium alloy crankcase, the 90 degree V8 featured chain-driven twin overhead camshafts, two valves per cylinder and, on a compression ratio of 11:1 with four Weber 48IDA carburettors, gave 421bhp at 6500rpm and developed 386lb.ft. of torque at 5000rpm in its first development stage. The engine, in its initial guise, had featured the proven combustion chamber design and valve gear, as well as the cylinder bore and stroke dimensions of the previous straight six. The figures rose to 450bhp and

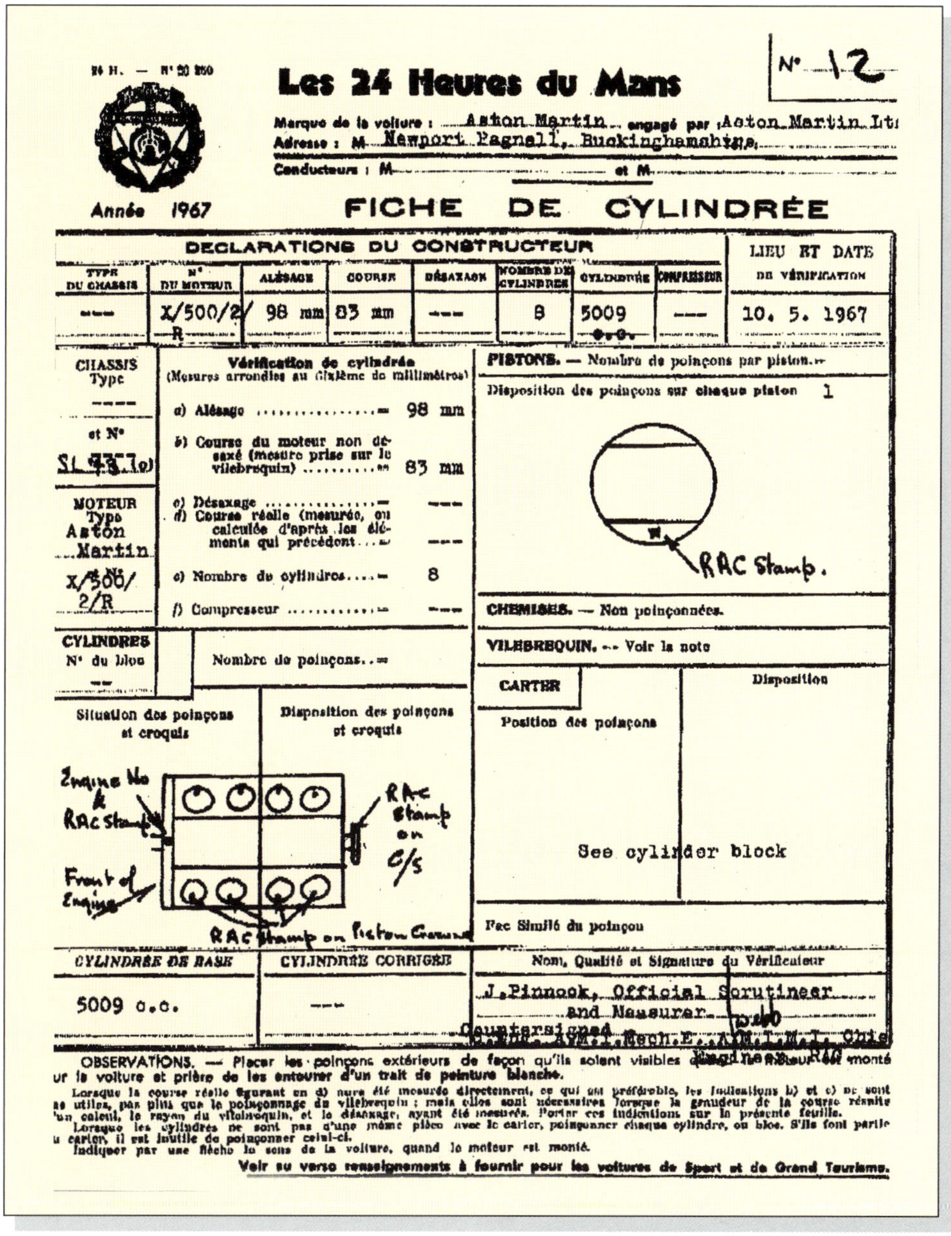

N° 12

Les 24 Heures du Mans

Marque de la voiture : Aston Martin engagé par : Aston Martin Lt
Adresse : M. Newport Pagnell, Buckinghamshire.
Conducteurs : M. ... et M. ...

Année 1967

FICHE DE CYLINDRÉE

DECLARATIONS DU CONSTRUCTEUR

Type du chassis	N° du moteur	Alésage	Course	Désaxage	Nombre de cylindres	Cylindrée	Compresseur	Lieu et date de vérification
---	X/500/2/R	98 mm	83 mm	---	8	5009 c.c.	---	10. 5. 1967

CHASSIS Type ---- et N° SL 73/121(o)

MOTEUR Type Aston Martin et N° X/500/2/R

Vérification de cylindrée (Mesures arrondies au dixième de millimètres)

a) Alésage ... = 98 mm
b) Course du moteur non désaxé (mesure prise sur le vilebrequin) ... = 83 mm
c) Désaxage ... = ---
d) Course réelle (mesurée, ou calculée d'après les éléments qui précèdent ... = ---
e) Nombre de cylindres ... = 8
f) Compresseur ... = ---

CYLINDRES N° du bloc --

Nombre de poinçons .. =

PISTONS. — Nombre de poinçons par piston. =
Disposition des poinçons sur chaque piston 1

RAC Stamp.

CHEMISES. — Non poinçonnées.

VILEBREQUIN. — Voir la note

CARTER

Position des poinçons

Disposition

See cylinder block

Situation des poinçons et croquis

Disposition des poinçons et croquis

Fac Similé du poinçon

Cylindrée de base	Cylindrée corrigée	Nom, Qualité et Signature du Vérificateur
5009 c.c.	---	J. Pinnock, Official Scrutineer and Measurer. Countersigned ... A.M.I.Mech.E., A.M.I.M.I. Chief Engineer RAC

OBSERVATIONS. — Placer les poinçons extérieurs de façon qu'ils soient visibles quand le moteur est monté sur la voiture et prière de les entourer d'un trait de peinture blanche.

Lorsque la course réelle figurant en d) aura été mesurée directement, ce qui est préférable, les indications b) et c) ne sont pas utiles, pas plus que le poinçonnage du vilebrequin ; mais elles sont nécessaires lorsque la grandeur de la course résulte d'un calcul, le rayon du vilebrequin, et le désaxage, ayant été mesurés. Porter ces indications sur la présente feuille.

Lorsque les cylindres ne sont pas d'une même pièce avec le carter, poinçonner chaque cylindre, ou bloc. S'ils font partie du carter, il est inutile de poinçonner celui-ci.

Indiquer par une flèche le sens de la voiture, quand le moteur est monté.

Voir au verso renseignements à fournir pour les voitures de Sport et de Grand Tourisme.

The entry form for one of the two Lola Astons for the Le Mans 24 hours, 1967.

413lb.ft. of torque in the engines which were slotted into SL73/101 and SL73/121 for the semi-works team which had been set up by John Surtees in conjunction with Eric Broadley. The prefix SL, incidentally, indicated that the car had been built in the new Slough factory, rather than the earlier set-up in Bromley.

SL73/121 was tested by Michael Scarlett of *Autocar* and the result reported in the May 8th issue. Scarlett started the article by asking the reader: "What does it feel like to recline in the upside-down goldfish-bowl of a vehicle weighing a shade over 17.5cwt with the option of 418bhp at the end of a length of a throttle cable?" He added to this rhetorical question by saying that to drive the T70 coupe was the equivalent of a learner driver being allowed to drive an E-Type Jaguar for the first time ... on ice!

Scarlett tried 121 at Silverstone and quoted its gear ratios as giving 79, 104, 128, 147 and 173mph at 7000rpm, and then commented on the child's tricycle-type bulb horn which had replaced the electric horn in the interests of lightness. Cockpit drill started with pumping the brake pedal to make sure there were some brakes (!) followed by switching on the ignition and then the fuel pumps. One prod on the accelerator pedal to squirt the eight accelerator-pump jets, press the starter button and, with luck, the engine started quite quickly.

Scarlett then wrote that first gear was engaged "with a bit of a crunch and you move off along Silverstone's pit lane by letting the Borg and Beck clutch plates touch only occasionally. Passing slowly by other cars being attended to, you wonder how close your wings are to them as it's all so wide and far to the sides from where you're sitting. Assuming the track's clear, you drive out onto it and tentatively press the pedal. There's this marvellous thrust in the back, much more noise and you're rushing forwards towards Copse. Something strikes you as vaguely familiar, a feeling that you've been somewhere like this before. The view ahead is of Tarmac streaming at the pronounced vee between the two high peaks of the front wings, all seen through a near-semi-circular strip of screen which is across and partly around you.

"You put [the gear lever] awkwardly into second (not used to

Right - SL73/135, the Sbarro modified Mark III built up as a road car. SL76/138, the Sid Taylor Mark IIIb coupé, can be seen in the background.

Below - In the late 1960s Tamiya produced an excellent model of a Mark III coupé.

right-handed gear changing and the movement is rather stiff and notchy) and carry on.

"The T70 steers in direct proportion to thought, rather than needing noticeable movement, though the steering isn't excessively low-geared and neither is it in the least twitchy. It just goes where you put it, rigidly, decisively, with the slightest suggestion of roll visible at the tops of the wings. It has complete straight-line stability.

"My turn quickly taught me that although the Lola's behaviour is faultless and its balance seemingly perfect, you have to treat 475-odd bhp per ton with care - a touch too much and that great turned-up tail starts to move. It is a most wondrously responsive beast.

"Ride seemed very good, which did surprise me greatly. It is on the firm side, of course, but not nearly as much as I'd expected. All this conspires to make you confident (famous last words), though you sit so low you don't really know how fast you're going. Only the gathering noise as the revs rise behind, the way the grass on the outside of the exit from Chapel Curve comes narrowing obliquely across to confine you and that pushed feeling in the back tells you. Brakes seem dead after servo-assisted touring cars and you shove hard for Stowe. As far as driving on a private track is concerned, the Lola T70 is a most wonderful experience: it's when others are around that you aren't so happy.

"I still don't know how people in Lola T70 GTs see anyone behind. There's precious little view to the side. The wing mirrors allow one to check for newspapers, race

programmes, birds nests, *etcetera*, blocking the big cooling intakes on each side. The central mirror performs a similar service for the gauze covers over the carburettor throats. Jackie Epstein carefully made sure I never got in anyone's way by delaying our foray to the end of the day, which was a very good thing."

A Mark III coupé, SL 73/113, awaits shipment to America.

The T70 as a road car. This is SL73/135, the last Mark III made. It was modified by Franco Sbarro with air-conditioning, silencing and even a radio. It was then displayed to the 1969 Racing Car Show in London.

As the factory geared up for its 1968 production run, in late 1967 a bombshell was delivered by the CSI, the sports governing body, which decreed that Group 4 cars would have to be made in batches of twenty-five and powered by engines of no more than 5 litres in order to limit speed. The CSI was concerned about the ever-increasing speeds of endurance racers, such as the 7-litre Ford GT40, and this new ruling was a knee-jerk reaction.

This ruled out Lola's intention to count-in the previous spyder production to qualify the T70 coupé for Group 4, and yet, ironically, the ruling was to lead to the fastest sports prototypes ever seen, the Porsche 917 and Ferrari 512.

T70 Mark IIIs in production at the factory in 1968.

6

RACING IN 1967

Doug Serrurier carried on the Springbok series of races in South Africa with SL70/5 after purchasing the car from Roy Pierpoint, and won a twenty lap race at Kyalami on January 2nd with ease. Unfortunately, whilst in the lead five days later at Killarney, Capetown, he had the misfortune to lose a wheel and the car hit a tree, fortunately with no damage to the genial South African but quite a lot to the car. He did have the satisfaction of having set a new lap record three seconds faster than the old one.

Back in England, Robin Darlington had bought Charles Bridge's T70, SL71/27, but commenced his time with the car by messing up the start of the Guards Trophy heat at Brands Hatch. After pulling the Lola up to fifth place, Darlington lost it on some oil and spun into the ditch at Clearways, fortunately with little damage.

Oulton Park, his local circuit, saw him redeem himself with a win in a ten lap race on Good Friday. He then lent the T70 to Peter Gethin who, although unfamiliar with the big car, calmly stroked it to victory in the Formula Libre event.

The big Lola news for 1967 was, of course, the imminent arrival of the Mark III GT coupé for international endurance racing. It

January 6th '67. Doug Serrurier leads the Porsche 906 of Mike de Udy and the rest of the pack at the start of the sports car race at Killarney, Capetown. The car, SL70/5, led until half distance when the front suspension failed and Serrurier crashed. (Courtesy Autosport).

Robin Darlington in SL71/27, Silverstone, 1967.

Old Hall corner, Oulton Park, March 24 1967. Peter Gethin gets an early taste of V8 power as he pilots Robin Darlington's ex Brian Redman car to victory in the Formula Libre race that afternoon. (Courtesy Autosport).

August 13 1967, Croft. The start of the second heat which David Hobbs went on to win. In the lead is Denny Hulme in SL73/102 whilst Mike de Udy can just be seen in between two Porsche 906 Carreras entering the corner. (Courtesy Autosport).

had been a sensation when displayed at the Racing Car Show: *Autosport* opined that if the engines, Aston Martin or Chevrolet, could be made to hold together, the car could prove invincible; especially as John Surtees was doing the development work. Team Surtees was formed with Howard Marsden, who was previously Alan Mann's general manager.

The new coupé's racing debut was inauspicious. At Sebring in March a Chevrolet-powered example was entrusted to Buck Fulp and Roger McKluskey. It arrived late and the suspension was damaged in practice so did not start. This could have been SL73/102 which was later sold to Sid Taylor. Ron Bennett remembers: "We got 102 part way through the year because prior to that we ran a GT40. Eric Broadley 'phoned Sid up and said 'I've got a white Lola here, just do [for] you, Sid.' Now, the thing was, in those days we never bought a car, they were always given to us. Sid was in motor racing when I joined him for about six or seven years before he had to buy tyres. Nothing was bought, it was always given. Things have changed a bit, haven't they? Broadley got him onto a Lola, says 'get rid of that bloody Ford, you must have this.' 'Cos I don't think Eric was too pleased with Ford anyway."

When the entry list for Le Mans was published, there were indeed three Lola T70 GTs entered. Two were Aston Martin-powered Team Surtees cars, and the third a Chevrolet-powered example for the Charles Vogele Racing Team. They did not, however, participate in the race itself, probably due to the works being unable to supply them with a car, such were the orders coming into the factory at this time.

John Surtees tested SL73/101 at Goodwood and the engine lasted up to fourteen hours. David Hobbs, meanwhile, was testing at Silverstone and soon got down to a time of 1min. 27secs, which would not have disgraced the current 3-litre Formula One cars!

Now fitted with the first LG600 5-speed Hewland gearbox and painted with the Surtees' team white arrowhead edged in red, the car went to the Le Mans test weekend on April 10th and was third fastest in the dry against Ferrari P4 and Ford Mark II and IV (7-litre) opposition. In the dry conditions of Saturday, Surtees wound up third fastest at 3min 31.9 seconds with the engine refusing to rev to more than 6000rpm, whilst on the Sunday in wet conditions he was over six seconds faster than any of the opposition. The car displayed a longer, more teardrop-shaped rear body made in aluminium, the intake trumpets were faired over, and larger than standard trim tabs were fitted - all in the quest for more speed on the Mulsanne straight. The Lola team was already learning that, whilst the new coupé gave outstanding roadholding due to a certain amount of downforce created

In later years one of the Lola-Astons (SL73/101) shows off its excellent handling. (Courtesy Autosport).

The policeman on the left seems singularly unimpressed at the sight and sound of the Epstein/Hawkins Mark IIIGT coupé at Spa-Francorchamps in 1967. (Courtesy Autosport).

April 1967 and, on a streaming wet Spa-Francorchamps road course, Paul Hawkins hustles SL73/112 past Lodovico Scarfiotti in a works prepared Ferrari P4. He took fourth place in the race which was the coupé's first international competition appearance. (Courtesy Autosport).

SL73/112, ex Jackie Epstein/ Paul Hawkins/Mike de Udy, seen today after a complete and perfect restoration by Peter Denty.

by the body shape, that same shape militated against outright top speed. By the end of the session, although expressing satisfaction, the team did not mention that the engine was running hot and there was a suspicion that a valve problem had arisen.

Jackie Epstein took delivery of SL73/112 on the last day of April and promptly trailered it to the Belgian circuit of Spa-Francorchamps to share the driving with Paul Hawkins. They were joined there by the first customer car, SL73/105, this being ordered by one Michael Grace de Udy, a South African who lived in London. This car featured twin 'periscopes' mounted on the cockpit roof in an attempt to funnel cool air into the cockpit. Whether they succeeded in this is open to question but they certainly seemed to help to extract the hot air. Poor De Udy had the misfortune to crash his car at the slow hairpin at La Source; not very badly but the suspension was too damaged to allow him to take part in a rain-soaked race that Jackie Ickx, in the Gulf Mirage, dominated.

This was, however, the first time that a T70 coupé was driven in anger and Paul Hawkins made the most of it. He loved the car. With it he posted fifth fastest time in practice whilst, in the race itself, held in the aforementioned appallingly wet conditions, he was up to fourth by lap ten. Soon after, he had the Lola up to third place overall and was challenging for second when he had to stop for fuel and to hand over to Epstein. Jackie Epstein was not as fast as Paul and the T70 fell to seventh place by half distance. Hawkins took over again

Lola-Aston SL73/121 at Le Mans for the 1967 race. Note the Marchal decal behind the front wheelarch. Surtees shared the car with David Hobbs who is standing on the left of the picture.

Surtees in SL73/121 during the 1967 Le Mans race. Note the high spoilers mounted at the rear of the tail.

and, towards the end of the race was menacing Mike Parkes in a works Ferrari P4 for fourth place. Hawkins got by and then had to stop again for oil and fuel but the P4 had to pit and Scarfiotti replaced Parkes. Although the experienced Italian had a one and a quarter minute lead, Hawkins whittled it away to pass him and take fourth place "in an enormous slide at the kink before Stavelot" (*Autosport*).

Epstein took his Lola to Sicily to compete in the Targa Florio but he split a bag tank and the two more he ordered did not arrive. He elected to practice with one tank only and he and Dibley, his co-driver for this occasion, had time to familiarise themselves with the long and twisty circuit. Come race day, Epstein was in the pits on the first lap complaining of gear selection problems and overheating. On the fifth lap the car was retired, lacking third and fourth gears and using an ominous amount of oil.

May 28th saw the Lola-Aston's race debut at the Nürburgring in the 1000 kilometre World Championship event, and the Lola was second in practice, eight seconds in arrears of Mike Spence in the Chaparral 2F coupé, but thirty seconds better than the nearest Ford GT40. The car's race itself lasted only seven laps. On that lap a rear wishbone broke at the Fuchsrohre and Surtees was fortunately able to bring the car to rest with no further damage.

The sad story of the Lola-Astons at the 1967 running of the Le Mans event is quickly told. The two cars entered, SL73/101 for Chris Irwin/Peter de Klerk, and SL73/121 for John Surtees/David Hobbs, never gave the co-drivers a chance to climb into the driver's seats. In qualifying the cars kept blowing their head gaskets and the Lola mechanics, there to look after the chassis, found the fuel injection timing to be 180 degrees out. John Surtees fitted Marchal sparkplugs under a bonus agreement and was blamed by Aston Martin when both cars retired: Surtees with a holed piston on lap three, and Chris Irwin with a cracked crankshaft damper

SL73/121, one of the two Lola-Astons, as seen in 1990. It has belonged to its present owner for twenty three years and he remembers going on picnics in it! Note the light to illuminate the rear race number for Le Mans.

SL73/121 at Le Mans with the nose removed showing the front-mounted oil tank for the dry sump and the fluid reservoirs.

after forty-five minutes. It was a fiasco and the cars were swiftly re-engined with Chevrolet units upon their return to the works.

The Rheims twelve hour race, starting at midnight, had long been a traditional follow-up endurance grind to Le Mans. For it Ford loaned Jo Schlesser and Guy Ligier a Mark II 7-litre car which would go on to win after four T70 GTs had retired, but not before putting on a show of speed which left the crowd gasping. John Surtees and David Hobbs were down to drive the car they had used

On the grid at Silverstone, the ex-Brian Redman/Red Rose Team Mark II. Robin Dartington awaits the start in October 1967.

SL73/121, the second Lola-Aston as it is today, now carrying a Chevrolet engine of the type that was used after Le Mans 1967.

1968. Denny Hulme at his best, hustling a big, powerful sports prototype through Silverstone's fast bends. It's April 27th, and Denny led from start to finish with Sid Taylor's first Mark III, SL73/102, to take the Players' Trophy.

Here they come! The start of the 1967 BOAC 500 at Brands Hatch with John Surtees already leading the pack in SL73/121 with Hulme to the left. Just look at those photographers; they don't get so close now! (Courtesy Autosport)

at Le Mans, complete with its aluminium tail and spoiler, but now with a 5.9-litre Chevrolet and sidedraught Weber carburettors. Sid Taylor had his new coupé (SL73/102) for Denny Hulme and Frank Gardner fitted with a 5.5-litre engine.

It was the first time that Denny or Frank had driven the coupé and Ron Bennett recounts: "Rheims, that was the twelve hour race, the only one that started in the dark. In practice, Denny came in, he was grinning from ear to ear. I said 'What's up?' He said, 'Bloody fabulous, absolutely fabulous!' So Frank Gardner had a go, he was pulling 185mph past the pits towards the first corner. He came in and he says: 'needs a touch of downforce at the front' so we put the ears (front tabs) on, and I said 'what do you think?' And Denny says, 'Do what you like, I'll bloody drive it all day!' He was thrilled to bits with that car, he called it just wonderful."

SL73/102 also had some modifications of Ron Bennett's own: "The alternator on the crossmember was my modification, as was the oil cooler on top of the oil tank. Of course, the car(s) used to go back to Lola every now and then, usually for bodywork to be done, and Eric (Broadley) saw it and those modifications came out on the later 3B coupé".

Paul Hawkins was again co-driving Jackie Epstein's car. Mike de Udy was sharing SL73/105 with Hugh Dibley and they also used a 5.5-litre engine.

From the start it was Hawkins and Surtees who set the pace, chased by the Ford GT40 and then Hulme. Within two laps, all four Lolas were in a solid leading block, blasting by the pits at frightening speed. Poor Dibley was black-

SL73/121 poses outside a past owner's home. Visible are the Le Mans lights on the rear race number patch and original Firestone tyres.

Firestone

A pit stop at Brands Hatch during the BOAC 500 and John Surtees directs refuelling whilst David Hobbs stands waiting to climb back into SL73/121.

Mike de Udy in SL73/105 during the BOAC 500 at Brands Hatch, July 30th 1967.

flagged at the request of his pit crew as he had a headlight not working. Once this was fixed, the rear lights went out! He lost considerable time in the pits. Paul Hawkins was setting such a fast pace that John Surtees was dropping back. After one hour in the dark, Hawkins had broken the outright lap record for the circuit set up by Bandini in a 3-litre Formula One Ferrari.

Just after 2am, de Udy's car had to be retired with electrical trouble, and an hour later Surtees was out with a broken crankshaft. It's possible that the 190mph straight had caused over-revving as Epstein had had a very high top gear specially cut for this race. One minute later, Hawkins called at the pits for Epstein to take over but Jackie couldn't select a gear. When the mechanics examined the car closely they saw that the bell housing had pulled away from the engine. The Lola was promptly retired.

Paul Hawkins was disappointed and told *Autosport*: "That car's capable of 2mins 7sec in the dark; I was only stroking it." In an article for that magazine at the end of the season, Paul reflected: "After eleven laps I broke the outright lap record at about 147mph - and that was in the dark on full tanks. You can't afford to relax at all in these big fast cars, because you daren't risk getting the car even a foot out of position - especially through the long fast bend after the pits that you take at around 180mph!"

Denny Hulme kept his white and green Lola in the lead until 2am when the car came in with a broken fan pulley. De Udy's car provided the spare part and the car resumed, now in sixth place. Just after 2am it was back in the pits with overheating problems; after a few more laps it was retired with head gasket failure. Said Ron Bennett: "We used to run 'V' pulley belts in those days instead of toothed belts and the things used to flex. The crank pulley broke and on a Mark III it's inaccessible. I had to chisel through the bulkhead to get at it and we pinched one off De Udy's car and put it back but the heads had

David Hobbs, lights ablaze in the gloom of a very wet day, comes from the back of the grid in SL73/121 to win the second heat of the Wills Trophy at Croft in August 1967. (Courtesy Autosport)

already cracked and so we retired in a cloud of steam some laps later but we were way ahead, I remember." The crowd applauded as the last Lola coupé was pushed away. The Rheims circuit was closed shortly after and Paul Hawkins thus left the lap record at a staggering 149mph.

A meeting which was to cause Eric Broadley and Lola problems was held on 12/13th June in Paris at the CSI headquarters. Called at extremely short notice, with no previous agenda available, the meeting decided some swingeing changes to the regulations, primarily a reduction in the Group 4 engine capacity to 5-litres, and 3-litres for Group 6 sportscars. Thought to be in response to the very high speeds achieved at Le Mans with the 7-litre Ford GT40s, the measure provoked astonishment and outrage from most of the constructors. Eric Broadley had had the T70 Mark III coupé lined up for homologation in Group 4 later that year in 5.9-litre form and now faced having to build extra cars with 5-litre engines, obviously not a task suited to a comparatively small manufacturer.

Whilst the factory was mulling over the implications of this rule, Sid Taylor's car went to the Norisring for Frank Gardner to drive in a two-heat race of one hundred miles each. Although chased hard by Paul Hawkins in a GT40, Gardner won both heats. Jackie Epstein, his Lola apparently down on power, was happy to finish fourth.

"It was the biggest and best line up of GT sportscars and drivers ever seen in England," Bruce McLaren commented on the BOAC 500 being held on 30th July at Brands Hatch. With works cars from Ferrari, Porsche, Mirage, Chaparral and Lola, plus Ford GT40s, Chevrons and Lotus 47s, it promised much and did not disappoint. The Lola contingent was represented again by John Surtees, co-driving this time with David Hobbs, while Sid Taylor's car was present for Denny Hulme and Jack Brabham, and Mike de Udy's car was being shared with Peter Westbury.

Denny Hulme was in fine form and put his boss's car on pole position with a 1:36.6 recorded. Brabham had only the second session in the wet with which to familiarise himself with the track. John Surtees wound up alongside Denny with the same time, and the eventual winner, the Chaparral driven by Phil Hill and Mike Spence, completed the front row. John Surtees made the best start and led immediately, Denny Hulme lagging behind but holding fifth by the end of the first lap. Surtees soon fell back with fuel pressure problems and Hawkins took over the lead in a Ferrari P4. Denny was soon up to third and then took the lead from the Ferrari and pulled away to such effect that he set the fastest lap of the race at 1:37.2 on the seventh round. Forty minutes of the race were run when Hulme broke a rocker and came into the pits to have it replaced by Ron Bennett. He recalled: "We had some good drivers, Hulme, Gardner, Redman. Brabham once, at the BOAC 500 at Brands in 1967. Well, he was going to drive but Denny screwed the clutch!

"There's always been, off and on, odd spates with rockers on those things, on the Chevys. We had the latest kind and one broke so Denny bought the car in, misfiring and you'd see a lump under the rocker cover and you'd think, another one gone. I pulled the rocker cover off, stuck a new rocker straight back on, and Denny went back out, and found, after a couple of laps, that the clutch was going, I could hear it round the back. He came in, he got out and said: 'Clutch has gone.' I put it in gear and Denny says, 'I'm telling you, the clutch has gone!' and it rolled with the damn thing in gear, just moving down the hill, you know, in the old pits at Brands. I

The new Lola assembly line at Slough in April 1967. In the foreground are two of the the lightweight Mark IIIb spyders destined for that year's Can-Am series. Three GT coupés are next in line. Note that the furthest carries the Team Surtees arrowhead and a race number. (Courtesy Autosport)

said 'Oh, Jesus, it can't be clearance and it definitely can't be crud, the damn thing was cleaned out'. Denny says 'No, it's my fault, I was in that much of a hurry, I went out in third, I thought I was in first so I thought I'd got wheelspin but, Jesus, I'd cooked the clutch!' He admitted it, he was always straight, Denny was."

For the Lolas that was effectively the end of the race. Despite magnificent driving by Surtees and Hobbs which saw their car into seventh place, the car later retired with piston damage, probably caused by the fuel pressure problems and the de Udy/Westbury car stopped out on the circuit with a loose passenger door. After shutting it fully, de Udy was unable to restart the engine and had to

John Surtees in his lightweight Mark IIIb spyder, SL75/123, in the 1967 Can-Am series.

Top: Mark Donohue in Roger Penske's Mark IIIb spyder, SL75/124. The car today features coupé bodywork.

Middle: SL75/124 - Mark Donohue's 1967 Can-Am challenger - today in America after being restored in the 1980s.

Bottom: SL75/124 again. One of the lightweight Mark IIIb spyders, this car was converted to coupé bodywork before it was restored.

collect a new battery from his pit. The car retired before the end with a broken crownwheel and pinion.

August 13th saw four T70s out for the fifteen lap qualifying and fifty lap final heat races for a national Group 4 and 6 Wills Trophy race at Croft. Denny Hulme was to drive Sid Taylor's white and green coupé, whilst David Hobbs was in the Team Surtees car SL73/121. Max Wilson made an appearance for practice in the ex-Team Surtees SL73/101, though he destroyed the crown-wheel and pinion and, shortly thereafter, left for home. Mike de Udy was in SL73/105. The only other big Group 6 car was David Piper's beautiful Ferrari P3/4.

Although Denny was fastest in all three practice sessions, he had no real opposition in his qualifying heat as both Piper and Redman retired leaving de Udy to take second place. Poor David Hobbs did not start as his Lola also destroyed its crownwheel and pinion. It was a different story in the final, however, as Hobbs was allowed to start from the back of the grid. The rain now came down in torrents and, although Denny led at the start, by the end of the first lap David Hobbs was already in eighth place, having made an astute guess where tyre selection was concerned.

Vic Elford used the Porsche 901's handling to advantage and caught and passed Denny. Even though he spun on the second lap he still kept his lead! By the second lap, Hobbs, using his wet weather

This is Mark Donohue's 1967 USRRC winner. In the same year it was driven in the Can-Am by George Follmer and still retains the repairs to its monocoque from a crash at Mosport.

Firestones to best advantage, was in third place and on lap four passed Denny to take second. Next lap he was in the lead, even though Elford hung on grimly in second place. Denny got the message of a waved tyre from his pit crew and came into his pit on lap ten to exchange his Goodyears for the same tyres as Hobbs, after which he set off in pursuit even though he had lost a lap. Ron Bennett remembers: "Oh, yes, that was where Sid Taylor nearly got knocked out! It was raining that much Sid put his old crash helmet on. We couldn't get Denny in for tyres; he just kept going around on dries. I'm holding a wheel and a hammer over the pit for four or five laps and then in he came. Well, it was the old days; it was me, it was Sid and it was Denny. So I set to with the front quick lift jack and when a car comes in it squats down, you have to tip it to get it [the jack] under, but not Sid. He tried to force the jack under and missed and the handle went whack! and hit him on the head. He staggered around and I put the jack under the front, took the wheel off, rolled it away and thought 'no-one'll let this go, someone will stop it' and I put the other one on and out Denny went. Marshalls were running everywhere after these wheels I'd taken off. I mean, you daren't let 'em go!"

Denny now showed why he was a Formula One champion and began catching Hobbs at the rate of two seconds per lap. On lap thirty-one Denny unlapped himself and, fourteen laps later, overtook Elford to become official leader. There was no gainsaying Hobbs, however, who held on to win the heat even though he did not quality for an award for the combined race result.

Once again, this race demonstrated the lovely Lola coupé to be master of any contemporary car as long as it could be made to endure. This seemed more of a certainty in the shorter national races in which it participated although, sadly, the same did not apply in the long-distance international events. An example of this was the last international race of the European season when Max Wilson entered SL73/101 in the Paris 1000km race held on the old banked circuit at Montlhéry. His co-driver was David Hobbs. Although the car was second fastest in practice, to David Piper and Jo Siffert, it wore through its sump under the loadings applied on the banking. After repair, the car held an initial second place but was retired after fifteen laps when the problem showed again.

The nemesis of the Lola T70 in open spyder form was announced to the press in the third week of August. Looking squat and purposeful the two orange McLaren M6A cars featured 5.8-litre engines with Lucas fuel injection on a crossover manifold with magneto ignition. Although the bonded and riveted magnesium and aluminium monocoque was state of the art, it was the design of the body's aerodynamics which really showed the attention to detail these cars had received. That, and the fact that they had already carried out an enormous amount of testing. Denny Hulme had lapped Goodwood at an average speed of 117.71mph, far quicker than the official lap record or any Formula One car of the period.

Meanwhile, Eric Broadley had been developing the Mark III spyder to bring it onto competitive terms with the McLaren M6A for the Can-Am series and he built four lightweight versions for Team Surtees, Roger Penske (for Mark Donohue) and Dan Gurney's All-American Racing Team. These cars were called IIIb roadsters but had nothing in common with the IIIb coupés which were to follow for 1969.

The car featured a tub with heavily drilled bulkheads which was 100lbs lighter than the Mark III spyder. Its suspension was redesigned to take 9 inch and 12 inch wide front and rear tyres respectively, but, due to all his other projects, Broadley had no time to test and develop the design.

The SCCA had run eight races in its 1967 USRRC series which had witnessed a Mark Dononue walkover in the Penske team T70 Mark III: he had won six out of seven races entered, was third in the seventh and set fastest lap and race records regularly. Imagine the shock of the competitors, then,

Parnelli Jones with the Bignotti-owned Mark III spyder in the 1967 Riverside Can-Am Race. The engine was a 4ohc Indianapolis Ford, first in 4.7 and later 5.0-litre capacity.

when Bruce McLaren and Denny Hulme were faster by ten seconds a lap in their McLaren M6As at the first Can-Am race at Road Atlanta!

Denny held fastest practice time until the last minutes of the final session when Bruce McLaren pipped him by one tenth of a second for pole position. John Surtees was seventh fastest after being timed at the fastest overall speed on the straight, but his Traco engine let go and he lost more time with gearchange problems. George Follmer qualified fourth with a small block Chevrolet fitted in the Lola in which Donohue had won the USRRC series. Follmer was in front of Mark Donohue who was running an aluminium 7-litre engine. Dan Gurney was third on the grid with SL75/122.

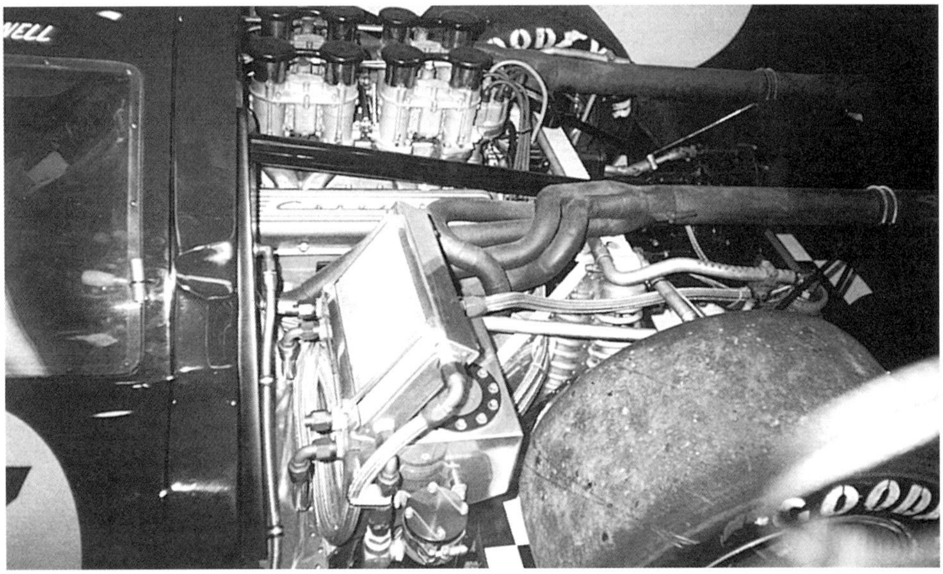

The engine compartment of SL75/124.

From the off it was Hulme all the way, with Bruce holding second until his car's oil system failed and the engine ran its bearings. Gurney pitted with numerous problems and Surtees was up into second place from Donohue. Such was the superiority of the McLarens that Denny lapped even the Chaparral 2G in fourth place, as did Surtees and Donohue. Five laps left and Surtees spun, avoiding a back marker, and Donohue nipped through the gap to take second place, twenty-five seconds ahead of 'Big John'.

It was a repeat showing two weeks later at Bridgehampton, except that this time, Bruce's car held together to give him second place to Denny. A lap later came

This was Peter Revson's 1967 Can-Am car. Rebodied as a coupé, it was raced in England before being sold in Holland. Sold again, it races in Group 4 events today.

The 5-litre Chevrolet - with Weber carburettors - of SL73/119.

George Follmer with John Surtees fourth. Neither Mark Donohue nor Dan Gurney finished, although Dan had been third in practice. Penske's mechanics had now fitted a small block Chevrolet engine to Donohue's car; it did little good, however, as it let go right in front of team mate, Follmer, in the race and caused him to spin!

Mosport Park was the next McLaren-dominated race, made even more impressive by the fact that McLaren's car was found to be suffering a leaking fuel bag on the formation grid. In thirty-five minutes his team had replaced it and, despite starting a minute behind the rest of the field, Bruce passed them all, including Dan Gurney in second place (who retired just before the end of the race with his Gurney-Weslake-Ford 351 engine losing oil and water). Denny's practice time, incidentally, was fully two seconds faster than that which Jim Clark had posted in qualifying for the recent Canadian Grand Prix!

The Penske team had a bad time. In practice Mark Donohue's car lost a wheel and crashed, bending the tub, whilst poor Follmer spun off after his car went 'light' at 150mph over the brow of a hill. Fortunately, George was unharmed. His mechanics performed a sterling job to ready the bent monocoque for the next day's race where Follmer brought the Mark III into sixth place. Donohue's Lola, although repaired, retired from the race itself, and John Surtees also withdrew with a misfiring engine.

George Follmer remembers his drives in T70s with affection: "I had two Mark IIs in 1966 and then went on to drive Mark III and IIIb spyders for Roger Penske in 1967 and later.

SL73/119. A spyder fitted with a coupé body.

They weren't bad at all; very good, in fact. They handled well, were very stable, didn't fly too easily (especially after we fitted even bigger spoilers!) and didn't scare you. I updated and improved mine to make it a very nice race car. I remember that I didn't think it was cheap, though! I recollect they cost around $15,000 but you could put one onto the grid for $25,000. In USRRC events you could win $6500 and $12,000 in Can-Am. It sure paid for Bruce McLaren, Denny Hulme and John Surtees to come over here!"

Laguna Seca on October 15th saw the Monterey Grand Prix run, and it was the first non-win by Hulme. He retired whilst in second place on lap eighty-one with camshaft failure. Dan Gurney led for the first seven laps but then retired with a blown engine. Jim Hall came in second to Bruce McLaren. The temperature in the shade reached eighty-eight degrees, playing havoc with cooling systems. The most interesting T70 development came with Parnelli Jones, whose mechanic, George Bignotti, had inserted an Indianapolis four-cam Ford V8 enlarged to five litres into his Mark III spyder. The car qualified fourth just behind Denny Hulme.

Jones closed up on the McLarens but then suffered fuel vaporisation in the ferocious heat and fell back to retire. John Surtees (now in an ordinary Mark III T70 as he had become fed up with the IIIb) and Lothar Motschenbacher (also Lola mounted), collided and retired, whilst Donohue's engine let go on lap seventy-four. George Follmer came in third.

Bruce won again at Riverside Raceway in the Los Angeles Times Grand Prix, but this time he had to work really hard as Jim Hall's Chaparral 2G finished just two seconds behind after the pair duelled furiously and alternated the lead for the last ten laps of the race. For once Dan Gurney got his Lola on pole position and it did look as if the McLarens were up against some serious competition. Parnelli Jones qualified equal fifth fastest with Peter Revson. Jones first of all kicked a tyre marker into the front of Denny Hulme's McLaren, putting that car out of contention, and then inherited the lead when Gurney's engine blew on lap three. Bruce McLaren then overtook Jones for the lead until Hall moved up to challenge Bruce on the tenth lap. By lap thirty-one, both the McLaren (exceeding its rev limit) and the Chaparral had lapped John Surtees. Also lapped were Mark Donohue and Parnelli Jones, in third and fourth places respectively.

John Surtees won the last race of the series, the Stardust Grand Prix, held, once again, in Las Vegas. Mark Donohue ran out of fuel when leading at the last turn and Surtees, driving the same car that he had used the previous year, finished a delighted winner in that race and third in the series.

The competition was getting tougher for the McLarens, although it was too late to stop Bruce being first in the series with Denny second. In practice, Denny couldn't better fifth fastest, alongside Peter Revson, and John Surtees and Mark Donohue were in the next two rows. Bruce McLaren was on pole with Jim Hall alongside. Two T70s were on the second row, both Ford-engined. Gurney was faster than Jones by one tenth of a second.

Parnelli Jones jumped the start but his gearshift failed on lap four and he was out. At the end of the first lap eight cars were out in a big mêlée. Hulme stopped to change a punctured tyre and Bruce McLaren retired with oil leaks. All this mayhem left Jim Hall in the lead with Dan Gurney second. Both were soon out, however: Hall with engine oil leaks and Gurney with a broken crankshaft damper. This left Mark Donohue in the lead and John Surtees second: Donohue had to drop back after losing the use of second and third gears. Denny Hulme had by now carved his way through what was left of the field to unlap himself, but he was fated not to finish as his engine let go after fifty-two laps.

In summary, 1967 saw the beginning of the 'Bruce and Denny Show', with John Surtees finishing third in the standings. The lack of development of the Mark IIIb when compared to the McLaren was evident, and it was a situation that continued as far as Can-Am racing went.

Bruce Burness, who was crew chief for George Follmer at this time, remembers: "Quite a few of the drivers preferred their previous Mark IIs to the later Mark III. George could definitely drive through some of the faster turns with more ease in his Mark II than the later car. My theory is that the Mark IIIs used double adjustable Koni dampers, whereas the Mark IIs used Armstrongs. I think the Armstrongs suited the car better, that's all I can think it was."

By September, S7L73/112 had been sent to Australia where it took part in a twelve-hour sports car race at Surfers Paradise raceway. Despite taking on huge amounts of oil and changing the brake discs, Hawkins and Epstein managed to bring the dark green coupé into second behind a Ferrari 275LM. Jackie Epstein then sold the car to Paul Hawkins who painted it bright red, won some club races and then shipped the car to South Africa for the Springbok series.

In the first race of that series, the *Rand Daily Mail* nine-hours at Kyalami held in November, Paul shared the car with John Love, a Rhodesian driver who had won the South African Formula One Driver's Championship for the past four seasons. Doug Serrurier and Jackie Pretorious were once again campaigning SL70/5, and Sid Taylor entered a roadster for Dave Charlton/Roy Pierpoint. Frank Gardner and Mike Spence drove SL73/102 and Mike de Udy and Hugh Dibley shared SL73/105.

Jackie Ickx and Brian Redman won overall in a Mirage coupé, but Hawkins and Love came second, thirteen laps behind, with niggling battery problems and a rough-sounding engine. All the other Lolas retired with a variety of problems.

Hawkins had his engine sounding right on December 3rd for a twenty lap sports car race at Kumalo, Rhodesia, and, after two laps, pulled away from the field, looking an easy winner. Alas, it was not to be. Hawkins pitted on lap ten when the oil pressure disappeared. It turned out that somebody had sabotaged his car as cotton wool was found in the oil tank.

Driving single-handedly for three hours Paul took the 5.9-litre-engined coupé - now converted to a dry sump lubrication system and with its engine woes cured - to victory in the Lourenco Marques race held on December 16th. Mike de Udy actually led at one point but retired after first a rocker arm broke and then a core plug blew out.

The last race of 1967 in the southern hemisphere was the December 26th Roy Hesketh three hours at Pietermaritzburg and the circus of competitors gathered again. Present for the Slough team were Paul Hawkins (driving solo) in his Lola, and Doug Serrurier/Jackie Pretorious in their Lola T70 Mark I spyder. The only real opposition to an outright win came from Ed Nelson and Mike Hailwood in one Ford GT40, and David Prophet in another. Rollo Fielding was down to drive the Drummond-entered Ferrari 275LM.

From the start the two Lolas battled for the lead for the duration of the race, the lighter weight of the roadster allowing it to keep up with the greater power put out by Hawkins' larger engine. With ten minutes to go the roadster took a decisive lead whilst poor Paul Hawkins' engine promptly put two conrods through the block! He was, however, classified second ahead of the Group 4 Ford GT40 of Edward Nelson and Mike Hailwood, even though they had passed Hawkins in the dying moments of the race.

Whatever befell the Lola drivers, they were looking forward to continuing the battle in the southern sunshine of 1968 ...

T70

7

RACING IN 1968

If 1967 is regarded as the development year for the T70 coupé, 1968 should have been the year it all came good. It did not, however,

F.I.A. Recognition No. 240

Group 4 Sports

ROYAL AUTOMOBILE CLUB

31, Belgrave Square, London, S.W.1

Form of recognition in accordance with appendix J to the International Sporting Code of the FEDERATION INTERNATIONALE DE L'AUTOMOBILE

Cylinder-capacity 4940 cm.³ 301.6 in.³

Manufacturer Lola Cars Limited — Model T.70 Mk III

Serial No. of chassis/body SL73/101 — Manufacturer Lola Cars Limited

Serial No. of engine RAF 8 — Manufacturer Chevrolet

Recognition is valid from 1st February 68 — List 68/2

The manufacturing of the model described in this recognition form started on 19th February 1967 and the minimum production of 50 (fifty) identical cars, in accordance with the specifications of this form was reached on 31st January 1968

Photograph A. ¾ view of car from front

F.I.A. Stamp

R.A.C. Stamp

First page of the homologation papers for the Mark IIIGT coupé. The car featured is the first Lola-Aston.

SL73/101 receiving attention at Silverstone in 1968. Jo Bonnier directs operations whilst standing by the driver's door. Note the NACA intake duct on the sill which was peculiar to this car.

and there were two main reasons …

Due to sheer pressure of work, Lola Cars itself never ran a works team. After the debacle of the Lola-Astons at Le Mans, John Surtees, Lola's most capable development driver, had turned away in disgust. In truth, there was just not enough money to make the programme work properly. The car was built to sell to the privateer racing teams and they, with their limited budgets, did as well as could be expected at a time when the works opposition comprised such powerful companies as Ferrari, Porsche and Ford, and professional rivals such as JWA Automotive.

Secondly, the Chevrolet V8s which powered the cars were not reliable in the long distance races for which the coupé was designed. They ran compression ratios up to 12.5:1 in order to develop their best horsepower and in their home country would have run on petrol with an octane rating of well over 100 RON (up to 116 RON on occasion). With this high-octane fuel, the racing versions of the engine, as built by Traco, Bartz, Ryan-Falconer, *etc.*, were perfectly happy. But put them on the best fuels in Europe and they could never live long. It is doubtful if the highest octane number reached in Europe at the time was 101 RON. Eric Broadley himself has recorded how nearly every engine he saw stripped down after a race showed signs of detonation.

Whatever, Hawkins' spare engine, a 4.9-litre unit, was put into his Lola for the first race of 1968, the January 6th meeting which was a two heat affair supporting the Formula One race at Killarney, near Capetown in South Africa. He used it to good effect to win both heats convincingly from the T70 roadster of Serrurier.

From the left: Denny Hulme, Ron Bennett, "Le Patron" Sid Taylor, Mo Nunn and Brian Vaner - a winning combination - with their first Mark III coupé, SL73/102. (Courtesy Ron Bennett).

Right, top: Sebring 12-Hours, 1968. Mike de Udy's Mark III, SL73/105, with its distinctive "periscope" cooler. He retired with miscellaneous problems.

Mike de Udy knocked off a water pipe in the first heat and suffered an oil pump scavenge failure in the second. A week later, using the highest gear the Hewland gearbox would accept, he went out and broke the South African land speed record, averaging 191.8mph over two runs.

At the last race in South Africa, de Udy broke down on the other side of the circuit to the pits so he walked back to his road car and promptly went to sleep! No-one else saw him and his mechanics spent an anxious hour walking the circuit trying to find him.

Back at home on January 12th, Mr. Peter Clarke wrote to *Autosport* pointing out that the T70 Mark III would become homologated in Group 4 on February 1st. "How, why, when, where and whodunnit?" he asked, and enquired if other readers were as curious as he to find out, since he was sure there weren't twenty-five Lola T70 coupés made. No replies were printed in the next issues. The real answer was that Jackie Epstein, as works manager at Lola, had called in as many customer's cars as possible, lined up all the tubs then in the works' possession, placed sets of bodywork at the far end of the line and walked the CSI representative quickly past the 'assembly line' after a very good lunch! Only in this way was the Lola T70 coupé accepted into the Group 4 category as Eric Broadley had always expected the spyder production to be taken into account by the sport's governing body. It's shock announcement at the end of 1967 that it would only homologate cars up to 5-litre capacity in batches of twenty-five had worried him a great deal, considering the investment he had made in the new coupés. Until then, only eleven Mark III coupés had been built.

The Lola racing action now switched to Florida where the Sebring Twelve Hours was run on March 23rd/24th and where no less than four T70s were entered. From Europe came the familiar light green SL73/105 of Mike de Udy/ Hugh Dibley, and Bonnier/Axelsson were entered in the ex-Team Surtees SL73/101. James Garner's AIR team put Scooter Patrick/David Jordan and Dick Gulstrand/Ed Leslie in SL73/117 and 131. Patrick and Jordan were the fastest Lola drivers in practice at 2.50:8, only 1.4 seconds slower than the pole-sitting works Porsche 907 of Hermann/Siffert. In the race itself this Lola reduced its lap time to 2.49:0 and led the pack for the first two hours until the steering broke. By the time Scooter Patrick collected tools from his pit and repaired the car, it had lost too much time and was out of contention. It later retired when a piston broke. The other three Lolas also suffered various problems and none finished. Poor Bonnier had the worst luck: it was discovered that the fuel he was using was contaminated, causing a persistent misfire and the car was retired.

April 7th and the BOAC 500 at Brands Hatch heralded the start of the World Championship for

Right, middle: Scooter Patrick driving hard in the early stages of the race in one of James Garner's Mark III coupés, SL73/131.

Right, bottom: Sebring 1968. With its distinctive twin cooling 'periscopes' on the roof, Mike de Udy hustles SL73/105 through a corner. Co-driving with Hugh Dibley, he retired with various problems after showing well. (Courtesy Autosport).

S
11

S
9
GOODYEAR

S
11
GOODYEAR

Brands Hatch, 1968. Ulf Norinder in SL73/132, the first of two T70 coupés that he owned.

Below: A Chevron B8 moves over as Bonnier's SL73/101 attempts to get by at Druid's Hairpin. Bonnier/Axelsson finished 6th in the 1968 BOAC 500 at Brands Hatch.

Prototypes and Sports Cars. Against strong works Porsche and Gulf-sponsored Ford GT40 opposition, three familiar Lolas were present. They were the Jo Bonnier car, he being partnered by Stan Axelsson for this race, Sid Taylor's SL73/102 driven by Dave Charlton and Craig Fisher, whilst Jackie Epstein had now bought the 'other' Lola-Aston SL73/121, (now Chevrolet powered) and was sharing the British racing green entry with Ed Nelson.

In practice, Ickx and Redman in the Gulf GT40 did 1:36.8, whilst the surprise third fastest on the first practice day was the Howmet turbine car driven by Dick Thompson. Jo Bonnier was the fastest of the Lolas at 1:38.4 (seventh fastest), whilst the new Ford F3 of McLaren/Spence qualified second fastest at 1:35.4 in the second session.

Charlton was the best placed in the early stages in Sid Taylor's car, holding sixth. It was not to last, however, as gear selection problems eventually forced the car's retirement, after it hit a bank. The new Ford retired after breaking a driveshaft doughnut whilst in the lead, but Bonnier and Axelsson drove a steady race throughout to finally finish sixth overall. Epstein and Nelson were eighteenth after having to refuel every half hour as one bag tank had split. Winners by twenty-three seconds over six hours of racing were Ickx and Redman in the GT40 over Scarfiotti and Mitter in a works Porsche. If only John Wyer had done a deal with Lola for T70s instead of GT40s!

Brian Redman scored a second victory in a week, this time at the wheel of Sid Taylor's repaired 102 at the Guards Spring cup, a one hour race held at Oulton Park on April 12th. From pole position, Brian lapped the field - including three GT40s - up to second place to cruise home and described his race as "A pleasant Sunday afternoon drive"!

Mike de Udy in the BOAC 500 at Brands Hatch in 1968.

Denny Hulme was in his place in the same car for the Group 4 race at Silverstone on April 27th and, after a tussle with Bonnier, romped away to victory again. Bonnier hung on tenaciously, though, and the leading pair lapped even third place man Paul Hawkins in a GT40, 'JoBo' breaking the lap record by four seconds!

Jackie Epstein and Eric Liddell did well to finish tenth at the Spa 1000km held on May 26th in a race dominated by Jacky Ickx driving the Gulf Ford GT40 to victory in the wet. Such was Ickx's mastery of his home circuit in the pouring rain that he finished the first lap over thirty seconds ahead of the second placed car.

August 17 1968 and Jo Bonnier fends off Mike de Udy (just) on his way to second place in the Speedworld International Trophy at Oulton Park. His car, SL73/101, is fitted with a red painted nose borrowed for this race after Pedro Rodriguez damaged the original at Karlskoga the week before.

Meanwhile, back at home, Sid Taylor, enjoying a drive in his own car for a change, finished second in a Formula Libre race held at Mallory Park and he won the special GT race at the same meeting whilst lopping 4 seconds off the GT lap record, something the Mark III Lolas seemed to make a speciality of! The same Lola came out again on June 3rd, this time driven by Denny Hulme, for the thirty-third RAC TT race held at Oulton Park over one hundred and ten laps, a distance of 303.6 miles. Sid qualified the car in the middle of the third row as Denny was returning from Indianapolis and, at the start Richard Attwood screamed away to lead in the Ford F3 whilst Denny ended the first lap seventh, still acclimatising himself to the Lola. On lap thirty-six, he took a lead he was not to lose except for one refuelling stop whilst Piper put Attwood into his Ferrari for the final stint. Richard Attwood quickly overtook Paul Hawkins for second place and Denny's lead stood at forty-five seconds with one hundred and one laps to go when he started having difficulty selecting gears. Attwood tried all he knew but the World Champion held him off to win by ten seconds at the finish. It was the third Sid Taylor/Denny Hulme/Ron Bennett TT team win in four years.

Sweden, Jo Bonnier's homeland, saw him a comfortable victor in a Group 4 race held at Anderstorp shortly thereafter, and Paul Hawkins took his red GT40 to a lead which lasted just six laps into the one hour race. That was

Denny does it again. Driving SL73/102, Denny Hulme wins the 1968 Tourist Trophy at Oulton Park.
(Courtesy Autosport).

1968. It's March in Florida and it's Sebring time. The Scooter Patrick/Ed Leslie Air Team's car which, after leading, having its steering damaged and repaired, finally retired with a blown piston.

One of Mike de Udy's Mark IIIGT coupés photographed in 1968.

when Bonnier shouldered by in his faster car. Paul finished second ahead of Stan Axelsson driving Sid Taylor's car, hired for this race. Ulf Norinder had a good dice with Eric Liddell in another GT40 until that car retired when its fuel tank split.

June 24th at Mallory Park, and Frank Gardner in Sid Taylor's well known car won the Guards International Trophy for Group 4 cars. He had to work hard, though, to overtake Paul Hawkins in his continually uprated GT40 and then go on to win.

The Watkins Glen six hour race saw four works Porsche 908s entered but three retired and the best the remaining one, in the hands of Hans Hermann and Tetsu Ikuzawa, could manage was sixth. Ickx and Bianchi won in a JW GT40, from David Hobbs and Paul Hawkins in a similar car. The only Lola entered was Bonnier's (shared

1968. May, and Sid Taylor swings down through the Devil's Elbow at Mallory Park in SL73/102 on his way to another victory.

Another photograph of Jo Bonnier in SL73/101 at Oulton Park in 1968. Mike de Udy is right behind him.

with Axelsson) and it finished tenth after holding fourth at the halfway mark.

John Woolfe bought SL73/102 from Sid Taylor and took it to the Vila Real road race in Portugal where it arrived with only three of its five gears intact after a race at the Norisring, a testimony to 5.5-litres of Chevrolet torque. This was a real 'Road Race' in the classic sense, through villages, over bridges and out on the local main roads. From the start Mike de Udy, with his distinctive twin 'periscope' cockpit cooling ducts on the roof, led throughout the twenty-five lap race, finishing one minute and eleven seconds ahead of David Piper, with Paul Hawkins third in his GT40.

That fast German circuit, Hockenheim, saw the International Solituderennen run on July 21st. Bonnier again competed, finishing fourth behind Paul Hawkins' GT40 after a late pit stop. David Piper took his glorious-looking and sounding Ferrari P4 to victory.

Sid Taylor now had another Mark III built up at his team headquarters. This was to be SL73/134 and it was entered for Denny Hulme to drive in the Martini 300 at Silverstone. This Lola, only completed the day before the race, qualified for pole position at 1:29.2. Mike de Udy's Lola was not handling well and could only manage 1:31.6,

1968. Jo Bonnier looks on from the right rear of SL73/101 as his mechanics grapple with a misfire at Sebring. The problem turned out to be water in the fuel and Bonnier retired in disgust.

A Mark III, SL73/ 113 today. Originally a spyder, this car featured a B.R.M. V12 engine fitted in 1969. It was re-bodied and owned and driven then by Max Wilson. Today, it is driven by Brian Redman in American historic races.

whilst Jo Bonnier's yellow car (SL73/101), now fitted with fuel injection, missed official practice as the injection was playing up and he had to start from the back of the grid with a ten second penalty. Hobbs, sharing Epstein's T70 (SL73/121) posted 1:33.4 to start from the second row. In the race itself, he was T-boned by Ron Fry's GT40 and the car went back to the factory for repairs to the monocoque.

From the start, Denny got involved in a tremendous dice with the Ford holding the lead. On lap thirty-five Denny spun under braking for Beckets and carried on unharmed, but Gardner was now fifteen-plus seconds ahead. Then the Ford's oil pressure sagged, Frank parked the car and Denny cruised home to victory, having lapped the field twice! Behind them, Bonnier had finally got his car going well and was lapping like the wind to try and catch up but, on lap twelve, the fuel pressure played up again and he was forced to retire some laps later. Mike de Udy held third until the distributor points broke on lap twenty-two and he pulled off to retire, leaving Paul Hawkins to claim second in his trusty GT40.

Poor Mike de Udy crashed 105 at Crystal Palace on August 4th after sliding off on oil and rain, deranging the left front suspension and tub. Remarkably, he did not wear a seatbelt and was lucky to be unhurt, although he did leave the imprint of his crash helmet on the windscreen!

Mike promptly bought the ex-Hawkins, ex-Epstein SL73/112 and scored victory straightaway in the sports car race at Oulton Park on

The Jackie Epstein/Eric Liddel Mark III, SL73/121, the ex-Surtees Lola-Aston now with Alan Smith Chevrolet power as it hustles along in the wet in a very rainy Spa-Francorchamps 1000 Kilometre race. The car went on to finish in tenth place overall.

1968. This is how to wave at the crowd in style! Ulf Norinder in SL73/132 on his cooling down lap after the Guard's International Trophy in which he placed second.

August 19th after a race-long duel with Jo Bonnier. Bonnier's car was fitted with a spare red painted nose after Pedro Rodriguez had had an 'off' in Sweden at the previous race and he shot into an immediate lead. However, Mike led at the end of lap two and had already put 8.5 seconds on Paul Hawkins, on this occasion driving Ulf Norinder's Lola to third place ahead of Ed Nelson in a GT40 who was delayed by a door refusing to close properly.

Sid Taylor's new Lola was the victor at the Guards International Trophy race held at Brands Hatch on September 2nd when it was driven by Frank Gardner. This was the deciding round of the RAC Sports Car Championship, and no less than six Lola T70 GT coupés

SL73/101, Jo Bonnier driving, during the Player's Trophy, Silverstone in 1968. Bonnier went on to finish second.

were there. What a sight and sound they must have made! Present were: Gardner in SL73/134; Ulf Norinder in SL73/132; John Woolfe in SL73/102; David Prophet in SL73/101 (fuel injected); Mike de Udy in SL73/112 and David Hobbs in SL73/121. Opposing them were five GT40s and two Ferrari 275LMs. And this was just a national race!

Bill Bradley in a 2-litre Porsche actually won the championship as he was ahead on points in his class. Paul Hawkins, the only driver capable of beating him, suffered a puncture near the end and slipped down the running order in his red GT40. Mike de Udy and John Woolfe missed practice due to engine bothers and started from the back of the grid, as did Ron Fry in his GT40. Gardner led the fifty lap race from start to finish, challenged only by the Chris Craft Chevron and the Paul Hawkins Ford, but John Woolfe retired on lap two with clutch failure and David Prophet pitted continuously with misfiring problems. At the end it was Norinder in second place after an excellent drive, whilst de Udy, who had passed him at one point, spun off and damaged the sump so had to retire. David Hobbs had started on wet tyres and stopped to change them which dropped him out of contention completely and he finished twenty-first.

Jo Bonnier and Mike de Udy met again on September 15th at Zeltweg, Austria, for the Austrian Grand Prix, though this time they were outclassed for final victory, facing the might of the Porsche works team. Bonnier's Lola was under-geared in practice but he still managed a position on the inside of the second row, whilst Mike de Udy's oil pressure failed after qualifying on the third row. After fifteen laps, Bonnier was in third place with Paul Hawkins pressing hard in the GT40, but, shortly after halfway, Bonnier retired as his fuel tank had split. De Udy's Lola retired on the first lap as the oil pump drive sheared yet again. The Porsches were first and second.

Le Mans was held in September that year, due to the student unrest in the summer, and Epstein and Nelson were entered in SL73/121, now freshly rebuilt after its Martini shunt, and carrying a set of deep purple body panels. There was so little for the mechanics to do that they cut out a large tinplate key and placed it on the roof of the car. Just before the start, Epstein, to the huge delight of the crowd, pretended to 'wind up' the car. They lasted until the seventeenth hour when the coupé ran out of gears and retired. This was a lot longer than Ulf Norinder's car, which ran out of petrol early in the race and was disqualified.

Norinder and his car featured again on October 13th at the Paris 1000km at Montlhéry, where he and Jean Michel Giorgi had the only two Lolas entered. Seventeenth place at the end of the first lap was the best Giorgi could do, whilst Robin Widdows, co-driving with Norinder, was in trouble with gear selection from the start, losing several laps before making it back to the pits for attention. After this he drove well until an oil line burst, covering the left hand rear wheel with oil and sending the big car spinning down the track at near maximum speed. The car finally stopped with a crumpled rear and was retired. The other Lola's gearbox oil disappeared when a bolt fell out of the casing!

The story of the Can-Am series in 1968, as far as Lola T70s is concerned, is easily told. By now, McLaren had achieved almost total dominance, bringing out the M8A and winning the first race in the customary one-two, with Denny beating Bruce. Surprise of the opening meeting at Elkhart Lake, however, was a Lola T70. Driven by Mario Andretti, this was the same Mark III that Parnelli Jones had campaigned in 1967, still featuring the Indianapolis four camshaft Ford V8, now bored out to five litres. It held third place for most of the race before the engine expired.

Carl Haas, the Lola importer, entered a new car for Chuck Parsons, a 7-litre T160 which featured a much lighter and stronger tub than the Mark III T70. It retired in the race and the first Lola home was in eleventh place.

Eighth on the grid was Mario at the next race at Bridgehampton. By now, John Surtees had joined in with a T160 fitted with a Weslake-headed aluminium 7-litre engine and with an aerofoil acting on the hub carriers. He started in tenth position. A McLaren still won, this one driven by Mark Donohue after Bruce and Denny had retired, but a T160, driven by Swede Savage and with 'only' five litres, did manage fourth place in a race of severe attrition. Surtees retired with broken pushrods.

At Edmonton, for the Klondike Trail 200, the Lolas were not in the picture. Denny and Bruce finished in their usual one-two, but surprise victor at Laguna Seca was John Cannon in an elderly McLaren M1C. In a race dominated by torrential rain, he proved to have the best wet weather equipment and won by over a lap from Denny Hulme. Skip Scott in a T160, in seventh place, was the best placed Lola.

It was back to the same misery for Lola at Riverside: best finisher was Chuck Parsons in eleventh, although Sam Posey went well in a

Scooter Patrick at the Sebring 12 hour race in 1968. He led the race until put out with damaged steering.

much lightened T160 until his engine ingested the wire mesh over the intake stacks. Surtees did run as high as fifth place until the water pump pulley became detached.

Final race was, as usual, the Stardust Grand Prix at Las Vegas, and Denny took his McLaren to a win and victory again in the championship. Behind him, though, there had been a tremendous pile-up on the first lap, through which came Andretti in the good old T70. The moment, however, was short lived: he suffered a puncture and retired when it was discovered a fuel line had chafed through. Surprise second place was George Follmer in one of Roger Penske's old T70 Mark IIIbs.

The European sports car drivers arrived for the Springbok series in South Africa and Rhodesia and it commenced as usual with the Kyalami nine-hours. Jackie Epstein had taken 121 with co-driver Dave Charlton, whilst Doug Serrurier and Jackie Pretorius entered their old Mark I spyder (which was later converted to a formula 5000 car). They faced a mixed bag of cars including the 5.7-litre JW Mirage Ford for Jackie Ickx and David Hobbs, and two Ferrari P3/4s; one entered by David Piper, who had won the event no less than five times previously. Also competing was the ex-Can-Am Open Group 7 Ferrari for Paul Hawkins and South African champion John Love. The first Lola home was that of Mike de Udy and Frank Gardner in SL73/112 in fifth place.

In the next race, the Capetown three-hours, Jackie Pretorious in the open Lola T70 was first away but Hawkins went by on the second lap. Pretorious held on but the Lola then burst a brake pipe and crashed on lap six. De Udy started third, had a puncture and a slight 'off' but finished 7th (and won his class) with Epstein's 121 running steadily to take eighth place.

Mike de Udy next scored an outright victory at the Rhodesia Grand Prix at Bulawayo in the fifteen lap event, beating Hawkins who oiled a plug on the line. Mike also claimed a sports car lap record. In the twenty-five lap event held earlier, Hawkins had won easily in the big Ferrari. Only one week elapsed until they were at it again. This time the venue was in Mozambique for another three hour race and Mike led after his crew had rebuilt the 6-litre engine and changed the differential. Unfortunately, he retired after twenty-three laps with a suspected broken piston leaving Mike Hailwood and Malcolm Guthrie to win in the Mirage. In this series, incidentally, it seemed that anything which could roll could enter; such diverse machines as three Renault Gordinis and even Volvos took part.

The last race of 1968 was at Pietermaritzburg over another three hour time distance and Mike de Udy led from Paul Hawkins at the end of lap three but was demoted to fourth after a spin on lap twelve. He slowed thereafter with brake problems but, after hitting a backmarker, really got into his stride and lapped faster than anybody else as rain started to fall. At 4.20pm Mike's right front wheel came off and, although his mechanics went out and fitted another, the tyre was wrong and the car retired next time around. Doug Serrurier's Mark I only lasted five laps as a conrod then exited the block and 'Hawkeye' won yet again in the Group 7 Ferrari, although there was contention over the lap scoring system. According to some, David Piper actually won!

The end of 1968 saw the end of T70 Mark III production. The new Mark IIIb coupé was about to be introduced for 1969. The works sold off all its spare Mark III parts to Franco Sbarro of Switzerland who built several exotic 'road burners' in the coming years.

Note: The T160 was jointly developed with the T70 Mark IIIb: you'll find the story of the T160 in chapter 11.

8

1969: THE LOLA T70 MK IIIB COUPÉ

With the Mark III coupé homologated into Group 4, Eric Broadley developed the Mark IIIb coupé for the 1969 season. His reasons were simple: he now knew that he could raise the torsional stiffness of the monocoque tub, lighten the whole car, and give better controlled suspension movement in a completely new package.

Although the car that resulted, the IIIb coupé, looked similar to a Mark III (except the four headlight nose), under this beautiful skin, all had changed. The new all-alloy monocoque bore more resemblance to the T160 (see chapter 11), the 1968 works Can-Am car, than the old Mark III. Bonded and riveted, it employed two detachable magnesium castings behind the cockpit area to assist in changing the engine and gearbox unit. Only the left hand sill unit now contained the fuel, although some teams used a double filler system which was, for want of a better description, a 'bolt-on goody'. Thus, thirty-two gallons of fuel could be delivered to the engine via twin Bendix electrical pumps. Above these pumps, situated behind the cockpit unit on the left, was the oil cooler for the gearbox, whilst a similar cooler, mounted on the opposite side above the large oil tank for the dry sump lubrication system, cooled the engine oil.

With torsional rigidity now up to five thousand pounds feet per degree, this new T70 (or T76 as its drawings and chassis number prefix made it) could now make use of the T142 running gear which it featured. (The T142 was the contemporary F5000 car). New cast magnesium uprights were held in Eric Broadley's twin wishbone suspension system, with self-aligning roller and ball joints at the front, whilst the rear suspension employed a reversed bottom wishbone, top link and top and bottom radius rods, the bottom pair located on the engine mountings. The steering rack was, once again, a BMC part from an 1100, but great care had been taken to ensure that bump steer could be adjusted minutely.

Brakes were radially-ventilated 12in by 1.1in, mounted on light alloy bells with four pot aluminium full-area long-distance pads fitted. The radiator was mounted at the front of the car, with the top canted forward, and an air box channelled the cooling air from the elongated slot in the nose section. Alongside this box on each side ran brake cooling hoses which linked up to aluminium castings attached to the uprights to aid brake cooling. At the rear, this air was ducted in through intakes in the top of the rear bodywork, allowing the air to pass down alloy 'periscopes' to the brake discs.

The car's bodywork was the first to make use of carbon fibre strengthening strips which were laid in a 'grid' fashion inside the nose and tail sections, helping to keep them lighter and stronger than the Mark III units. The rear bodywork

The specification sheet for the Traco 304 cu. in. Chevrolet V8 fitted to many IIIb coupés.

LOLA

SLOUGH 27341

LOLA CARS LTD · 839 YEOVIL ROAD · TRADING ESTATE · SLOUGH · BUCKS

TRACO 302 5 LITRE CHEVROLET ENGINE

GENERAL SPECIFICATIONS:

ENGINE MAKE:	Chevrolet
Bore:	4"
Stroke	3"
Maximum engine speed:	7,500
Oil Pressure:	Min. 40 -- Max. 80
Type and/or grade of oil:	Mineral 40 or 50 Weight
Recommended filter element:	Paper
Recommended Spark Plug:	Champion J 83 Y J 86 Y [illegible]

CRANKSHAFT AND CONNECTING ROD TORQUE SPECIFICATIONS	FT LBS.
Standard Chevrolet connecting rod bearing cap bolts ⅜"	45
Billet steel connecting rod bearing cap bolts (Warren)	65
Crankshaft bearing cap bolts (No. 1 - 5)	60
4-Bolt main bearing cap side bolts only (⅜ Allen Bolt)	45
CYLINDER HEADS:	
Cylinder head to block bolts	65
FLYWHEEL:	
Flywheel to crankshaft bolts	60

BEARINGS:	Std	.001	.002	.010
Standard Main Bearings No.	3912038	3912039	3912040	3912041
Standard Rear Main Bearing	3912030	3912032	3912033	3912035
Standard Connecting Rod Bearing	3910555	3910556	3910557	3910558

CLEARANCES:

Connecting rod bearing clearances	.002 to .003	
Connecting rod bearing side clearance	.014 to .025	
Crankshaft end play	.002 to .006	
Crankshaft main bearing journal clearance	.002 to .0035	
Camshaft end play (roller cam only - with front cover and water pump in place.)	.005	
Top compression piston ring end gap. (Ramco)	-020	-030"
Second piston ring end gap	-020	-030"
Top compression ring clearance in groove (side clearance)	.003 to .005"	

TAPPET SETTINGS:	INTAKE	EXHAUST
Roller Cam no. 251	.012" Hot	.014" Hot
Flat Tappet No. 3927140	.022"	.024"

FIRING ORDER : 1--8--4--3--6--5--7--2

SPRING HEIGHTS:

Roller Cam: Approximate spring height 1.750 -- New Springs 145 lbs - 155 lbs on seat cam lift on valve plus .060 min., before coil bind. Used springs 130 lbs - 140 lbs on seat, same coil bind, max. of .090 shim under spring.

Flat Tappet: Approximate spring height 1.800 -- New springs 125 lbs - 135 lbs on seat cam lift on valve plus .060 min before coil bind. Used springs same as new, Max. .090 shim under spring.

was wider than that of a Mark III, to accommodate ever-growing tyre widths; wheel width options were 8 or 10.5in at the front, 10, 14 or 17in at the rear. Track varied between 54in and 57in depending on the wheels and tyres fitted, but the wheelbase remained the same as a Mark III at 95 inches.

The doors were now forward hinged, it being felt that this was safer for emergency driver exit and also to prevent loss of the doors at speed which had happened on occasion with the gullwing type of the Mark III.

The nose section was completely altered, being brought down much nearer to the ground to provide extra downforce. The opportunity was also taken to add another pair of headlamps behind longer perspex covers. In effect, the bottom lip of the radiator intake now became a splitter, forcing air away from the flat underside of the car.

At the rear, adjustable trim tabs were fitted to provide the same aerodynamic trimming as on the previous Mark III coupé. The cockpit section had the familiar bonded windscreen and a roll-hoop behind the driver's head. Weight was now down to 860 kilogrammes but the factory stated that re-homologation would be sought at 800 kilogrammes. The standard (!) engine offered was a Traco-modified Chevrolet V8 of 304 cubic inches (5-litres) breathing through four 48mm downdraught Weber

SL76/138, the second Mark IIIb coupé made at the 1969 racing car show. The car - already painted in Sid Taylor's colours - was to be driven by some of the best drivers of the day. Inset: David Piper.

David Piper, that doyen of racing car drivers, bought a Mark IIIb coupé, SL76/150, in 1969 and describes it thus: "The Lola T70 was such good value as a long distance sports racing coupé at that time. It was a big step forward in all areas over the Ford GT40 against which it was measured. The car was comfortable and easy to drive with no vices at all; it was very forgiving in the handling department, the steering being so light. That was unheard of in a car with such huge rim widths but, of course, Eric Broadley had been very clever in ensuring that the main width of the wheels was inset. This, no doubt, contributed to the feeling that so big a car could be made to feel so light.

Of course, the Achilles heel of the car was the iron heads on the Chevrolet engines; today that's all been cleared up. Indeed, the engine's now probably the most reliable part of the car! In summary: a cracking car, just terrific and, even today, people remark on just what a beautiful car it is".

Sid Taylor entered Lola T70s in both spyder and coupé form for such luminaries as Denny Hulme, Brian Redman and Frank Gardner. He remembered the T70 well: "One of the best cars ever made. Very simple and straightforward to run. It came out at the same time as the Lotus 40 and early McLarens and beat them easily. Of course, McLaren got his act together in the Can-Am from 1967 on and beat the Lolas but, 'till then, ...! The coupés were beautiful, too, just as easy and cheap to buy and maintain. We had the first car to lap Silverstone at 120mph and the first to lap Mallory Park at over 100mph. Great days."

LOLA TYPE 70 Mk.3b.GT. GROUP 4 (5 litre)

SEASON --- 1969

The Type 70 GT was homologated for Group 4 Racing in January 1968, and a new series of cars is under construction for 1969.

These cars incorporate detail modifications that have been found to improve their racing performance. Also various changes to improve accessability, maintenance and reliability.

The principal differences are:-

1. Availability of alternative wheels with 14" and 17" rim widths for the rear, and 11" and 12½" for the front. It being possible to fit these wheels on the 1969 model without body modification.

2. The fitting of cooling ducts to both front and rear brakes, found necessary because of shrouding by the wide rims.

3. Improvements to the brakes including full area thick pads for long distance running, as standard equipment, and "Redman" couplings on the brake bells to improve disc life.

4. The radiator and oil cooler ducting has been re-designed, resulting in greater radiator efficiency with reduced weight.

5. The luggage space has been re-located behind the rear wheel arches so that access over the engine is unrestricted, and there is space for a more efficient exhaust system.

6. The rear chassis hoop now incorporates a detachable cast Magnesium cross member.

7. The doors have been hinged to open forward, contrasting with the existing "gull wing" type, which in practice have been found difficult and slow in operation, particularly at Le Mans starts.

8. Engines will be equipped with dry sump lubrication.

9. The Hewland transaxle will have a new crown wheel and pinion to eliminate the odd failure encountered in the transmission.

10. Careful consideration has been given to the question of weight reduction, and the intention is to re-homologate the car at 800 kilos. when 25 have been built to this weight.

Both pages: The specification sheet for the Mark IIIb GT coupé.

LOLA TYPE 70 Mk.3b.GT. GROUP 4 (5litre)

SPECIFICATION

CHASSIS	Light alloy monocoque structure, bonded and riveted, providing a tortional rigidity of 5000 lbs.ft.per degree.
BODYWORK	Lightweight glassfibre panels, colour impregnated to choice. Front section quickly removeable by withdrawing four "pip pins", giving good access to front suspension, and cooling system. Tail section similarly removeable for access to engine, transmission, and suspension. Doors hinged to open forward. A roll-over bar is incorporated into the cockpit roof section. The laminated glass windshield is bonded in.
FRONT SUSPENSION	Independent with upper and lower wishbones on self-aligning roller bearings and ball joints. Koni shock absorbers, adjustable for bump and rebound, and co-axial springs.
REAR SUSPENSION	Independent with double wishbones and radius rods on self aligning roller bearings and ball joints. Koni shock absorbers adjustable for bump and re-bound, and co-axial springs.
STEERING	Rack and pinion with lightweight leather covered 11" diameter steering wheel.
BRAKES	Ventilated discs 12" x 1.1" mounted on light alloy bells with aluminium "4 pot" full area thick pad calipers.
ENGINE	"TRACO" built and tuned 304.6 cub.in. (5 litre) V-8 Chevrolet engine. Bore 4.020, stroke 3,000. Includes 4 bolt main bearing caps, fully counterbalanced crankshaft, light alloy flywheel, forged pistons, heavy duty connecting rods, ported, flowed, and polished cylinder heads, special valves, double valve springs, light alloy rockers on needle roller bearings, and high lift race camshaft with roller followers. Fitted with four Weber 48mm downdraft carburetters.

TRANSMISSION — Hewland LG 600-5 speed and reverse transaxle, supplied with the following ratios:-

	Gear	O/a Ratio
1st	24-50	6.87
2nd	28-47	5.54
3rd	31-43	4.58
4th	33-39	3.90
5th	37-38	3.39

A wide range of alternative ratios can be supplied, covering all possible circuits and conditions. The gear ratios can be changed individually by removing the back section of the casing and withdrawing the complete gearbox assembly, thus allowing the ratios to be changed easily and quickly.

CLUTCH	Borg and Beck 7¼" - 3 plate
DRIVE SHAFTS	Roller spline
FUEL SYSTEM	Flexible fuel cells incorporated into the monocoque structure. Large single filler arranged for rapid filling. A surge tank is mounted at the rear of the car, incorporating a non-return valve. Feed is by two Bendix electric fuel pumps.
COOLING SYSTEM	Water: Fully ducted radiator mounted at the front of the car. Oil: Two light alloy coolers, ducted and mounted on the centre bulkhead.
ELECTRICAL SYSTEM	Either a lightweight Varley dry battery or a larger capacity lead/acid battery for long distance racing. Lucas alternator mounted on the gearbox. Four headlights fitted into the body nose section, behind perspex fairings. Direction indicators, tail and brake lights etc. All necessary wiring built into a strong loom.
WHEELS	Cast magnesium 15" diameter - Front 8" Rear 10" rim widths. Alternative sizes available. Front 10½" Rear 14" or 17"
TRACK	Front: 57" with 8" rims; 54" with 10½" ". Rear: 57½" with 10" rims; 54" with 14" or 17" rims
WHEELBASE	95 inches.
WEIGHT	860 Kilos. 1930lbs. Including oil and water.

carburettors. Transmission was via the, now usual, Hewland LG600 5-speed and reverse gearbox fitted with a three plate Borg and Beck clutch. Large roller-spline driveshafts were employed to cope with the 480bhp the engine's builders claimed for it.

Twelve cars were laid down at the end of 1968; sixteen would eventually be delivered by the end of 1969.

SL76/139 was the first car actually delivered (to Roger Penske on 30th December 1968) whilst SL76/139 was shown, painted in Sid Taylor's colours, at the 1969 Racing Car Show where it received unanimous approval.

Lola T70

9

RACING IN 1969

The big news for 1969 as far as Lola racers were concerned was the new IIIb coupé. Until the advent of the Porsche 917 later in the season, there is little doubt it was the fastest big sports car around, but, with the exception of Roger Penske's racing team at Daytona and Sebring only, no team had the resources to compete against the might of Ferrari and Porsche in long-distance events. Still, Penske's efforts did show what might have been.

Speculation was rife at the beginning of 1969 as to what would be happening in Group 4 in the season.

Patrick McNally, writing in *Autosport*, commented that the current rumour in motor racing circles was that Paul Hawkins would be employed to drive a works-supported Lola T70. This did happen but, once again, there was not enough support, either financially or logistically, for Paul to overcome the bugbear of engine reliability problems.

1969 saw a good start for Paul. The final round of the Springbok Challenge in South Africa saw Mike de Udy's old faithful come out noseless for the race at East London: poor Mike had gone off the road in

Paul Hawkins in characteristic pose in SL76/142 at Snetterton for the Guards Trophy, 4th April 1969. He went on to overall victory. (Courtesy Autosport)

Mark Donohue with SL76/139 in the pits.

practice due to a puncture and, in an effort not to let the sponsors down, Mike's mechanics laboured to repair the car for the start. Mike actually led into the first corner but waved Hawkins and Piper past to hold third. After the unfortunate demise of Piper's Ferrari (burnt out before David could reach the pits after a collision with Hawkins) Paul cruised home first.

Various privateers, like Ulf Norinder, Mike de Udy and Jo Bonnier, showed the Lola to be very competitive in certain European medium-distance races, but it had yet to be proven a reliable long-distance runner. However, the Lola T70 Mark IIIb started its competition life in a blaze of glory. It won the Daytona 24-hours and showed what could be achieved with the right preparation.

Roger Penske ordered two cars and Mark Donohue and Roy Gaine picked up the first, SL76/139, on New Year's Day 1969. Two Traco-Chevrolet 305 engines on Lucas fuel injection had been ordered and the team spent the next three weeks installing the engine and gearbox and preparing the car, which included plumbing, making an exhaust system, painting, *etc*. Mark Donohue commented: "It was a monumental job. The team spent eighteen hour days continuously on the task. It was one of those 'We're gonna drag it out of the woods' type of things." The beautiful coupé was painted dark blue with gold lettering and was to be driven by Mark Donohue and Ronnie Bucknum.

For the race itself, Ulf Norinder entered his new IIIb (SL76/141) for himself and Jo Bonnier, as Jo's new car was not yet delivered. If Sid Taylor had come to terms with the organisers over travelling expenses, SL76/138, the Racing Car Show exhibit, would also have entered. James Garner's AIR Team entered two Mark III GTs driven by Scooter Patrick/Ed Leslie and Dave Jordan/ Lothar Motschenbacher (SL73/131 and 117). They were running wet sump engines on carburettors.

At 3pm under a cloudless blue sky, the race got underway and,

Brian Redman takes SL76/138 to victory in a two heat Group 4 and 6 race at the Norisring in 1969. (Courtesy Autosport).

Below: Daytona 24-Hours, 1969. One of James Garner's (far right) AIR T70s, SL73/117, in the pits.

from the start, Donohue held second behind the works Porsche of Siffert, with another Porsche, that of Elford, in third place. Donohue soon fell back with fuel pick-up problems and Bonnier and Norinder retired their car after two brushes with back markers and then the wall.

The two AIR Lolas held 9th and 10th places at the end of the first hour but Leslie then lost time with a broken throttle spring. Donohue, sharing the Lola with Chuck Parsons (a last minute driver change after Ronnie Bucknum broke his thumb in a motorbike accident), started moving back up when the works Porsches began encountering problems with splitting exhausts. At the two hundred lap stage Penske's Lola was fourth with the fuel consumption improving. The Patrick/Leslie Lola was holding eighth. Then, after two hundred

Ulf Norinder with his T70 coupé, SL76/141, at Sebring for the twelve hour race in 1969.

and forty laps the Penske Lola suffered a pit stop lasting an hour and nineteen minutes as the exhaust manifolds began to break up. This dropped it right down the field. Most people didn't believe they would last the distance anyway.

However, by three hundred and thirty laps the Penske car was up to seventh place with the Jordan/ Patrick Lola sixth and the Leslie/ Motschenbacher car eighth. The Sunoco IIIb was then elevated to third as the leading cars retired in the early morning. On lap four hundred and sixty-nine the remaining GT40 of Ickx broke part of its suspension and retired, leaving Donohue and Parsons in second place behind the sole surviving Porsche which went a further thirteen laps before retiring with an intermediate shaft failure, the same problem that had caused the other 908 retirements.

So, the Lola ran out a splendid winner, despite spending an inordinate amount of time in the pits. To cap it all, Lothar Motschenbacher and Ed Leslie brought one of the two Mark III GT coupés home in second, with Scooter Patrick and Dave Jordan coming home in seventh place with the sister car.

Still in Florida, the Sebring twelve hours was next on March 28th and the Daytona winning car was entered again for Donohue and Bucknum. This time, in the quest for reliability, it sported Weber carburettors instead of injection. This lowered the quoted horsepower by forty to four hundred and twenty-five. The weight was quoted at 917 kilogrammes. The car qualified just 0.78 of a second behind the pole sitting 312P Ferrari of Amon/ Andretti. The two AIR Mark IIIs were entered again, as was the Norinder/Bonnier IIIb coupé. Ranged against them were no less than six Porsche 908s and two JW Ford GT40s.

The flag was dropped by the Starter and, this time, Donohue swapped the lead in the opening laps with Siffert/Redman in their works 908. Scooter Patrick blew up the AIR Lola's engine after fifteen laps, whilst the Norinder/Bonnier Lola was retired after a radius rod pulled out of the monocoque. By the three hour mark the Penske Lola was leading the Amon/Andretti Ferrari 312P but, by 3.34, the Lola was a shock retirement with the same problem as the Norinder/ Bonnier car. The two Jackies, Ickx and Oliver, won the race in the Gulf-sponsored GT40, and the best Lola finish was Leslie/ Moschenbacher in sixth place.

Roger Penske had been going to contest all the big endurance races in Europe in 1969 but the Lola and its transporter were stolen from outside a truck stop on the way back to Pennsylvania. It was several weeks before Donohue, after offering a reward for information, was able to track down the thieves and retrieve the equipment. Unfortunately, by that time, the car had been so cannibalised that the Penske team gave it all up as a bad job. They turned 139 into a road car, complete with air-conditioning, and sold it. Mark Donohue reported that they kept getting calls from the customer in California wanting the mechanics to travel there to tune the engine for him!

Back in England, round one of the RAC Group 4 championship was held at a very wet Silverstone at the end of March and seven T70s were entered. They were: Chris Craft in a 1967 Techspeed-entered Mark III (SL73/134) who was quickest in practice at 1m 29.4, followed by Brian Redman in SL76/138, Sid Taylor's new acquisition. Ron Bennett remembered: "March 30. Silverstone. Brian lost a wheel in practice, I know there was a screech as he was coming into Woodcote, and it was one of those sessions where there weren't many people out. You can always hear a Chevy coming. Well, there was this screech ... the noise stopped and a cloud of

Jo Bonnier in SL76/143. Note the covered over headlights and the tube for carrying cooling air to the cockpit.

blue smoke came into sight! Then Redman trickled into the pits. 'I've lost a bloody wheel,' he says, 'it's trundling down the track!"

Team Elite had entered their Lola to be driven by Trevor Taylor (SL76/144), and Paul Hawkins had his new IIIb, SL76/142. Jo Bonnier (SL76/143) was on the second row with his IIIb alongside David Piper's new Lola (SL76/150), whilst the line-up was completed by Denny Hulme in John Woolfe's ex-Sid Taylor Mark III GT (SL73/102).

Rain fell as the race started and Trevor Taylor took an immediate lead, with Redman holding second and Hulme third. On lap five Taylor understeered into the bank at Copse and two laps later Hulme overtook Brian Redman who, thereafter, tried everything to get by. Matters resolved themselves on the last lap when the gearbox bung blew out of Hulme's Lola, covering Redman's screen in oil. Both cars slowed but maintained enough speed to finish ahead of Paul Hawkins' car with Chris Craft fourth and David Piper fifth with a leaking head gasket.

Paul Hawkins' Lola had had its first track testing at the Le Mans practice days and he had posted a very respectable time of 3:35.2, the third fastest. Ominously, it was the new Porsche 917 which had been fastest overall at 3:30.7, even though it had weaved its way down the Mulsanne straight at somewhere around 240mph! To achieve his time, Paul had used special 'longtail' bodywork which Eric Broadley had produced. Hawkins announced himself delighted with the result.

Round two of the RAC Group 4 Championship was at Snetterton on Good Friday. Brian Redman headed the first practice session but Bonnier equalled it in the second, thereby giving Brian pole position alongside Bonnier in the

A wet Silverstone with Brian Redman in Sid Taylor's new Mark IIIb coupé, SL76/138, ahead of Denny Hulme in Sid Taylor's second Mark III coupé, SL73/134.

Sid Taylor's Mark IIIb GT, SL73/134, pictured in 1969.

Ulf Norinder at the BOAC 500, Brands Hatch, in 1969. The car is SL76/141.

middle with Hawkins on the outside. At the start of the fifty lap race Hawkins swept into the lead immediately ahead of Redman, Bonnier and Attwood. By lap eight Hawkins had lapped all the smaller cars except for Charles Lucas in a Porsche 910 whilst, on lap eleven, Redman set a new record as he reeled in Hawkins. Four laps later they were together and fighting hard. Try as he might, Brian Redman could not get the better of Paul Hawkins and the battle had the crowds on their toes. On lap twenty-two Redman was through but he spun three laps later and Hawkins took back the lead which he held to the finish. Jo Bonnier was second, twenty seconds adrift, whilst the other Lolas all retired with sundry engine problems.

Next in the Championship was Thruxton on Easter Monday and, following so closely on the previous race, Chris Craft and Richard Attwood's cars were withdrawn as they could not be repaired in time. Ron Bennett well remembers arriving there. He and Sid were late: "I'm in the back of the transporter with Sid driving and I'm doing the carburettor balancing on the way down. It gets a bit fumey in there! It was the old Dan Gurney transporter we used, you couldn't open the

Silverstone, March 30 1969 and Denny Hulme, in SL73/102, just pips Brian Redman driving Sid Taylor's SL76/138 for the first time. The occasion was the first round of the RAC Group 4 Championship.

tailgate on the move. We got to the track and, of course, it was closed 'cos everybody was going round, we were that late. Well, the guy's there with the flag and he says 'there'll be a gap in a minute, get ready!' and he waved his flag and we drove across into the paddock and the crowd were cheering like mad 'cos the announcer had said 'the stars are here!"

This time Redman took pole ahead of Bonnier, with Taylor, Hawkins and Gardner following. At the start Bonnier elbowed the big Lola into the lead ahead of Redman, Gardner and Hawkins. Gardner's clutch went over centre and he lost all his gears, whilst Redman outbraked Bonnier into the chicane. So hot was the pace that Hawkins was lapped on the penultimate lap!

For the BOAC 500 race at Brands Hatch, all the new IIIb coupés turned out, including the very latest, Jo Bonnier sharing the Scuderia Filipinetti car (SL76/145) with Herbert Muller. Ulf Norinder shared his new IIIb with Robin Widdows, Paul Hawkins shared 142 with Jonathan Williams and David Piper and Roy Pierpoint drove SL76/

In line ahead formation, no less than five Mark IIIb coupés exit Thruxton's complex with Bonnier leading Redman and Hawkins.

BOAC 500, Brands Hatch 1969. Paul Hawkins in SL76/142 leads another Mark IIIb coupé whilst one of the Gulf Mirages tucks in. (Courtesy Autosport).

150. Two Mark IIIs were entered; the Techspeed car of Chris Craft/ Eric Liddell, and the ex-de Udy car for David Prophet/Ed Nelson.

Fastest Lola in practice was the Filipinetti car for Bonnier/Muller, this being third behind a 908 Porsche and the Amon/Rodriguez Ferrari 312P. Disquieting cracks in the rear damper mountings were found on both Hawkins' and Sid Taylor's cars, and these were reinforced.

From the start, Bonnier held third behind the Porsche and Ferrari until he had to pit after a water pump drivebelt became detached. Thereafter, the Lolas suffered a stream of troubles including punctures, oil leaks, *etc.*, but Hawkins was sixth at the two hour mark, with Craft seventh. Ulf Norinder's car broke a rear wishbone and the mechanics set about repairing it.

At the halfway mark Sid Taylor replaced Revson with Denny Hulme

Embassy Trophy race, Thruxton in April 1969 and Bonnier in SL76/143 is chased by the eventual winner, Brian Redman in SL76/138.

Jo Bonnier, hotly pursued by a GT40, takes the new SL76/145 of the Scuderia Filipinetti through a bend during the BOAC 500 at Brands Hatch in 1969. Later on he lost control and wrote off the car. He was lucky to emerge unscathed ...

Below: The Mark IIIb coupé of Trevor Taylor, SL76/144, during the BOAC 500 of 1969 at Brands Hatch.

but then attention shifted to Jonathan Williams, driving Hawkins' car. A rear wishbone snapped as he was flat out in fifth gear through Pilgrims Drop. By a miracle the Lola missed everything after an enormous double spin but was retired at the pits. By now the GT40 of Hobbs/Hailwood had a lead it was not to lose, but the final Lola drama took place when

Jo Bonnier in SL76/145, the Scuderia Filipinetti car, at the BOAC 500 at Brands Hatch.

Bonnier, who had been really pressing on whilst at the tail of the field, ran wide through bottom bend and launched himself at some 100mph along the Armco. Bonnier was fortunate to emerge relatively unscathed, but Eric Broadley immediately asked the team managers of the remaining IIIbs to bring their cars in for inspection. Norinder carried on but Taylor and Piper both retired when their rear wishbones proved to have hairline cracks. Norinder finished twenty-first, whilst the older Mark III of Craft and Liddell was eighth.

At Monza for the 1000 kilometre race, the big attraction for the partisan crowd was Mario Andretti paired with Chris Amon in a Ferrari 312P. T70s entered were David Piper's car, shared with Paul Hawkins, Jo Bonnier's personal T70 (SL76/143), shared with Herbert Muller after wrecking the Filipinetti car, and Ulf Norinder's car, shared with Robin Widdows. Frank Gardner was sharing Sid Taylor's car with Andrea de Adamich. Ron Bennett recalled the race: "Old Frank [Gardner], he's got a dry wit: he only ever thanked me once ... We were at Monza in 1969 and he had a bit of a coming together with an Alpine on the last lap. That was when we used the banking, and Frank, in qualifying, went round and round: he wouldn't let de Adamich in. Well, near the end he had to, of course, to let the guy qualify with half a dozen laps but while he was out, Frank said 'I kept him out as long as I could, Ron. You know what Eyeties are like in bloody Italy, they think God's watching them!' De Adamich came in, as on the banking a big piece had come out of the right front tyre and it frightened the life out of him!

"That IIIb coupé was funny, 'cos that was the first time out on a really quick circuit at Monza and Frank came in, he says 'Jesus, what a beast, I can't hold it straight - it's jumping all over the road, I'm really having to drive it down the straight.' We went back and checked the toe steer, ride height, tracking, angles, everything. Everything was alright. 'There's something funny,' he says. So we looked again and, on a IIIb, there's a sort of half-spoiler on the side of the tail. Frank says 'It must be air spilling off the brake cooling ducts and hitting that.' So I put aluminium plates inside and cut the side spoiler off and taped it over. Frank went out and he comes back and says 'You wouldn't believe it, you can drive it down the straight with just your finger and thumb on the wheel now, it never moves: just keep quiet and say nothing to the other teams.' That was it, after that it was good everywhere we went. Frank was timed at 196mph on the straight but Frank said it ran into a brick wall then. He said you could fly by most cars in the corners but whilst he stayed at constant top speed, some of the other cars would inexorably close up!"

All the IIIbs had boxed-in rear wishbones and stronger damper brackets. Two Mark IIIs, Craft/Liddell and Troberg's car, were entered, but Troberg's transporter was delayed for fourteen hours by a wreck in the Simplon Tunnel.

Forty thousand spectators turned out on race day to see Andretti make a demon start in the Ferrari 312. At the end of the first

June 1 1969. Jo Bonnier takes SL76/143 away at the start of the Nürburgring 1000 kilometres ahead of a GT40 and a Porsche 917.

lap Craft and Piper were tenth and eleventh, Robin Widdows and Frank Gardner both pitted after tangling with one another and Bonnier stopped briefly with overheating problems. By twenty laps David Piper's Lola was leading the Group 4 class in eighth place overall but retired later when a front wheel bearing broke. Bonnier also retired due to head gasket failure with twenty laps to go. The T70s of Craft/Liddell and Norinder/Widdows both went out with crownwheel and pinion failure, but Frank Gardner, in sorting out an enormous 'moment' on the last lap, just failed to catch the fourth placed GT40 by 1.20 seconds. The Group 4 category went to Kelleners/Joest in the Ford.

Jo Bonnier and Herbert Muller - with SL76/151, the brand new Filipinetti car built to replace the car Bonnier had wrecked at Brands Hatch - were the only T70 entrants

Brian Redman in SL76/138 leads Jo Bonnier in SL76/143.

Paul Hawkins in SL76/142 in the Spa 1000kms in 1969. The car led from pole position until its engine failed toward the end of the race.

in the Targa Florio in Sicily on May 4th. Although Herbert Muller was delayed with ignition problems at the start, he fairly rocketed around the twisty course on the first lap, passing no less than sixty cars! He was then unfortunate enough to collect a puncture and limped around to the pits to change the wheel. Bonnier took over but suffered a huge 'moment' whilst reputedly doing two hundred and four miles per hour on the seven kilometre straight. 'Handling disorders' was put down as the reason for retirement ...

By now the international season was in full swing and the daunting Spa Francorchamps circuit in Belgium next on the agenda on May 11th. Three T70 Mark IIIbs were entered: Paul Hawkins/David Prophet in SL76/142; SL76/151, the Scuderia Filipinetti car, for Bonnier and Muller; and SL76/148 for Picko Troberg and Bjorn Rothstein.

The new Porsche 917 was fastest in wet practice, in 3:41.9, with Hawkins second at 3:42.5, "throwing the big Lola around with gay abandon" (*Autosport*). Bonnier missed most of practice with a defective coil, but when they got down to it the Swede/Swiss partnership earned themselves a place on the second row lapping only 1.10 seconds slower than the best Ferrari time. Bjorn Rothstein, who had raced nothing larger than a Mini before this, posted a very creditable 4min. 18sec. on a soaking track.

Hawkins made a tremendous start and led the field at the end of the first lap with Bonnier fifth and Rothstein ninth. Second time around, Siffert in the Porsche 908

With the VDS Team Alfa Tipo 33 keeping clear, Paul Hawkins sweeps past in SL76/142. In the 1969 Spa-Francorchamps 1000kms, after leading at the start, the car's engine failed when it was lying 4th. Hawkins shared the drive with David Prophet.

caught up sharply to Paul but Bonnier was past Ickx in the Gulf Mirage to claim fourth whilst Rothstein was now seventh! By lap three Hawkins was demoted to third by Siffert, and Rodriguez and Bonnier back to fifth by Elford's 908. The 917 driven by Gerhard Mitter had been retired with an over-revved engine at the end of the first lap.

In the next few laps, the leading trio pulled well away from the rest as Bonnier lost six places due to an over filling of engine oil, whilst Rothstein was all over Ickx trying to take fifth place. After Rodriguez clipped a back marker in the Ferrari, Hawkins moved up to second place. He offered no challenge to Siffert until the leader pitted for fuel and

Brian Redman in SL76/138 chases Jo Bonnier in SL76/143 in the second of two heats at the Norisring in 1969. Bonnier retired with an overheating engine shortly after this picture was taken.

Brian Muir driving SL73/101 at the 1969 Nuremburg 200, followed by a Mark IIIb coupé. Muir went on to finish 14th.

to hand over to Brian Redman, whereupon Hawkins led for a lap until he, too, had to pit for fuel. After thirty-five laps, the Hawkins Lola was fourth, Bonnier was seventh, and Troberg tenth. With only one and a half laps left, poor Hawkins lost all oil pressure and abandoned the car out on the circuit. He was still classified eighth, however, and this gave Bonnier and Muller fifth and victory in Group 4.

The Martini Trophy at Silverstone on May 17th was also round five of the British RAC Group 4 championship. Entered in IIIb coupés were Paul Hawkins, David Piper, Brian Redman in Sid Taylor's car, and Trevor Taylor in the Team Elite car. In Mark IIIs were Chris Craft, David Hobbs and David Prophet. Max Wilson had entered a Mark III spyder fitted with a BRM V12 engine and T160 bodywork. This was chassis number SL 73/113.

The pouring rain made conditions for the race abysmal. After a few laps, Trevor Taylor decided the whole thing was pointless and went home. Brian Redman said things were so bad that 3000rpm was enough to spin the Lola, and David Hobbs' car had to be pushed off the back of the grid after having shorted its battery. Hawkins led away but spun at Abbey and rejoined. Piper now led, Redman spinning at Woodcote! Chris Craft pulled up to second whilst Hawkins had regained fourth. Redman spun again, this time at Abbey, the door flying open and cracking the screen. He got going again without losing a place. He was now third. Craft overtook Piper for the lead and started to pull away. Hawkins did the same and set out after Craft,

A snapshot of David Piper's SL76/150 at Oulton Park for the Tourist Trophy, 26 May 1969.

overtaking him on lap ten. Craft did not let up, however, and by now Redman was in third place even though he spun again at Stowe and then again at Woodcote. Meanwhile, Craft spun at Stowe and rejoined only to go off at Abbey and give Paul Hawkins the lead. Hawkins then spun at Chapel!

Lap forty-seven out of sixty-five and Hawkins was in the pits with his throttle linkage in disarray. After two stops to fix it he rejoined in fourth but by now Chris Craft had an unassailable lead and deserved his hard-fought victory. Redman splashed home in second, with David Piper coming third.

Gathered for the Tourist Trophy on May 26th at Oulton Park were Trevor Taylor's Team Elite car; David Piper in SL76/150 and Brian Redman in SL76/138. John Woolfe had entered Richard Attwood in his new IIIb (SL76/146). Mark IIIs entered were: John Woolfe/Digby Martl; Jack Oliver in the Techspeed car; and David Prophet in the ex-de Udy car. Practice saw Bonnier and Hawkins joint quickest at 1m 35, and then it started to rain. David Piper posted the fastest 'wet' lap at 1m 45 dead - two seconds quicker than Bonnier, Redman or Hawkins who all posted 1:47.2. Paul Hawkins took the lead and led the second place man, Herbert Muller, by 3.30 seconds at the start of the second lap with Redman, Taylor and Piper following.

After eight laps Muller had become familiar enough with Oulton Park to overtake Paul Hawkins at Old Hall and then begin to pull away. Redman also overtook Hawkins, who was clearly not happy with 142's handling (he was also passed by Trevor Taylor on lap twenty-four). Hawkins stopped two laps later to have a front wheel changed. One lap later he was in again to have his mechanics inspect his front suspension. Muller extended his lead and got down to 1m 34 but then went off the road at Druid's, doing enough damage to force his retirement.

By lap forty Redman held a comfortable lead over Trevor Taylor, followed in third and fourth places by Piper and Attwood. Brian Redman then spun 138 at Island bend and, though new bodywork was fitted, he went off again due to a puncture at Knickerbrook. A sudden rain shower now wetted the track and tyre changes were the order of the day, with David Piper, Trevor Taylor and Paul Hawkins all pitting. The rain stopped and Paul Hawkins pitted to change back onto dry covers. Now in seventh place, the Australian carried on driving as hard as ever to regain places, but, on lap sixty-five he slid wide at Island bend and the red Lola spun across the road and hit a tree, catching fire. Paul Hawkins died instantly and the wreckage that blocked the track forced the race to be aborted with results declared as at the stoppage.

After this, the Nürburgring 1000km on June 1st was almost an anti-climax. Siffert and Redman won yet again in Porsche 908s and only three Lolas ran. These were the Bonnier 'Bongrip' car, shared with Herbert Muller, Picko Troberg/ Bjorn Rothstein in their IIIb, and David Prophet's Mark III. In practice, Bjorn Rothstein lost Troberg's Lola on Friday and went off the road at around 150mph. Rothstein was lucky to emerge almost unhurt but the car was totally demolished, although a new car with the same chassis number appeared from the factory only six weeks later. David Prophet retired his car with ruined bearings.

Come race day, a rolling start

was employed and Siffert led by the end of the first lap. Bonnier pitted at the end of that lap and then set out to chase the Kelleners/Joest GT40 for the Group 4 lead. He got close but was forced to retire with a broken universal joint halfway through the race.

The big race of 1969 for sports cars was, of course, Le Mans. After Hawkins' death, the only Lola runner was Jo Bonnier, this time teamed with Masten Gregory. They qualified fastest of the Group 4 cars, at 3m 36.2 but, come the race, the Lola only lasted until 11pm when it crawled into the pits with severe overheating. Not to be beaten, the mechanics changed both cylinder heads in three hours. The car lasted until the twelve hour mark when the engine failed on the Mulsanne straight.

Even though the works Porsches had now officially retired with their agreement for JWA to run their cars in 1970 sealed, three 908s were at hand for the Watkins Glen six hours on July 6th. For Lola, there was the Scuderia Filipinetti entered SL76/151 for Bonnier and Muller, whilst opposition included Johnny Servoz-Gavin and Rodriguez in a Matra, and a Mirage for Ickx and Oliver.

Bonnier was fourth on the grid at 1:11.10 with the pole-sitting 908 of Siffert and Redman recording 1:8.47. From the start it was Siffert and Redman with a lead they were not to lose. On the third lap, rain came sweeping in but Bonnier was up to third place. For most of the race he stayed in this or fourth place until Muller retired the car after three hours with a head gasket gone.

The next day Bonnier had the car entered in the Can-Am race so he inserted a 5.9-litre engine and qualified at 1:8.08. He had better fortune in this race of two hundred and three miles, finally coming in seventh behind Siffert in a Porsche 908.

Hitler's old saluting base at Nuremburg overlooked the Norisring where fifty thousand spectators gathered in late June to watch the 'Nuremburg 200', a race for Groups 4, 6 and 7 cars run in two heats. There was a works-entered 3-litre Alfa Tipo 33 for Ignazio Giunti, and David Piper had brought along his Lola as well as his Ferrari P3/4. Redman was driving Sid Taylor's car, Bonnier was in SL76/143 with a 5.7-litre engine and Trevor Taylor came with his 5-litre car.

Bonnier was fastest in practice, at 1m 19.5, until Giunti in the Alfa achieved 1m 18.7. Meanwhile, David Piper had swapped cars with Richard Attwood, obviously preferring his Ferrari to the Lola. In the first heat Bonnier led at the end of lap one by two seconds, with Giunti second, Elford and Stommelen third, and Brian Redman fifth. By lap six, Bonnier was lapping the 2-litre Alfa 33s and, by lap fourteen, Elford had found his way past Giunti to second place. Prophet had retired earlier, as had Taylor, due to overheating and a broken tappet, respectively. By half-way, Bonnier led Elford and only five cars were on the lead lap.

Brian Redman now used all of the 6.2-litres installed in his Lola and carved his way through to challenge Bonnier, who found he had to keep to 6000rpm to prevent overheating his engine. By the end of the first heat Redman was only point six of a second behind Bonnier, having set fastest lap at 1:17.3. At the rolling start of the second heat, Redman made no mistake and shot into the lead but Bonnier overtook on lap five having disregarded the rev limit of his engine. Two laps later he retired with a dropped valve leaving Redman fending off Elford who, in turn, was being challenged by Richard Attwood's Lola. Attwood spun but managed to stay ahead of Stommelen's 908 for a while. At the finish Brian Redman was 1.4 seconds ahead of Elford, with Stommelen third, Piper fourth and Atwood fifth. On aggregate, Redman won overall from Elford, and the crowd had seen the previously all-conquering Porshes defeated. Ron Bennett remembered the scene at the prizegiving: "Norisring, that was a laugh, we were all there, Trevor Taylor, Chris Craft, Redman, one or two others, and at the end of the meeting, at the trophy presentation, Trevor and Brian are standing arms raised in acknowledgement to the crowd and an official says; 'We don't do that any more here!'"

For the superb Vila Real road race on July 6th in Portugal, only two T70s appeared. These were the IIIb of Mike de Udy, sharing the drive with Frank Gardner, and the T70 roadster of Max Wilson fitted with a BRM V12 engine, this car having been completely rebuilt since its crash at the Nürburgring. Mac Daghorn was its second driver. Sid Taylor had been going to enter 138 but defaulted to prepare the car for the international race at Croft the following week. Also withdrawn were the Lolas of Techspeed, Team Elite and Picko Troberg. Main opposition came from Alain de Cadanet's Porsche 908 spyder, driven by David Piper and Chris Craft, and T33 Alfas from the VDS team driven by Bourgoignie/Gosselin.

De Udy led away at the start and kept the lead until David Piper got by and pulled away at the one and a half hour mark. However, with Frank Gardner replacing an exhausted de Udy, the Lola closed up so that at the three hour mark (half-way) the 908 had only a ninety second lead from the Lola, but it was enough. By the end of the race the 908 had lapped the Lola, which had been suffering a bad steering vibration for some time making it difficult for Gardner to steer with precision.

The privateers turned out in strength at Croft for the two heat Wills Trophy on July 13th, with Frank Gardner driving Mike de Udy's car, Trevor Taylor in SL76/138, Chris Craft in the orange Techspeed car, and Digby Martland in SL76/146. Piers Forrester entered SL73/101, but a cylinder liner collapsed in practice. Chris Craft was fastest in practice at 1:07.8. Gardner and Taylor were next but couldn't break 1:08, whilst Martland could only post 1:10.8, though this was still fast enough to keep him ahead of the fastest Chevron! In the first heat, Craft led away ahead of Gardner and Martland. Taylor was twelfth, as he had had to start from the back of the grid because his engine had refused to fire until the very last minute. By lap four he was third but then had to pit with a loose exhaust. Gardner had, by now, forced his way past Craft, although his car faltered on lap fourteen, allowing Craft to win with Gardner second and Taylor third.

Frank Gardner started the second heat with new tailpipes, though they were of no avail as the car expired shortly after the start with clutch failure. Taylor made a sensational start from the third row and led Chris Craft who, knowing he had a lap in hand, allowed the Sid Taylor car to cruise away in the lead. Digby Martland swiftly drove from the back of the grid to third place and, at the end Craft was the winner on aggregate.

The Gran Premio del Mugello comprised a forty-one mile road circuit which had Sid Taylor lending his T70 to Nino Vaccarella and Andrea de Adamich that July. In the race, held in scorching heat, Merzario's Abarth was in the lead after doing 31:32.5, whilst de Adamich had passed thirty-one cars to record 31:41.9 to take second (shades of Muller in the Targa Florio!). Toivonen retired the 908 as he could not stand the extreme heat and, by lap three, Merzario had established a six minute lead over the second Abarth with the Lola thirty seconds behind that.

On lap four the Lola pitted for five minutes to replace a broken rear anti-roll bar but, despite this, it still led its class and finished third overall.

The Österreichring, a six kilometre circuit constructed in less than twelve months, played host to the 1000km race held on August 10th. Porsche, although there in an unofficial capacity, entered two 917s, this time with rear wheel widths up to 15in and all anti-dive taken out of the suspension. There were also three 908s on tap from Porsche Salzburg, backed up by three more 908s privately entered. To combat this might there were only three Lolas: SL76/151, the familiar Filipinetti car for Bonnier/Muller, SL76/150 for David Piper and Dieter Quester, and a new Mark IIIb, SL76/147, for Louis Morand and Gerard Pillon.

Bonnier was on pole after Muller damaged the car in practice. Piper and Quester were faster than the 908s and wound up ninth on the grid. In the race itself, Jo Bonnier led off from the grid but Jo Siffert's Porsche 917 and Jackie Ickx's Gulf

Mirage passed him on the back straight. By lap eleven Bonnier was fourth, having been passed also by Masten Gregory in a 908, whilst David Piper was eighth in his car. By the time the first fuel stops had taken place at the forty lap mark, Bonnier was back in second behind Ickx, although, twelve laps later, he dropped to fourth behind the Servoz-Gavin/Ahrens Porsche 917. Cracked heads, caused through overheating, saw the retirement at fifty-two laps of Piper's car, and Muller dropped 151 down to sixth place.

Fortunes then turned dramatically in the Lola's favour, when a series of retirements and crashes put it back into second place behind the Siffert/Ahrens 917. Unfortunately for the striving Bonnier, the Porsche had a faultless last pit stop but it had been a very close run thing, and Bonnier and Muller could be very proud of their second place, bringing the essentially 'private' Lola in close behind the mighty works Porsche.

That was the end of the classic long-distance FIA races of 1969, but some national ones of note remained. Thruxton on August 10th witnessed the last round of the Group 4 Sports Car championship where Chris Craft had his Mark III, as did David Prophet. Denny Hulme was there in Sid Taylor's car and Frank Gardner led from pole in heat one in Mike de Udy's car with Craft second and Denny third. The positions were reversed at the end when Frank Gardner's Lola suffered a leaking head gasket and Craft a down-on-power engine. David Prophet had already retired with a broken water pump belt.

Heat two started with Craft leading again but Gardner was past by lap two and so was Hulme. The heat finished with Frank winning by 9.8 seconds but Denny was overall winner on aggregate.

Oulton Park was the venue for a Group 4 race in August but, with the finish of the championship, entries were sparse. Bonnier was in the red Filipinetti car and Gardner was there in de Udy's Mark IIIb. Another protagonist was Piers Forrester in Jim Beach's Mark III joining in the over two litre class. Bonnier took pole in 1m. 33s. which was substantially faster than Herbert Muller's previous record of 1m 34.4 set in the TT in the same car. For some reason Bonnier didn't start, and Frank Gardner drove the nineteen laps well off his practice times to lap everyone by the end.

As a change for the drivers, the Nordic cup - a series of races held in Scandinavian countries - was next, and the first round was held on August 31st after an abortive try at Keimola which was cancelled when the start/prize money was lowered. At the start it was Redman in SL76/138 with the Porsches of Leo Kinnunen and Chris Craft chasing hard. Kinnunen had been fastest in practice. Muller was fourth with Piper and Bonnier sixth and seventh. Practice times told and, on lap four, Kinnunen shouldered by Redman to take a lead he never lost. Redman spun the big Lola a lap later and restarted in fourth place. Undeterred he clawed his way back to third place until he damaged the rear suspension against a barrier. Although he restarted, he was subsequently forced to retire.

Anderstorp was the venue for race two. The entry was similar to the one at Mantorp Park with the exception that Ulf Norinder's car was driven by Jackie Oliver as Ulf was racing his F5000 car elsewhere. The result was another re-run of Mantorp Park, although Brian Redman did finish in second place this time! Kinnunen was to go on to a works Porsche team contract in 1970, as was Brian Redman. The sensation of the race, though, had been Chris Craft who had carved five seconds off the lap record after being push-started from the back of the grid. Unfortunately, his engine failed towards the end. On the same weekend in England, Alastair Cowin, driving David Prophet's T70 Mark III, came second to Roger Nathan in a combined Groups 4 and 6 race at Crystal Palace.

Ron Bennett remembered the series: "Nordic Trophy, 'More Dick Trophy', the drivers called it ... There was some good competition there, some racing as well ... ! They were a good group, I suppose they are in T70s today in historic racing. Brian came in, he couldn't get rid of the Porsches and I opened the door and he said 'I can't go any quicker, I just

can't go any quicker!' Dickie Attwood came up and he says 'go out there and drive' and slammed the door. Afterwards Brian said, 'when I went out, I was in a red haze.' He knocked two seconds off his lap time, though. Put it on pole. He says 'Don't ever do that to me again, I hate to drive like that!' I saw him at the Silverstone historic meeting recently and we were reminiscing about the old days. It was good."

It was to Holland on September 27th that David Piper took his Lola next where he came a commendable second to a very 'on form' Gijs van Lennep in a Porsche 908 at the Trophy of the Dunes at Zandvoort. David had led for the first half of the race before van Lennep got by, but Piper "flinging the big Lola around like a Porsche" (*Autosport*) regained the lead only to lose it again two laps from the end. Barrie Smith entered his Lola but a spin and two punctures saw his retirement.

Now very much towards the end of the season, the Montlhéry 1000km took place on October 13th near Paris. Three Lolas were entered, these being the Filipinetti car for Bonnier/Muller, David Piper's car driven by Richard Attwood/Michael Parkes, and the ex-John Woolfe IIIb, now bought and run by the Belgian VDS racing team for Teddy Pilette/Taff Gosselin. This car, unfortunately, broke its drive belt to the oil pump in practice and didn't start.

Even with the world class cars and drivers entered, Bonnier led for the first fourteen laps until passed by the two Matras which went on to win. Richard Attwood lost his rear anti-roll bar on the banking and continued at reduced pace, although Parkes drove the car with exuberance when his turn came, to take tenth place. The Filipenetti car finished in eighth place after breaking rockers towards the end.

Bonnier's next race was a farce as fog fell at Hockenheim and the three hundred mile race was held over the short course. Bonnier finished second to Jurgen Neuhaus's Porsche 908, David Piper's Porsche 917 was third, and Hans Hermann, in Piper's Lola, was fourth despite having finished without fourth and fifth gears and having to hold second in.

Springbok time again! Everybody who could now went to South Africa to grab some sunshine and racing. Kyalami was first with three Lolas entered: Bonnier's SL76/143 for himself and Reine Wisell, Brian Redman and John Love in SL76/138, and Mike de Udy and Frank Gardner in SL76/148. Doug Serrurier and Jackie Pretorious were out again in SL70/5.

Bonnier held second place at the start to David Piper's Porsche 917 (shared with Richard Attwood). Although pole position holders Brian Redman and John Love started badly, Brian soon usurped that position 24 minutes into the race until he pitted for broken rockers to be replaced whilst Bonnier proceeded to demolish his car against a bank (he was unhurt). After six hours, John Love retired the, now orange, Sid Taylor Lola with a broken differential. After nine hours, the Piper/Attwood car won,

Brian Redman, a professional who drove in the works teams of Porsche, Ferrari, JWA Ford, B.R.M. etc., remembers the Lola T70 with fondness. He started in a Mark II and remembers his first race at Oulton Park in the Lola: "I had gone straight from a lightweight E-type Jaguar to the Lola and had thought the Jaguar fast but, with the Lola, the straights at Oulton became long bends when the throttle was applied! It was raining in that first race and I applied the loud pedal coming through lodge in the same place as I had the E-type. The Lola swapped ends and I came onto the pit straight backwards. I can still see Charles Bridges' white face now.

I drove Sid Taylor's Mark IIIb coupé in 1969. That was a great car. I [and a lot of other drivers - JS] didn't realize then just what a part aerodynamics played through fast bends until I drove the Porsche 917. That's when I realized just how good the IIIb coupé was with its advanced body shape.

Whether we ran 5.0 or 5.7-litre engines we were told that they delivered 'about 500 horsepower'. I don't believe they ever did, and remember remarking to Sid Taylor towards the end of '69 that somebody else had been using the engines first!

I drive a Mark III coupé in Historic Racing in America these days. It's got around 600 horsepower (American) and it's very nice, very well balanced, although the brakes aren't up to IIIb standard.

Memories? Passing Jo Bonnier under braking into the Chicane at Thruxton on the last lap on one race. Yes, the T70 was a really great car."

A Lola T70 Mark IIIb coupé today.

with de Udy and Gardner finishing second. This, despite the car's crankcase having to be welded up before the race as cracks had been discovered.

At Lourenco Marques for the three hour race, John Love led away from the front row and Serrurier was second after a demon start. De Udy was sixth after being slow off the line. By lap four he was second and passed Love shortly thereafter. He retired after a while, though, with blown head gaskets. Frank Gardner took over the leader's car but suffered a puncture which dropped him to third behind Richard Attwood in the Mirage and Alistair Walker in a Ferrari P4. Frank really turned on the pressure and took two seconds a lap off the Ferrari;

with half an hour to go he regained the lead. Frank cruised comfortably to victory ahead of the Ferrari, with the older Lola in fourth place. Ron Bennett remembered the events leading up to that race particularly well: "South Africa, Frank came into the pits in practice and said 'Memory check. Did you put any oil in the diff?' 'Course I did,' I replied. 'Well, it's talking to me,' says Frank. I fitted three diffs in it: we'd had a batch of incorrectly treated pinions from Hewland. I had to tow it from the track, then I slept in the car until 6am when de Udy arrived and I set to and built a new gearbox from his spares and we were ready with about ten minutes to go. It's a good job you don't get jobs like that every day!"

John Love finally reversed the fortunes of SL76/138 at the Bulawayo three-hours, winning with de Udy finishing second yet winning the series overall. At one stage, de Udy had led until a spin and then a puncture occurred.

And so finished the year that should have seen the T70 come good. That it didn't is no reflection on the car; it had always needed more time and money spent on it to sort out its niggling failures. With the coming of the Porsche 917 and the Ferrari 512 with their purpose-built racing engines, its chance had passed and it could only look forward to defeat on the international scene.

10

RACING IN 1970

Despite the emergence of such superior cars as the Porsche 917 and Ferrari 512 with their purpose-built overhead camshaft alloy racing engines, the T70, mainly in IIIb coupé form, soldiered on well into 1970.

South America was the continent the Lolas visited first, the Buenos Aires 1000 kilometres race attracting the VDS team's SL76/146, driven by Teddy Pilette and Garcia Vega, with Bonnier and Wisell in SL76/151, Jack Oliver and Carlos Reutemann in SL76/141, and Peter Gethin and Trevor Taylor in SL76/138. SL76/147 was crashed in practice by Gerard Pillon and SL76/152 was black flagged in the race itself after colliding with, and forcing out, the leading Porsche 917.

Although Jean Pierre Beltoise and Henri Pescarolo won in a Matra, with Porsche 908s second and third, the VDS car came fourth, Peterson and Cupiero seventh, and Oliver and Reutemann eleventh. Not bad for a bunch of old ladies!

At Daytona and Sebring, the odd T70 was entered but did not figure in any result sheet. Then came the European season.

In a national Group 5 and 6 race at Thruxton in late March, David Piper's car started from the front row and held second until he pitted after hearing something behind him break. It turned out to be the alternator belt. He rejoined but had lost two laps and had to settle for fifteenth place. In contrast, Bonnier took SL76/143 from almost the back of the grid to third overall behind Siffert in a 917 and Brian Redman in a Chevron B16, with Barrie Smith driving his T70 to fourth place.

April 12th was the date of the BOAC 500 race and Bonnier did well again, sharing his yellow car with Reine Wisell to take a well earned seventh overall. He was the only one of three Lolas entered to finish, however, as Sid Taylor's car (he had bought SL76/144 from Trevor Taylor) and Mike de Udy's ex-Sid Taylor SL76/138, both retired (how troublesome can a motoring historian's life be?).

At the very fast Monza 1000 kilometres race held on April 25th, the best Lola T70 home was the VDS entry in sixteenth place. Suddenly, dramatically, the car had fallen from favour and was now completely outclassed, not only by the seven works Porsches and three Ferraris, but also the privateer teams running these cars as their twenty-five necessary production run was sold off. *Autosport* wrote of the entry: "There seemed every chance that neither of these cars (SL76/146 and 147) would get within 90 per cent of the fastest time and would fail to qualify. The days of the T70 are over."

Spa was better (anything would have been!) with Bonnier and Wisell finishing in tenth place. They had held seventh in the early stages and Pilette had made a terrible start after the carburettor covers were left in on the grid before a mechanic noticed and removed them. Teddy Pilette managed to hold fourth until he retired after a puncture and damaged suspension.

David Piper carried on his policy of hiring out his Mark IIIb coupé when he was otherwise engaged and he let Jean Pierre Beltoise use it at Magny Cours in France for the Group 5/6 and 7 race on July 14th. Despite sterling opposition from Barrie Smith and Jean-Marie Jacquemin Rey in other Lola T70s, he romped home ahead of Piper's Porsche 917.

For the Swedish Grand Prix at Karlskoga, David Piper's Porsche 917 was beaten by a Lola T70 again, this time Reine Wisell in Bonnier's SL76/143. Bonnier himself beat Wisell and took third place in the new generation Lola sports car, the two litre T210. Barrie Smith and Teddy Pilette finished eleventh and twelfth respectively.

July 5th saw a happy victory for the team that tried so hard when the VDS T70 Mark IIIb driven by Teddy Pilette and Taf Gosselin won the Vila Real 500km in Portugal. The weather was so hot that the engine overheated in practice and so the team, unable to obtain any anti-freeze locally, filled the cooling system with red wine! (the boiling point is higher than water). Teddy Pilette drove for most of the race as Gosselin was suffering with food poisoning, and the Lola led from quite early in the race to the finish.

August 11th in North America saw the Watkins Glen six-hours where Bonnier and Wisell in SL76/143 came in a creditable eighth behind the all conquering Porsches. The following day saw Bonnier with an even bigger smile on his face. Most of the big sportscars took part in the Can-Am race and, mainly due to attrition amongst these cars, Siffert's Porsche finished second. Bonnier, driving solo, finished eleventh.

At Dijon the week following Vila Real, Richard Attwood drove SL76/146 to victory, and then Pilette and Gosselin took the car back to try once again at Le Mans. They lasted until the tenth hour and this time the clutch was the cause of their retirement. This particular car was campaigned longer than any other Mark IIIb in international competition: it appeared at Spa for the 1000km in 1971 and also at that year's Le Mans, where it lasted barely an hour before a piston let go. The car appeared at Thruxton in the first 'Interseries' event, on September 20th in 1970, driven by Teddy Pilette and finishing a distant seventh after thumping both ends in practice.

An interesting footnote to the T70 story is the use of several of them in the Steve McQueen produced film, *Le Mans*, arguably, the best film on motor racing ever made.

Solar Productions, McQueen's own company, bought or hired several cars to use some of them in the crash sequences of the film. Two Mark III coupés, Ulf Norinder's SL73/132, and the ex-Sid Taylor/Techspeed SL73/134 were damaged severely.

Norinder's Mark IIIb coupé, SL76/141, was dressed up as the Porsche 917 that was supposed to have been crashed by Steve McQueen (ever seen steam escaping from an air-cooled Porsche 917?). It was sold afterwards, repaired and sold again in England in 1971 to an owner who kept it for some twenty-five years.

SL73/132, was used as the 'guinea pig' in the radio control experiments for the film but ran out of transmitter range and was severely damaged. The pressures of film making meant there was no time to repair the car and so SL73/134 was purchased, fitted with Ferrari 512 bodywork and is the car seen vaulting over a bank and exploding in flames (lots of special effects!). The remains of 134 were exported back to England, *sans* bodywork, the chassis was repaired and the car is now in the process of restoration. This car, incidentally, had a tremendous race record in the hands of Denny Hulme and Chris Craft (see Appendix 1). SL73/132, meanwhile, acquired the bodywork of 134 and is, at the time of writing, in France again, with its identity crisis cleared up.

SL76/150, David Piper's own car, was hired for the film, and is the green Lola seen in a carefully orchestrated spinning sequence. David Piper himself was unlucky enough to suffer a huge accident in a Porsche 917 which resulted in severe injuries (see the film credit to David at the end of the film).

Barrie Smith took chassis SL76/148 to Argentina in January 1971 to compete in the Buenos Aires 1000km with Ed Swart. The car failed to finish, whilst David Piper used SL76/150 to compete in a race at Thruxton in April, and Richard Attwood won a race at Montlhéry in the car.

Jo Bonnier inserted a 'Big Block' engine, which Heini Mader says was 8.4-litres (!), into the Filipinetti car, SL76/151, and went money-hunting in the half-hearted interseries races in Europe in 1970-72, with a couple of other Mark III coupés, sometimes cut down to spyders. They posted a singular lack of success.

And that was really the end. By now, the cars were getting very old and were no longer competitive. They vanished from the international scene but a new life was just beginning.

T70

11

T160/162/163/165
1968-70

Although the T160 does not share the T70 designation, it fits into the T70's story as being the direct precursor of the T70 Mark IIIb coupé.

In 1968, Eric Broadley realized that to combat the McLarens in the rich Can-Am series, his cars would need more power, and the only way to achieve this in the American series and for the American market was to utilise the new 'big block' Chevrolet engine of 427 cubic inches - the immortal 7-litre.

Apart from lack of power, the T70 Mark III had some other disadvantages. In particular, the one-piece rear bulkhead, which supported the rear suspension, made changing the engine a laborious and time-consuming task; detachable top and bottom crossmembers would make engine changes a lot simpler, add torsional rigidity, and give the further benefit of overall simplification. It's important to realize that through all of this period, racing cars were becoming ever more powerful, wheel rim widths growing almost by the day, and slick tyres were starting to be introduced: the car with the stiffest chassis and suspension best able to utilise these colossal changes in power and grip would be king.

First tested in May 1968 by John Surtees, the T160 was more angular in shape than the T70 it superseded. The T160 was also almost two and a half times stiffer in terms of torsional rigidity than the T70 Mark III, even though its bare weight was a mere 130 pounds, and its simpler and lighter tub was skinned in 16swg alumimium. The Mark IIIb T70 coupe of 1969 would feature an almost identical tub.

The suspension members followed the then current Lola practice of steel wishbone tubes brazed onto the sockets of the lower ball joints, with both balls in the uprights and Rose joints at the front upper and rear lower inboard mountings to permit camber and castor adjustment. Dampers were Koni double adjustable, and adjustable anti-roll bars were, as usual, in use at the front and rear. 12 inch (305mm) diameter by 1.1 inch (28mm) thick ventilated discs with alloy calipers made in four pieces - each caliper having four brake pads - were mounted outboard all round (unlike the T140/142 Formula 5000 car) and a big block Chevrolet V8 engine of 7-litres was installed. John Surtees' own car's engine had Weslake heads.

Whatever engine was fitted, a Hewland LG600 5-speed plus reverse gearbox was fitted - the '600' denoted how many horsepower the gearbox could cope with oil coolers for both gearbox and engine mounted at the rear, above the gearbox. Two rubber fuel tank bags held a total of fifty gallons and fed a collector tank situated just in front of the left rear wheelarch. The dry-sump oil tank was situated on the other side of the chassis.

Wheel sizes were 15 inch

Right: The completed rolling chassis of the T160 prototype in the factory.

Cockpit area of the T160 prototype showing the gearchange linkage and instrument panel.

Chevrolet big-block 'mule' engine used before installation of the race engine.

The T160 immediately before being shipped to Carl Haas in America.

(381mm) diameter with 9 inch (228.6mm) wide fronts and 14 inch (355.6mm) wide rears - although the latter would swiftly become 17 inch (432mm) wide. Bodywork, as usual with Lola products, was by Specialised Mouldings. The wheelbase was 94 inches (2387.6mm), front track 56 inches (1422.4mm), and rear track - depending on rim size - 51 inches (1295.4mm). Weight was given as 1450 pounds (657.72kg) and its distribution as 40/60 front/rear.

Dan Gurney and James Garner of AIR both ordered T160s for the Can-Am series, whilst John Surtees bought one car, took it back to his own Team Surtees facility and extensively reworked it, renaming it the 'TS-Chevrolet'.

In 1968 the T160 was still unable to overcome the McLaren steamroller. The new Can-Am car was disappointing, due, primarily, to a lack of development following Surtees' departure. The best results were courtesy of the Simoniz car (SL160-9), driven by Chuck Parsons (race number 10) who gained a fifth at Edmonton and a fourth in the Stardust finale at Las Vegas where Follmer's T70 was second. Mario Andretti and Sam Posey/Skip Scott (Simoniz-sponsored, race number 26) also piloted T160s, as did David

1968. Skip Scott driving the 'Simoniz Special' T160 in the CanAm series.

'Swede' Savage, in Gurney's team car, but, at the end of the season, the T160 was only tenth in the points. John Surtees' car was a disappointment, too, but this was down to the Weslake-headed engine, failing in each of the three races John started.

Only two T162s were built, chassis numbers SL160-13 and SL160 14. The T162 chassis was identical to the T70 Mark IIIb then being designed; in fact, all of the mechanical parts are interchangeable between the two models.

Both the T162 and the T163 sported modifications to the suspension and body shape in an attempt to get on terms with the McLarens; in this they failed, but then so did everyone else in Can-Am until the advent of the Porsche 917/10 in the 1970s. The T163, additionally, had modifications to the bulkheads and fuel bags.

For 1969, the most successful regular driver was Chuck Parsons whose lightweight T163, powered now by a Chaparral-built Chevy, placed third overall in 1969 as the best of the rest behind the Kiwis who had eight 1-2 results in their McLarens in ten events. Parsons was second at Riverside and third at St. Jovitc and Laguna Seca. Other T163 drivers were Ronnie Bucknum and Peter Revson sharing the same car, and Mark Donohue in a Penske car.

In 1970, Dave Causey was fourth in the points in a T165. A mid-season flourish saw him gain a third place at Road America followed up with a second at Road Atlanta. His was the first Lola behind the Hulme, Motschenbacher and Gethin McLaren M8Ds.

Today, most of the T160s have survived, and several have been rebodied with T70 coupé bodies, notably SL160/1 and SL163/18, each with a Mark III body, and SL160/9 was used as a road car by a doctor in South Carolina and then Rod Leach, the owner of 'Nostalgia', a company which specialises in selling exotic cars - particularly Cobras. It's reasonable to suppose that with the ever-increasing popularity of historic racing, such 'road cars' will sooner or later be taken back to their original shape.

In the USA, Craig Bennett and his brother Kurt, under their father, Bud Bennett's direction, race a T163 which is regularly the class of the field in the popular Can-Am 'Vintage' races.

1968. John Surtees at Riverside in his Team Surtees-modified T160 with Weslake big block engine.

SL160/8 today. After not being used in its heyday, 160/8 was sold to John Littlechild, who used it enthusiastically until replacing it with Bob Akin's T70 Mark IIIb coupé. (Photo John Littlechild)

The T165 was an attempt to use wings on the T160 design, and was reasonably successful. (Author's photo)

T70

12

THE LOLA T70 IN HISTORIC RACING

In the years since the Lola was at its peak, it has suffered more than most historic cars. Parts, and even whole monocoque tubs, have been swapped around, giving the T70 historian a real maze in which to sort out the individual histories. Some people have even fabricated complete cars using gaps in the chassis number listings, or recreated cars which were totally destroyed.

In this respect, the early roadsters have fared worse than their coupé sisters. This is almost certainly because the coupés were chronologically later cars, and because the roadsters were gradually 'used up' in USRRC and Can-Am racing in America (until they were destroyed in racing accidents or became simply 'old race cars' pushed into a corner of someone's garage, robbed of their ever-useful V8 engines, and sometimes stripped of their suspension). Add to which the propensity of the alloy tubs to weaken with age and you can see exactly why a lot have vanished from sight.

Even though the coupés also suffered the above, their beautiful shape somehow marked them out as cars to keep. Indeed, quite a few T70 coupé owners have made them

SL76/148, a Mark IIIb coupé at Silverstone in 1993. It belongs today to David Piper.

Not many Marks I, II or III roadsters are seen racing today. Here is Tomi Drisi at Daytona in 1998 where he placed second overall in the 1-hour HSR race. Tomi kindly lent your author the Lola to drive in the 24-minute demonstration before the 24-hour race. It was a delight to drive. Tomi is in SL75/125, which he owned until selling it to Los Angeles-based Stephen Young, who races it in vintage events on the West Coast today. (Author's photo)

road legal in order to keep on enjoying them, one owner reporting using his car to follow his family on their weekend picnics! Furthermore, such was the popularity of the cars that Lola itself tooled up for and made five brand new Mark IIIb coupés in the early 1980s. Even as late as 1997, Lola was actively investigating building another batch of T70s. Only the fact that the FIA refused to allow them into historic competition brought the plan to nought.

Other enthusiasts took up the slack. No FIA papers showing a car to be 'genuine' are necessary in the United States, and there are at least four T70 Mark IIIbs actively racing, which are built up from parts with locally-fabricated monocoque chassis.

Although the T70's reign in national and international racing was over by 1972, a new fashion was beginning to attract the paying public to race circuits; the running of old cars, now past their prime, in what were loosely known as 'historic races'.

T70s featured almost immediately. Their direct opposition came first of all from Ford GT40s and, later on, Porsche 917s and Ferrari 512s. For a comparatively small sum, Lola T70s gave good value. Lots of parts were available, and cheap and powerful engines were to hand from the USA. T70s flourished in these events.

Somehow, the dear old Lolas escaped the sort of price inflation the 917s and 512s soon began to suffer, although SL76/138 could have been bought in 1974 for some £12,000 and was worth nearly £250,000 by 1989! Prices appear to have stabilised since then. Still, a Porsche or Ferrari would set the prospective purchaser back at least £1-2 million now.

SL76/148 - driven by Gerry Marshall - at an historic race in the 1980s.

One of the peculiar results of this price hike was that Lola T70s stayed out racing in greater numbers than their more illustrious colleagues.

T70s were developed season after season to outdo one another until, by the early '90s, engines of over 400 cubic inches were being shoehorned into chassis designed

Chris O'Neill following the author in his Mark IIIb coupé at the Nürburgring in 1992 in a heat of the International Supersports Race.

A T70 awaits its race at an American historic race meeting.

Ready for the fray. The author's T70 on the left, SL71/23 in the middle and SL76/137 on the right before the 1991 International Supersports race at Spa-Francorchamps.

for no more than 520 horsepower, instead of the 650 now being produced. This resulted in a number of final drive failures, as the Hewland gearbox could not take this amount of torque. Suspension stresses also increased dramatically, necessitating further modification.

In 1993, Group Four racing came into being in England, specifically to organize the class of racing in which Lolas could participate. One of the first rule changes that Jonathan Baker,

A Mark III, Mike Pendlebury's SL73/112, lines up with the author's Mark IIIb coupé at Donington for an all-Lola race in 1991.

SL71/23 in Terry Smith's capable hands. He raced this T70 for many years.

Group Four's principal, instituted, was to set the engine limit back to the original five litres. He also specified treaded tyres. Despite numerous grumbles, this now turned T70s back into much more manageable race cars than they had become. It also increased the life of the differential. Clive Robinson, who specializes in the upkeep of T70s, reported that he was unable to sell the spare differential that he kept, 'just in case', for four years!

Incidentally, Jonathan Baker took your author's old T70 coupé to no less than sixteen straight wins in the Group Four series.

Despite the reduction in engine size, T70s are now lapping faster in Europe than they ever did with big engines fitted. Clive Robinson puts this down to "a much better balanced chassis. The cars no longer need the understeer that we had to dial into them before to cope with the excess power."

Nigel Hulme has owned and raced several T70s in his driving career and had this to say when asked about them: "Great cars! Having raced them for over twenty years, I can tell you that they are forgiving on a track, just as a proper racing car should be. They're also pleasing aesthetically, good to look at from every angle. It is a privilege to be able to race them."

In America, the 'big-engines syndrome' persists, although the

The monocoque chassis of a Mark IIIb GT coupé under restoration.

The shapely hull of a Lola coupé.

37
PLATIPUS
AWS

The view most competitors got when competing against Mark IIIb coupés! This is Nürburgring 1993. (Courtesy Gerd Paumann)

The front of a Mark IIIb with a new nosebox being fabricated.

The rear of a Mark IIIb coupé during restoration showing the engine bay.

The hubs and wheel bearings for a Mark IIIb.

fastest T70 driver there, Duncan Dayton, uses 'only' a 366 cubic inch NASCAR Busch engine fitted with just one, though huge, Holley carburettor. With this engine (and his press-on driving style), Duncan has embarrassed many later GTP

The brake discs, bells, light alloy calipers and cooling ducts of a Mark IIIb coupé.

You'd smile, too, if you were about to race a T70 at Silverstone! Nick Amey with SL73/110. Originally a spyder, this Mark III was converted to coupé bodywork some years ago.

Later life. SL76/138, the ex-Sid Taylor Mark IIIb coupé, under pressure from Colin Parry-Williams' Mark I spyder at the Osterreichring during the 1980s in a Supersports historic meeting.

Famous names. The signatures of Brian Redman and Denny Hulme on the monocoque of the author's Mark IIIb in 1991.

Steering, front suspension and brakes of a Mark IIIb coupé.

sports-prototype cars of the 1980-1993 period, regularly running as high as third and fourth overall.

Bob Akin, who rose to prominence in IMSA racing in America with a quartet of Porsche 935s, and then 962s, today races in 'Vintage' or historic events. For several years he raced a Lola T70 Mark IIIb coupé, SL76/149, which today belongs to John Littlechild.

Engine bay and rear suspension of a Mark IIIb coupé.

Bob commented upon the Lola thus: "Well, it's just a gorgeous car. Any angle you look at it, it's just great. And it's the same to drive. No vices. We've got a 410 cubic inch small-block Chevy on injection, and a Charlie Agg-modified Hewland LG600 gearbox, to take all the torque that the monster engine can put out. We can do 2:13s around Sebring, and I guess there's probably a 2:11 if I really got a clear lap." (Author's note: even some of

Right and below: Just some of the refurbished components of a Lola T70 during restoration. (Author's photos)

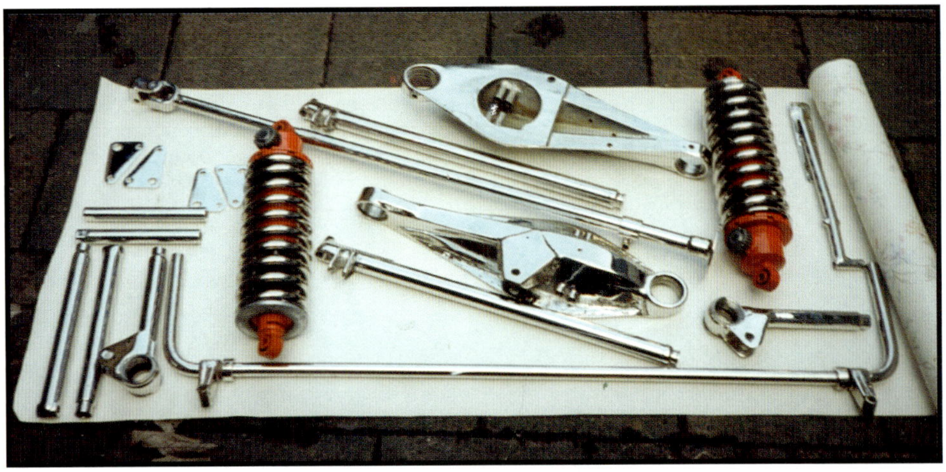

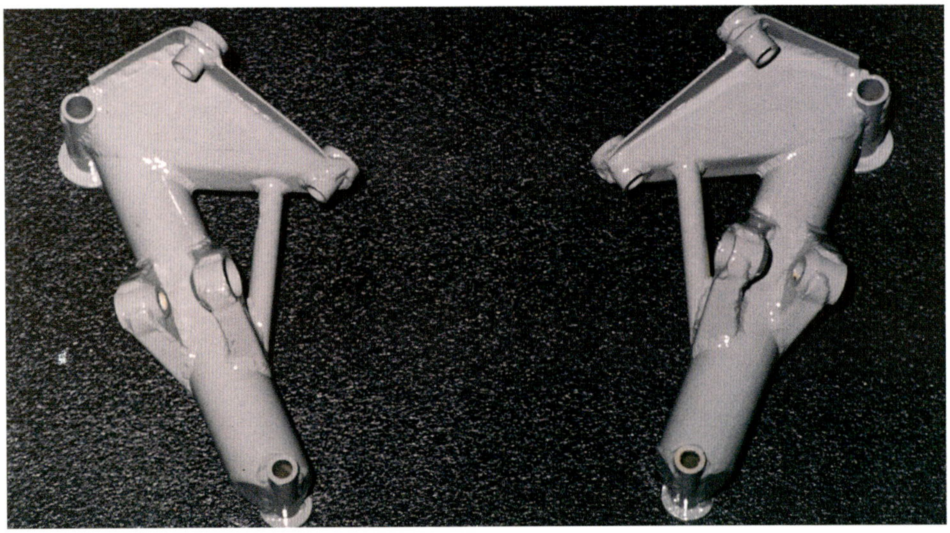

These are 'go-faster' engine mountings from Clive Robinson Cars in England. Basically, they allow the bottom radius arms to be mounted so that the whole of the rear tyres' tread is in contact with the track, rather than the usual three quarters of the width with the standard set-up. (Photo by Clive Robinson)

Left: Power pack. A 5.9-litre Chevrolet on injection with a Hewland LG500 gearbox ready for installation in the author's car.

the later 1981-1993 GTP cars can't get down to these times).

So there we have the story. A glorious-looking car which simply

The engine bearers with radius rods in situ.

ran away from the opposition when it was first introduced in 1965, and, with the wheel turning full circle, is doing the same again today. Long may it remain so!

The front suspension uprights of a Mark IIIb.

Restoration of a T70

The Author had his car restored during the winter of 1991-92. Some of the pictures in this chapter are, therefore, a record of a T70 Mark IIIb coupé 'under the skin'.

The steering rack, clutch and brake fluid reservoirs of the author's car during its rebuild in 1992.

SL76/138, the ex-Sid Taylor IIIb coupé when owned by Mike Wheatley in Europe for a historic race in the 1980s. John Sabourin, his mechanic, stands alongside.

This T70 Mark IIIb coupé is driven very effectively in HSR races in America by Duncan Dayton today. He won the Monterey historic race for Sports-prototypes in 2000 with it.

Jim Oppenheimer is an enthusiastic vintage Lola racer, racing a T296, a T192 and this T70 Mark IIIb coupe. (Author's photo)

13

TRACK TESTING THE LOLA T70

My thanks for the following track tests of T70 coupés go to the editors of *Classic and Sportscar* and *Classic Car* in the UK, and also to Dr. Jonathan Palmer.

1967 LOLA T70

"Heavens, time passes quickly. Looking back, I can barely believe it was 15 years ago that I was racing my Ford GT40, and in those days the car to have was a Lola T70. It was hundredweights lighter than the Ford, and the Chevrolet V8 engine that was invariably used was more powerful than the Ford unit in the GT40.

"However, I also recall that, although T70s would come flying past me in the corners and on the shorter straights, I would reel them in on a long stretch: the GT40 had a good 20mph on hand in the right circumstances. The T70s may have been lighter and more nimble but, in spite of that beautiful and apparently streamlined shape, they had relatively poor aerodynamics at the top end. They were also relatively fragile, too, with such assorted problems that they seldom won anything of consequence.

"To me, the GT40 was like a D-type: it was developed for Le Mans and was, therefore, a strong, stable machine. It was also quite heavy, though, with plenty of weight at the back, and if you hung the tail out and lost it the resulting spin seemed to go on forever!

"The T70 was much more of the lightweight, nimble, 'British School of Design'-type of car. Mind you, bear in mind that everything is relative. The Ferrari 512 that came four years later was much lighter again, and more powerful - it made the T70 seem rather lorry-like.

"Mike Wheatley's car is well-known on the circuits, always looking colourful and beautifully prepared. There have been several changes of sponsorship since I drove it in Uni-Petrol colours in 1983 - after spells carrying the identity of Ashdown Petroleum and Premium Pen it was painted in Agfa's vivid orange livery. Mike had always suspected that his T70 was one of Sid Taylor's cars, and this was confirmed when its original paint scheme was revealed during a strip and respray in 1984. He doesn't know precisely which Taylor car it was, but Mike Hailwood, Brian Redman, Hulme and Attwood all drove it. After that it passed to de Udy's Bahamas Racing and then to one Jack Le-Fort, before Mike acquired it in 1974.

"He has raced it continuously since then, and loves it so much that he says he'll never sell it. In an average year he races it about 14 times, in recent years invariably in the David Piper/Mike Knight SuperSports series, which takes him all over the world. Oddly enough, his first SuperSports win came in Britain at Donington in 1987. Before the advent of SuperSports, Mike had a good run in the HSCC GT Championship, winning it outright in 1979 and coming second for the following three years.

"Mike initially used a Morand-tuned Chevrolet engine, but problems obtaining parts caused him to turn to Mathwall Engineering, who have looked after his engines ever since. David Cottingham's DK Engineering prepared the car when I tested it in 1983, but since then John Sabourin has been responsible for fettling it. The efficiency of the operation is shown by the fact that, with a new engine, the car fired first time, completed several laps of the full Silverstone Grand Prix circuit with both Mike and myself driving in succession and, apart from some blanking tape over the radiators to warm things up a little (the test day was bitterly cold and windy), required no more work on it at all. The car was completely untemperamental.

"Compared to the GT40, the T70 is much easier to drive, much more forgiving and yet much more responsive, like a smaller racer. As I've said, if you hung the tail out on the GT40 you were in danger of being carried away by the weight of the engine behind you - the T70 was much more controllable.

"I was surprised at the amount of roll on the T70 - later it was confirmed that it was on a very soft setting. This is not necessarily a bad thing, since it makes for more predictability and a more gentle breakaway. It is set up for Mike's tastes, and he has shown how fast it can be. Were I to drive the car in a race I might well sacrifice some of the chuckability for a stiffer setting and thus perhaps corner that little bit quicker. But who knows?

"It is also a power-steerer: if you enter a corner on a trailing throttle the car will want to understeer off, so you have to keep the car balanced with the power, keep it smooth and on a good line. Do so and it rewards you with exhilarating cornering.

"The new 5-litre engine that Mike had just had fitted when I drove featured a 'softer' cam, one which perhaps doesn't give quite as much power at the top end - about 480bhp is the figure - but which has loads of torque lower down the rev range. A load of rubbish is often talked about power: a lot of power is fine, but if it's concentrated in a narrow rev range it's almost pointless. What is needed is usable power, and that is where this engine scores highly. Mike tells me that the 5.7-litre unit which he later installed - 'I needed to be more competitive against the agile stuff' - is even punchier throughout the range, peaking at about 560bhp. It is also fuel-injected, whereas the 5-litre used four Weber twin-choked carburettors.

"The 5-litre will pull cleanly and mightily from quite low revs so you can sling-shot out of a corner without falling into a power hole. This also gives better throttle response, allowing steer with the accelerator pedal and not wait for the urge to come in. There is, of course, a third advantage: you don't need to rev the engine to its limit, which would give a longer life. All in all, it's an impressive unit.

"The Hewland gearbox has the usual heavy change. It's not particularly pleasant, but if you expect it to be difficult and treat it as such, then it is no problem. This car, like some others I've driven, has something I hate: a gearlever that can rotate about its bottom ball joint - it's not fixed, in other words. You can't 'palm' a change, since your hand would just slip off the knob. You have to hold the lever firmly and feed it into each gear: thus, the third to fourth movement, across the gate, requires some concentration and firmness of action.

"The driving position is very good, although again, with the car set up for Mike, I was perhaps an inch or so too far from the pedals and steering wheel. This was no bother for a few laps, but I would probably have some padding, or the seat moved, were I to race. And, like the Aston Martin Nimrod I had driven a little earlier, the windscreen is quite far away from you, so the pillars intrude into your vision. The vision to the rear is very restricted.

"To sum up, I thoroughly enjoyed my time behind the wheel of the Lola. More sophisticated than the GT40, less so than the Ferrari 512, it filled a gap in my racing experience. A lovely looking car, a good, beefy, torquey engine, predictable handling and excellent roadholding and braking.

"Mike's record has shown that the T70 is a good honest racer which wins races, gives pleasure to driver and spectator alike (in fact, the day I drove was the first time Mike had seen it on a track in someone else's hands, and he was mightily impressed), and sums up an era."

[Unfortunately, a sad postscript has to be added to this track test, for Mike Wheatley suffered a horrific crash in his T70 at the time when the original edition of this book was nearing completion. He was racing with the SuperSports crowd in March 1988 at East London, South Africa, when a suspected suspension breakage sent the car out of control. Poor Mike suffered a broken leg and two broken arms: the car was written off.]

(From *Classic & Sportscar Book of Racing Car Track Tests* by Willie Green).

LOLA T70 MKIIIb COUPÉ

"Although the Lola T70GT can be called a GT40 development, it has always struck me as a considerably more fearsome projectile, something to be treated with much more respect than a good old GT40, which I have driven on road and track, wet or dry on a number of occasions. The Lola is lighter, faster and some four years on from the GT40.

"Once again, it was to be a wet track test, although light rain had only just started when I climbed into Richard Bond's 1969 Lola T70 MkIIIb. It is very much a standard sports-racer - a pair of seats between a pair of fuel tanks, heels on the stressed floor skin, with lower front wishbones coming into the cockpit. This one, with a background of long-distance racing and road car, is rather more instrumented than most - there was even a speedometer which had some figures on it, but I never saw whether it worked!

"It usually fires on the starter button, but little Varleys can get rather tired churning big Chevrolets on cold wet days, so three-man power was used instead. In second gear it soon fired with that ferocious roar of an F5000-type engine which is very audible inside, too; you are well protected from the engine by the official bulkhead and there is a clear plastic window at the forward end of that viewing tunnel on the rear deck, but the exhaust is still very evident.

"The reassuring thing about driving the car for the first time is that you can see some of the car ahead of you, like wheelarch tops and mirrors on them; on some overwedged cars like the LM Ferrari you see nothing beyond the screen and are very conscious that your legs are the nearest thing to the accident.

"A big 5-litre engine with a 6000rpm rev limit is still well blessed with usable torque from around 3500rpm upwards, so it isn't too hard to keep it on the cam at gentle speeds. With about 550bhp/ton on tap throttle response is instant and it is certainly very fast. It was a lap or two before I used full throttle in third on the straight; the big wet Goodyears took it all and shot the car forward as if it were on slicks and a dry track. The Hewland LHG600 gearbox was as short and precise in its travel as a much smaller box and it was no trouble to flick through the five-speed gate, still feeling tremendous acceleration comfortably over 100mph in fifth.

"Once the rain started to come down, the big single wiper coped admirably and I'm pleased to say that the tyres were as effective at transmitting brake torques as tractive ones. It's obviously a little difficult to comment on handling after a few wet laps, particularly when that much excess power is bound to spell oversteer, but it is set up to start with a reassuring amount of understeer which can easily be felt through remarkably light steering - not the sort of understeer that you have to counteract by a hefty boot on the throttle. Throttle response is gradual enough to keep it balanced without it biting; on the few dry occasions he has had to experiment with, Richard has found the handling very nice and predictable and has yet to discover the full limit despite a Club lap time of 58.7sec. What I found surprising about the car was that it felt so much smaller than it looked; it didn't really feel that much larger than the Chevron

B16 (a similarly-shaped GT) I had driven five years before with a 1.8-litre FVC engine.

"This particular car, chassis No. SL76/148, was completed on 12 March 1969, as one of the last MkIIIbs - the final number was 153. It was sold to Picko Troberg via Jo Bonnier with a 304 cu. in. Chevrolet engine. It went to the Nürburgring 1000kms in June 1969 wearing the PR for Men colours but was reduced to a 'horrible heap against the bank' (my own words when covering that race for *Motor*) by Bjorn Rothstein. The next we hear of it is back at Lola in August 1969 being rebuilt, which took about six weeks, and it was then sold to Barrie Smith. He took it to the Buenos Aires race in January 1970 and hit a dog which necessitated borrowing a nose cone from Sid Taylor, but he didn't finish in the results.

I'm not sure whether it performed again in Europe that year, but Smith took it to the Kyalami 9-hours in November to drive with Jackie Pretorius but didn't figure in the results. It hadn't been too successful by this time and in 1971 it was sold to a Mr. Farley, who converted it to a road car with some silencing and a more tractable state of tune and painted it blue. Mike Weatherill, who owned the Lotus 15 described elsewhere in this book, acquired the car during 1974 but didn't use it. Richard Bond, well known for his regular finishes as a privateer at Le Mans, bought the car in October 1974.

"By now it needed a complete rebuild which was undertaken by freelance race preparer Louis Lorenzini; the engine is basically a Traco F5000 unit with Alan Smith heads and develops around 440 reliable bhp. In five mostly wet races in 1975, Richard gained two firsts, a second plus a fifth and seventh with overheating problems.

"Since then it has joined the Historic racing fray where it is a regular front-runner alongside another T70GT and a GT40 which uses the 5-litre Gurney-Weslake version of the Ford V-8, quite like old times; however, as in former days the T70 has the legs of the GT40 in short sprints, but not surprisingly both are liable to be beaten by the lighter Can-Am equivalents.

"The T70 wasn't a great car in GT form, but if Broadley had managed to retain his Ford association and take advantage of the Ford development work for long-distance racing, it might have been - until the arrival of the Porsche 917s, that is."
(From *Track Tests - Sports Cars* by Michael Bowler, *Thoroughbred & Classic Cars).*

LOLA T70 MKIIIb COUPÉ

In the late 1980s, Doctor Jonathan Palmer track tested a Lola T70 Mark IIIb coupé which had been developed by Ray Mallock; Palmer's almost unique qualifications of having driven racing cars up to and including F1, made him an almost-unique judge of the cars. Here are some of his comments:

"Geoffrey Marsh's T70 had been re-engined with a newly rebuilt two-year-old Alan Smith 5-litre Chevrolet V8 running on carburettors instead of the usual fuel injection and was producing 440bhp at a mild 6500rpm.

"The T70 felt much more basic inside than a modern Group C car. A long gear lever complemented the old-fashioned cockpit, while even a handbrake and speedometer were included! Ray did a few laps to check out the engine before handing over to me. Bump starting was necessary owing to a jamming starter motor problem. On moving off, I found everything so much softer than a Group C car; the engine quieter, the long-throw gearchange seeming faster than its contemporaries. And the ride ... the ride was so smooth! Accelerating down towards Redgate corner at Donington, I could have been in a road car, the engine was that tractable, while the minimal downforce was obviously contributing to the featherweight steering.

"This was quite a new experience for me. The accelerator pedal travel was very long, and I thought I was using 90 per cent of it rounding my first lap, until I thought I'd get the last 10 per cent - and my foot disappeared into the depths of the footwell with a consequent satisfying surge of acceleration! Feeling at home very quickly, I was soon feeding in the power early enough to provoke satisfying power oversteering slides. This really was fun, one of those cars that bring out a big grin of childish satisfaction almost immediately!

"The chicane was, of course, second gear in the T70 and, although it would rev to 7000rpm, I changed up early, settling on just over 6000rpm before snicking the next cog to continue the steady surge of acceleration.

"The T70's handling was delightful on slow and medium speed corners. Its excellent turn-in ability, with no trace of understeer, enabled the Redgate apex to be clipped precisely so that the power could be fed in very early with the excellent traction, building up to maintain an easily controllable slight power oversteer attitude on the exit. Very satisfying. Sure, the car rolled much more than its modern counterpart but at this speed it was not a hindrance.

"The Craner Curves did show up the older car's limitations rather more, though. Although approaching it slower than in a Group C car, such as a Lola 610, quite a big lift, though no actual braking, was necessary for the left-hander down the hill and one was conscious of the car heaving over with the tail being on the verge of letting go.

"Settling the T70 down early for the old hairpin was important if one was to have any chance of turning in precisely, after changing down to fourth from using fifth down the hill. At this initial turn-in point the car did feel a fair bit slower than a Group C car, though its poorer grip meant a later turn-in point was necessary with a consequent tighter radius of turn. This was vital enough to get the power on early, which had the effect of neutralising the slight entry understeer as the exit kerb was brushed. Surprisingly, at this point the T70 was going faster than a Group C car. I was suspicious of this fact and double checked gear ratios and CWP ratios, but there was no reason to doubt the accuracy of the rev counter. The only point I would make was that I had, at this point, less experience of a Group C car.

"Again the softer, wallowy nature of the T70 limited it at high speed. After taking fifth soon after the old hairpin, it was not quite possible to take the uphill left kink flat; roll oversteer would set in. McLeans was taken in third gear, with similar handling to Redgate, and again the exit speed by the kerb was similar to a Lola T610 Group C car. As with the old hairpin, the entry speed felt much slower, although this shows the result of powering out of a corner early in a car with a torquey engine and good traction.

"Down the main straight it pulled 151mph, and though the brakes were superb for an elderly car, with a very firm pedal, twenty yards longer was required to knock the speed off for the chicane. Here the T70 was in its element, the soft suspension allowing the car to turn in quickly and cope with full throttle on the exit very early with, once again, a gentle power oversteer.

"The T70 finished up 4.5 seconds slower than a T610 I tried on the same day and, although it gave away 75 kilos and 100 horsepower to the T610, the maximum speed and exit speed from a corner were very similar and it is the entry speed to the corner which makes the difference between the two generations of car."

APPENDIX 1

HISTORY AND RECORD OF INDIVIDUAL T70 CHASSIS

INTRODUCTION

Over the last eleven years I have attempted to put together a history of the individual Lola T70s, both in their heyday and, as far as possible, following the cars to see what happened to them afterwards. It has proved a task both fascinating and frustrating in almost equal measure!

To find out which early spyders did what, where and with whom is difficult, as the majority went to America and were sold through Lola's agents there, firstly John Mecom and then Carl Haas. The records of these two agents covering this period have been lost with the passage of nearly thirty years and so sheer detective work has been employed in sifting through contemporary race reports and factory records in order to identify the individual cars. Quite a few race mechanics in the USA clipped off the chassis plates at the end of each Can-Am season and affixed them to their tool boxes!

Although I have advertised widely in the American car magazines for information, little has been forthcoming, and talking to today's owners has proved the only way to verify some of the cars' histories.

In this respect, I should thank Klaus Handeman of Germany. Klaus has long been working on a database of all the T70s' race results and was kind enough to let me have a copy. Working from it, I managed to add substantially to this appendix. Thank you, Klaus.

Due to the hurly-burly of USRRC and Can-Am racing, it's safe to assume that a fair few cars must have been destroyed and, with the passage of time, the earlier cars which had a lot of steel in their monocoque chassis must have corroded badly. To race one today one would need to be sure that the tub had been very thoroughly rebuilt/replaced.

As far as the coupés are concerned, the detail is simpler as most of these stayed in Europe, EXCEPT for the replicas which have been built subsequent to the original cars. I have attempted to ignore these cars and follow the continuous history of the cars wherever possible. As is common with old racing cars, several cars today claim the same chassis number where there has been a division of the parts used, usually after a crash, to rebuild the car(s).

In some cases, cars have been fabricated from scratch, usually with the builder copying a car he has had in his shop for restoration. Sometimes this has resulted in individual chassis numbers being used two, three or more times. Where possible, I have alluded to these anomalies in the chassis record.

So, should the reader be an enthusiast (I hope so!) who wishes to purchase one of these cars, please take care and don't regard the information I have given as a safe provenance for any car. The rule must always be to check out the car's history THROUGH DOCUMENTATION and with expert help. Remember, a chassis plate is only affixed by two pop rivets, so ... *Caveat emptor*!

Glossary of Terms

RU: Result unknown.
MIA: Missing in action.
DNS: Did not start.
DNF: Did not finish.
STPO: Sold to present owner.
GP: Grand Prix.
USRRC: United States Road Racing Championship.
Can-Am: Canadian-American Championship.

MARK I

SL70/1 (Photo at the bottom of page 27).
The first Lola T70.

1965:
22/1: Displayed at the Racing Car Show. Royal blue with a white stripe. Delivered to J. Burke of Eastleigh, Hants on March 20th. Team Surtees purchased the car for Jackie Stewart and Tony Maggs. Tested in March at Silverstone by Surtees where it equalled the outright lap record. Repainted in Team Surtees colours, red with green stripes. 4.5 Traco Oldsmobile, then 4.5 Chevrolet, then 5.9 Traco Chevrolet engines. SL70/1 was bought by John Mecom at the end of 1965 and perhaps raced. Afterwards, it went through the hands of several owners until today.
20/3: BARC Senior Service 200 at Silverstone. 25 laps. Race number 1.
In practice it was 2nd fastest to Jim Clark in Lotus 30. The race was held in pouring rain and stopped after eighteen laps out of twentyfive. Surtees led after Clark spun but then spun himself and Clark took over the lead again. Surtees 2nd.
05/5: Los Angeles Times GP, Riverside: Stewart; DNS.
15/5: Silverstone: Surtees; DNF - 3 laps from the end when leading.
05/6: USRRC Players 200, Mosport Park: Surtees. Race number 11. 1st overall.
29/6: Broke lap record at Silverstone whilst testing Firestone tyres, 1:28.3, (McLaren 1:31.6). 9.20x15Fr, 12x15R wheels.
24/7: Martini Trophy at Silverstone: Surtees; pole position but DNF.
30/8: Guards International Trophy, Brands Hatch: Jackie Stewart; 3rd.
25/9. Mosport: J. Stewart; withdrawn from Pepsi 100 after Surtees crashed in practice.
30/10: Riverside: Stewart; 2nd. Engine blew in consolation race; DNF.
Sold to John Mecom. Engine from Walt Hansgen's crashed car installed.

1966?: Sold to Lime Rock, Connecticut.
1967: Sold to Bob Lutzingen of New York, (December).
1969: Sold to Tom Shoral, an attorney in Pittsburgh. Then sold to Dave Walin of Buffalo, and then to John Krause who raced the car with a big block engine installed.
Sold to Larry Elting with crash damage.
Sold to Chuck Haines.
Sold to Dave Hankin of California, USA Original Mk I tub.
The car had a Mark II rear body plus a six-litre fuel injected Chevrolet engine. It also had a cooling slot behind each front wheel, which was only seen on the early Team Surtees cars. Armstrong dampers fitted. These were made to special order for Team Surtees in June, 1965. No chassis plate but this is probably SL70/1.

SL70/2 (Photo on pages 29 and 33).
Dark blue with a light blue stripe. Sold to Ian Yates of Long Melford, Suffolk on March 20th of Harold Young Racing for David Hobbs to drive. 4.7 Ford then 5.9 Chevrolet engine installed.
David Hobbs had a very good 1965 season, winning three races. The T70 was then sold to Monte Shelton who raced it through 1966 and 1967 although: "So many races, can't remember the results!"
In 1967, Monte sold the T70 through a broker who never paid him. The next owner kept the car for thirty years before selling it to Bob Erikson who has carried out a masterful restoration on the car.

1965
19/3: Goodwood. David Hobbs; 3rd. Unpainted.
01/5: Tourist Trophy, Oulton Park: Hobbs; 2nd. (Hobbs actually won the race on aggregate but the timekeepers got it wrong and the RAC refused to correct matters).
15/5: International Trophy, Silverstone: Hobbs; RU.
07/6: Guards Trophy, Mallory Park: Hobbs; pole 49.8s, 97.58mph. 2nd in 1st heat, 1st in 2nd heat, 1st overall.
15/8: Croft: 40 laps. Hobbs; 1st overall.
30/8: Guards International Trophy, Brands Hatch: 5.9 Chevrolet. Hobbs; race number 1. DNF due to gearbox problems.
19/9: Mont Tremblant-St. Jovite: Hobbs; 3rd overall.
10/10: North West Grand Prix, Kent: Hobbs; 6th in 1st heat, DNF in 2nd heat.
30/10: LA Times GP, Riverside: Hobbs; DNF.

1966
22/8: For sale in *Autosport* (offers).
Sold through Sid Taylor to Monte Shelton, Oregon.

1966 Can-Am races
USRRC, Kent: Shelton; 5th.
Riverside GP: Shelton; RU.
SCCA Nationals: Shelton; RU.
Newport, Oregon: Shelton; RU.
Rose Cup, Portland; Shelton; 2nd.
Laguna Seca: Shelton; RU.

1967
16/7: Kent: Shelton; 11th.
Sold to an unknown owner who kept it for 30 years.

1999: Sold to Bob Erickson.
2000: Restored with bodywork from original moulds.

SL70/3
Sold to John Mecom on 11th March, 1965. 4.7 litre Ford engine. Metallic blue. John Mecom was the Lola distributor in the United States and ran his own race team.

1965
15/3: Sebring 12 hour International Race: DNF (oil cooling problems).
11/4: Pensacola USRRC: Hansgen; DNF.
24/4: Stardust GP, Las Vegas: Hansgen; 2nd.
01/5: Times GP, Riverside: Hansgen; DNF.
02/5: Riverside USRRC: Hansgen; DNF.
09/5: Monterey GP, Laguna Seca: Hansgen, race number 11; 1st.
09/5: Laguna Seca, USRRC: Hansgen; DNF.
06/6: Players '200' USRRC, Mosport Park: Hansgen; crashed in practice and suffered chest injuries. The car was destroyed but the engine and gearbox were saved and used in SL70/6.

SL70/4 (Photo at bottom of page 25).
Sold to Hugh Dibley but returned to the factory as the chassis

was faulty. Not re-issued as number 4. See SL70/7.

SL70/5
Photo at base of P49.
Sold to Mike Taylor of Taylor and Crawley for David Cunningham. Ford 289 cu. in. engine.
David Cunningham raced this T70 just once without success. He sold it to David Good (Good International Racing) who hill climbed it (a withered arm prevented him from obtaining a racing license). Roy Pierpoint raced it for him both in the UK and in South Africa, where Doug Serrurier, after driving it with Pierpoint, bought the car and campaigned it successfully until 1969. Serrurier then converted the car into a T140 F5000 car using the running gear, engine, and gearbox, *etc*. This car was known as the T70/140. It was then crashed and sold to the Domingo brothers who sold the project on to Peter Haller. He turned it into a dragster but it was never used. The conversion was carried out by Delport. Johan van der Merwe acquired the "sorry remains", which were rebuilt into a T70 for Ivan Glasby in Australia.

1965
01/5: LA Times GP, Riverside: Hugh Dibley; 7th.
15/5: International Trophy, Silverstone: Cunningham, 7th.
01/7: Silverstone: Pierpoint; DNF.
12/7: Senior Service 25 laps,Silverstone. Pierpoint; DNF due to gear selection problems.
24/7: Martini International, Silverstone: F. Gardner; DNF.
30/8: Guards International Trophy, Brands Hatch. Roy Pierpoint; DNF.
8/11: South African 9-hours, Kyalami: Entered by David Good and driven by Pierpoint/Serrurier. Broke a pushrod after 6-hours, dropped a valve, and broke a piston. DNF.
28/11: Rhodesian GP, Bulawayo: Hawkins; 2nd.
4/12: Rand GP, Kyalami: Hawkins; 1st.
27/12: Pietermaritzburg 3-hours: Hawkins; DNF.
1965: Cape International 3-hours, Killarney: Hawkins; RU.

1966
May: Sold to Stirling Moss Auto Racing Team.
7/11: 9th South African 9-hours, Kyalami: Entered by Roy Pierpoint and driven by Pierpoint/Serrurier. Race number 1. Led until 88 laps when a pushrod broke again.
19/11: Cape 3-hours, Killarney: Pierpoint/Serrurier; 2nd overall.
17/12: Lourenco Marques 3-hours: Serrurier/Pierpoint; 1st.
27/12: Dickie Dale 3-hours, Roy Hesketh Circuit, Pietermaritzburg: Serrurier; pole position. 1m 16. Led at the start, DNF due to rear suspension breakage after 65 laps.
Sold to Doug Serrurier

1967
02/1: Kyalami Sportscar race, 20 laps: Serrurier; 1st overall. First over 100mph lap.
07/2: Killarney circuit, Capetown: Serrurier; DNF. Crashed at half distance due to front suspension failure when leading after rain fell. New sportscar lap record, 3 seconds faster than previous.
27/3: Roy Hesketh Circuit, Maritzburg: Serrurier; DNF (engine).
1967: Bulawayo GP: Withdrew from event.
1967: Rhodesian GP Sports car race: Serrurier; rear suspension trailing arm broke when leading.
08/4: Killarney circuit, Capetown: Serrurier; 2nd in both heats.
09/7: Roy Hesketh circuit, Pietermaritzburg: Serrurier; 2nd in 2 heats, 2nd overall.
7/10: Kyalami 12-laps: Serrurier; led until oil pressure forced retirement (broken piston).
04/11: Kyalami 9-hours: Serrurier/Jackie Pretorius; DNF due to piston failure.
18/11: Cape International 3-hours, Killarney: Serrurier/Pretorius, race number 3; 3rd overall.
16/12: Lourenco Marques 3-hours: Serrurier/Pretorius; DNF due to overheating.
26/12: Roy Hesketh Circuit 3-hours. Serrurier/Pretorius; 1st overall.

1968
09/11: Kyalami 9-hours. Serrurier/Pretorius; DNF due to a fractured oil pipe.
23/11: Killarney, Cape Town: Serrurier; Crashed when a brake pipe blew off at the end of a pit straight. Frontal damage.
08/12: Lourenco Marques: Serrurier; 3rd overall.

1969
08/11: Kyalami 9-hours: Serrurier/Pretorius; led from start then pit fire. DNF (slight damage).
27/12: Roy Hesketh 3-hour: Serrurier/Pretorius; left front suspension damaged in practice so DNS.
1969: Piermaritzburg: Serrurier; 1st.

Sold on since.

SL70/6
Sold to John Mecom on 28/4/65 for Walt Hansgen. (Rose Bud Racing Team, Houston, Texas for USRRC races). Grey (primer?). Now yellow with black stripes. Walt Hansgen successfully raced this T70 for Mecom's team in 1965 after destroying SL70/3. We don't know what happened to it after this until it turned up with Mike Smith in Florida in the late 1980s. He sold it to Dr. Wagner in Germany.

1965
July: Tested by *Road and Track*.
??/7: Galveston: Hansgen; DNF.
30/8: Guards International Trophy, Brands Hatch: Ford 4.7-litre fitted, Hansgen, DNF in 1st heat due to a fuel blockage. 4th in 2nd heat. 9th overall.
05/9: Elkhart Lake 500: Hansgen; DNF.
12/9: USRRC, Road America 500, Elkhart Lake: Hansgen; pole position in practice (2:27.8). Result unknown but pitted twice whilst lying 2nd then 3rd.
19/9: Bridgehampton 500: Hansgen; 4.7 Ford engine. Pole position (1:39;6); DNF after ten laps due to a broken rear upright.
10/10: Northwest Grand Prix: Hansgen; 1st overall (two heats).
17/10: Monterey GP, Laguna Seca: Hansgen; race number 17; 1st overall (won both 100-mile heats). Lap record: 97.01 mph.
30/10: Times Grand Prix, Riverside: Hansgen; 5th in the 1st heat.
14/11: Stardust GP Las Vegas: Hansgen; 2nd.
Sold to Dan Blocker, the actor who played Hoss Cartwright in the television show '*Bonanza*', for John Cannon and Jack Saunders to race.

Sold to Mike Smith of Florida.
Sold to Dr. Matthias Wagner in Germany.

SL70/7 (Photo on page 25).
Light green with dark green racing stripe. Tub only, as a replacement for SL70/4. Delivered to the Stirling Moss Auto Racing Team for BoverallC pilot Hugh Dibley on 13/4/65.
Hugh Dibley raced this T70 both in the UK and America in 1965. After this, he loaned to car to Scooter Patrick for a race, and then sold it to the Smothers Brothers for Hugh Powell to drive. The T70 was then used in the film *The Challengers*. Nose damaged. Sold

SL70/8.

through Chuck Haines to Jim Schield of Pomona who owned it for eleven years then sold it to Phil Schmitt of Californa in 1985. A tree, which had grown up in front of the barn where the car was stored, had to be cut down to remove it, and black widow spiders were living in the car! The car has been restored to 1968 specification and has Mark IIIb front from Dan Gurney's shop, and rear bodywork from George Follmer's Mark II Spyder, which was crashed at Riverside in 1968. 9 inch front and 16 inch wide Halibrand wheels are fitted. The present owner has raced the car in various vintage events for over 3000 miles and has now restored the car back to its original specification and in Hugh Dibley's livery.

1965
19/4: Easter Monday Goodwood Meeting: Dibley; 4th.
15/5: Silverstone International Trophy: Dibley; race number 26; 2nd.
06/6: Players 200, Mosport Park: Dibley; race number5; qualified 8th, DNF.
01/7: Silverstone: Dibley; DNF.
12/7: Senior Service 25 laps: Dibley; DNF due to a blown engine.
24/7: Martini Trophy, Silverstone: Dibley; DNF (the gearbox split when 2nd at 29 laps).
09/8: Guards Trophy, 10 laps, Brands Hatch: Dibley; RU.
15/8: Croft, 40 laps: Dibley; DNF (gear selector problems).
30/8: Guards International Trophy, Brands Hatch: Dibley; DNF.
19/9: Players Trophy, Mont Tremblant-St. Jovite: Dibley; DNF.
10/10: North-west GP: Dibley; DNF.
30/10: Times GP, Riverside: Dibley; 7th, race number 69.

1966
22/4: For sale in *Autosport*: £3600 with a 6.2 Chevrolet engine.
Loaned to Scooter Patrick in the USA.
30/10: LA Times GP, Riverside: S. Patrick; race number 53; DNF.
Sold to Hugh Powell with the Smothers Brothers.

1967
03/9: Can-Am round 2, Elkhart Lake 200: Powell; DNF.
17/9: Can-Am round 3, Bridgehampton: Powell; DNF.
15/10: Can-Am round 4, Monterey GP, Laguna Seca: Powell; qualified 31st, RU.
29/10: Can-Am round 5, Los Angeles GP, Riverside: Powell; qualified 35th, RU.
12/11: Can-Am round 6, Stardust GP, Las Vegas: Powell; qualified 28th, crashed in a first lap "coming together".
2001: Newly rebuilt Ford V8 installed.

SL70/8
Sold to John Klug of Newport Beach, California, on 28/4/65 (Pacesetter Homes). Bentley Blue. Gearbox number LG500/10. John Klug was an enthusiastic entrant, having had Dan Gurney race a King Cobra for him in 1964. He bought this T70 and had several drivers race it for him. The car had large streamlined air intakes over its sidedraught Weber carburettors, as did Fulp and Penske's cars. The 'Pacesetter Homes' Lola, racing in the USRRC and Can-Am series, was driven by Roger McKluskey, Bob Bondurant and Rick Muther.

1965
364 cu.in. Traco Chevrolet engine.
24/4: Stardust GP, Las Vegas: Bucknum; 4th.
01/5: Times GP, Riverside: Bondurant, race number 11; DNF.
08/5: Monterey GP, Laguna Seca: Rick Muther; 5th in first heat,

DNF in second.
27/6: Watkins Glen: Muther; DNF (broken oil line).
01/8: Northwest GP, Kent: Muther; 4th.
1965: Continental Divide, Co: Muther, race number 11; 2nd.
31/10: Los Angeles Times Grand Prix, Riverside: Bondurant; 8th in qualifying race. Main event: DNF due to a crash. Race number 11.
December: Nassau Trophy Race: Bondurant; race number 111; 8th.
December: Governor's Trophy, Nassau: Bondurant; DNF.

1966
Lancer-Lola entry? Had the streamlined carburettor covers.
24/4: USRRC, Stardust GP, Las Vegas: Skip Hudson; 3rd.
01/5: USRRC, Riverside: Hudson; 2nd.
08/5: Laguna Seca: Hudson; 3rd.
26/6: USRRC, Watkins Glen: Hudson; 4th.
30/7: USRRC, Kent: Hudson; 16th.
29/8: Mid-Ohio: Hudson; DNF.
04/9: USRRC, Road America 500: Skip Hudson; race number 9; 3rd.

1967: Driven at Riverside by Roger McKluskey. Race number 12. In 1967, the T70 was crashed at Riverside whilst giving rides, (driven by mechanic Roy Campbell) after the steering wheel was seized by a passenger. Burnt out, it was buried in Rubidoux, CA.

SL70/9
Sold to J. Fulp Jnr. (Buck) of Anderson, South Carolina, on 24/5/65. Royal blue. Chevrolet 5.3-litre engine. Buck Fulp's first T70, (he bought a Mark II to race later in 1965).

1965:
01/5: Times GP, Riverside: Fulp, race number 8; 1st.
27/6: Watkins Glen: Fulp; DNF.
01/8: Northwest GP, Kent: Fulp, race number 26; DNF.
19/9: Bridgehampton 500: Fulp; DNF (steering deranged?).
5/12: Nassau International Trophy: Fulp; DNF.
Sold to Dave Posey in the USA.

SL70/10 (Photo on page 45).
Sold to Carroll Shelby, Los Angeles, on 3/5/65. 305 Ford engine with Weslake heads. White.

1965
01/5: LA Times GP, Riverside: Grant, race number 8; DNF.
31/10: Los Angeles Times GP, Riverside: Jones, race number 18; DNF when in 4th.
14/11: Stardust GP, Las Vegas: Jones; DNF when leading race.

1966
24/4: USRRC, Las Vegas: J. Grant; DNF.
01/5: USRRC, Riverside: J. Grant; DNF.
08/5: USRRC, Laguna Seca: J. Grant; DNF.
22/5: USRRC, Bridgehampton: J. Grant; 1st.
04/6: Players 200, Mosport: J. Grant; DNF.
26/6: USRRC, Watkins Glen: J. Grant; 5th.
10/7: Mont Tremblant: J. Grant; DNF.
31/7: USRRC, Kent: J. Grant; DNF.
11/9: Can-Am, Mont Tremblant: J. Grant; DNF.
18/9: Can-Am, Bridgehampton GP: J. Grant; 7th.
24/9: Can-Am, Canadian GP, Mosport: J.Grant; DNF.
This car was crashed in a test session, by Chuck Jones when demonstrating the car to journalists, and was destroyed. The remains of the tub were cut up and put in the Orange County municipal rubbish dump. The car is presently being recreated in the USA.

SL70/11
Sold to Carl Haas (Greenwich Autos Inc.), USA. White. LG500 gearbox.
30/10: Times GP Riverside: P. Jones; race number 18; DNF.
14/11: Stardust GP, Las Vegas: Race number 18; DNF.

SL70/12
USA. John Mecom. Probably sold to R. Bucknum who raced it in a few USRRC races. If so:

1965
24/4: USRRC, Las Vegas: R. Bucknum; DNF.
01/5: USRRC, Riverside: R. Bucknum; DNF.
30/7: USRRC, Kent: R. Bucknum; DNF.
No other information but could have been crashed and re-tubbed with SL70/13.

SL70/13
USA. John Mecom. Spare tub.
The chassis number of this T70 is stamped into the top of the front bulkhead. Its early history is unknown but it was imported from Chuck Haines, via Ian Webb, in 1980(ish) into the UK. Sold to Nigel Hulme, sold to Colin Parry Williams who races it extensively still. In January 1997 the car was dismantled for a rebuild. The front and rear suspension mountings have anti-dive built in, and the whole tub has a nose-down attitude and is one inch shorter than a Mark II.
1997: Restored by Clive Robinson Engineering, UK.

SL70/14
To the USA. Sold to the Alpha Corporation. Ford 289 cu. in. motor. Delivered 12/8/65. Probably the car sold to Shermen Decker of Oneonta, New York.

1965
29/8: Mid-Ohio: Decker; DNF.
September: Mont Tremblant-St. Jovite, Sherman Decker rolled his Lola, "completely demolishing it" (*Autosport*). (Probably damaging it badly - Ed).

1966
22/5: Bridgehampton: S. Decker; DNF.

Used as a camera car for the film: *Grand Prix* and one other (unissued) film.
Owned by James Garner and driven by Dan Gurney.
Sold to Robin Spurrier in the early '70s. Fitted with Mark III bodywork and raced by him for several years.
Sold to Chuck Haines of Missouri in the late '80s.
Bought by Corrado Cupellini from America in 1985. For sale in Italy (2/93). Dark blue. Fitted now with a Ford 4.7-litre engine. Sold. Another car with this number exists in Britain. It has a genuine Lola T70 tub, and is really chassis number SL70/13.

SL70/15
Sold to Haskell Automotive Co., Hollywood, California, on 12/8/65.

1965
31/10: Riverside GP: Bondurant; DNF.
14/11: Stardust GP, Las Vegas: Bondurant; 4th.

1966
24/4: USRRC, Stardust Raceway, Las Vegas: Bucknum; DNF.

01/5: USRRC, Riverside: Bucknum; DNF.
31/7: USRRC, Kent: Bucknum; DNF.
11/9: Can-Am, Mont Tremblant: Bucknum; DNF.

1997: For sale in the USA, having been owned by the same person for ten years.
1998: Sold in the USA.

MARK II

Introduced June/July 1965

SL71/16 (Photo on page 43).
Sold to Team Surtees. Sent to the USA in July 1965. John Surtees' second T70. He was badly injured in this car at Mosport in September. It's possible that the suspension, brakes, engine and gearbox were built into a spare tub, SL71/17.

1965
30/8: Guards International Trophy, Brands Hatch: Driven by John Surtees, it won both heats, finishing more than 90 seconds ahead of Bruce McLaren. 1m.36s, 99.37mph, race number 4.
19/9: Players Quebec race, Mont Tremblant-St. Jovite: Surtees; 1st.
25/9: In practice for the Pepsi 100 prior to the Canadian Grand Prix at Mosport, Surtees suffered severe injuries when the front nearside hub carrier broke as he was testing the car for Jackie Stewart. The remains of the car were buried at Mosport and it is now under the parking lot of the Bowmanville shopping precinct. Note: This car may have been rebuilt in 1965 using the tub marked SL71/17. If so, it probably took part in the 1966 Can-Am as a Team Surtees car, possibly the one driven by Graham Hill. If so:

1966
10/4: Archie Scott-Brown memorial Trophy, Snetterton: G. Hill; DNF in the 1st heat due to differential failure.
14/8: Wills Trophy, Croft: Surtees; 1st.
30/8: Brands Hatch: G. Hill; 3rd.
03/9: Road America 200, Elkhart Lake: G. Hill; 3rd overall.
30/10: Riverside Can-Am: G. Hill; 3rd.

Jan 27 1967: Car advertised in *Autosport*, through Howard Marsden, as a Graham Hill car with a 364 Chevrolet engine.

SL71/17
Sold to John Mecom, according to factory records. Spare monocoque used to rebuild SL70/1. BUT, possibly to replace the tub of SL71/16 which had been badly crashed at Mont Tremblant-St. Jovite by John Surtees (see above).

1966
11/9: Can-Am, St Jovite: Surtees, race number 3; 1st.
16/10: Can-Am Round 4, Monterey Grand Prix, Laguna Seca, 2 heats: Surtees; 4th in the 1st. In the 2nd race, the steering failed after Surtees was hit by Jones. DNF. Surtees then swapped to using SL71/43.

SL71/18
Sold to John Mecom on 19/12/65.
Sold to John 'Buck' Fulp. Chevrolet engine. 58mm sidedraught Weber carburettors, small brakes.
Gearbox number: LG500-41.

Fulp's second T70 with which he won at Riverside and then badly crashed the car at Mosport. A spare tub (SL71/18), was used to rebuild the car. Fulp then won three races with the car.

1965
5/12: Nassau International Trophy: Fulp; DNF.

1966 USRRC series
"Bardahl" sponsored car for All-American Racers: 2nd in the championship. (22 points).
24/4: Stardust GP, Las Vegas: Fulp; DNF.
01/5: LA Times GP, Riverside: Fulp; 1st.
12/6: Mosport. Car badly crashed. New Mark II (SL71/18) built up in two weeks.
26/6: Watkins Glen: Fulp, race number 26; 1st.
31/7: Kent: Fulp; DNF.
Bridgehampton: Fulp, race number 26; 1st.
29/8: Mid-Ohio: Fulp; 3rd.
04/9: Road America 500: Fulp; race number 26; DNF.
Watkins Glen: Fulp; 1st.

1966
24/4: USRRC, Stardust Raceway, Las Vegas: Fulp; DNF.
01/5: USRRC, Riverside: Fulp; 1st.
26/6: USRRC, Watkins Glen: Fulp; 1st.
28/8: USRRC, Buckete Cup, Mid-Ohio: Fulp; 3rd.
04/9: USRRC, Elkhart Lake 500: Fulp; race number 26; DNF.
2/12: Governor's Trophy, Nassau: Fulp; RU.
4/12: Nassau Trophy: Fulp; 4th.

Perhaps:
1967: Sebring 2-hours: McCluskey/Fulp; race number 12; DNS due to suspension damage.
Sold to the East coast and then crashed at Lime Rock in 1977.
1988: Restored in Florida and sold to D. McKay.
1990: Sold to Jim Galucci.
2001: For sale.

SL71/19 (Photo on page 38 - behind race number 33)
Gearbox number: LG500-40.
Sold to the Racing Partnership Team (Jersey) in December 1965. Tony Sergeant/Hugh Dibley. Green.

1966
10/4: Archie Scott-Brown Memorial Trophy, Snetterton: Sargeant; DNF. Ford 4.7 engine.
11/4: Formula Libre, Mallory Park: T. Sargent; 1st. Chevrolet engine.
30/4: Tourist Trophy, Oulton Park: Dibley; 2nd.
15/5: International Trophy Race, Silverston: Dibley; 5th.
18/6: Formula Libre, Rufforth: Sargent; 3rd.
09/7: Martini Trophy, Silverstone: Dibley; 4th.
17/7: Supporting race to British GP, Brands Hatch: 5.9 engine. Dibley; 1st.
24/7: Gold Flake Handicap, Phoenix Park: Sargeant; DNF.
07/8: Sports-Racing Cars Race, Crystal Palace: M. Daghorn; 1st.
14/8: Formula Libre, Croft: Sargeant; 1st.
14/8: Wills Trophy Race, Croft: Dibley; 2nd.
21/8: Castle Combe: Dibley; 5th. Ford 4.7 engine.
30/8: Guards International Trophy, Brands Hatch: Dibley; DNF, CWP.
11/9: Crashed at the 1966 Can-Am practice at Mont Tremblant, St. Jovite, when it flipped onto its back after cresting a rise. Repaired.
24/9: Can-Am, Mosport Park: Dibley; 7th.
9/10: Kent: Dibley; 18th.
16/10: Can-Am, Laguna Seca: Dibley; 10th.
30/10: Can-Am, Los Angeles Times Grand Prix, Riverside: Dibley; 6th.

13/11: Can-Am, Stardust Grand Prix, Las Vegas: Dibley; 5th.
Nothing further known.

SL71/20
Sold to John Mecom on December 19th, 1965.
Gearbox number: LG500-39.
POSSIBLY the Bardahl car driven by Jerry Grant. Car used to replace SL70/10.

1966:
Watkins Glen: race number 8.
Bridgehampton: Grant; 1st.

SL71/21
Sold to John Mecom on 10/1/66.
Gearbox number: LG500-43.
The first T70 sold to Roger Penske for Mark Donohue. Big block Chevrolet, 427 cu. in.

1966
29/5: St. Jovite, FIA race. 427 Chevrolet. Donohue; spun, punctured the radiator, and the engine was damaged.
04/6: Mosport: Rebuilt engine. Donohue; DNF.
26/6: USRRC, Watkins Glen: Donohue; qualified 3rd, crashed and burned out. Dumped in trash.
End of 1965 production.

SL71/22
Sold to Rick Muther (USA) on 12/1/66. Gearbox number: LG500-42.

1967
29/10: Can-Am round 5: Muther; qualified 29th; DNF.

SL71/23 (Photo on pages 40 and 41).
Sold to Phil Scragg for hillclimbs only.
Gearbox number: LG500-52.
Philip Scragg had raced a lightweight E-type Jaguar in British hillclimbs and he used his T70 in the same type of events. In 1966/67, he had the car cut down to what amounted to Spyder bodywork with cycle fenders.

1966
23/4: Loton Park: Scragg; 9th.
08/5: Prescott: Scragg; 2nd.
21/5: Barbon Manor: Scragg; 5th.
Shelsley Walsh: Scragg; 8th.
Bo'ness: Scragg; 8th.
Prescott: Scragg; 6th (Gold cup awarded).
06/8: Great Auclum: Scragg; RU.
Craiglantlet: Scragg; 1st.
Shelsley Walsh: Scragg; 4th.
Harewood: Scragg; 6th.
Dyrham Park: Scragg; 8th.

1967
Converted to open wheeled bodywork by Williams and Pritchard.
22/4: Loton Park: 11th.
May: Prescott: 1st BTD.
5/8: Great Auclum: 1st in class 6.
9/9: Prescott: 1st in class 6.9th overall.
10/9: Harewood: 1st in class 6. 8th overall.
15/10. Loton Park: 1st in class 6.
Craigantlet: 4th with Ford 4.7 engine.
Sold to Tony Harrison of Little Aston, Birmingham, in July 1969.
Sold to Brian Classic. Sold to David Preece.
Sold to Terry Smith who rebuilt/rebodied it with IIIb coupé bodywork. 1995: Sold to Yvan Mahe of France, reverted to Mark 3 G.T. coupé front and rear bodywork.

SL71/24 (Photo on page 43).
Sold to John Mecom on 12/1/66. Ford engined.
Gearbox number: LG500-44.
Driven by Parnelli Jones. Fitted with a Paxton supercharged 4.7 Ford giving approximately 470bhp. George Bignotti, Jones' race engineer, later replaced the Ford engine with a Chevrolet unit. According to *Motor Sport* , a big-block unit.

1966
24/4: USRRC, Stardust GP, Las Vegas: Jones, race number 18; DNF.
11/9: Can-Am Round 1, Mont Tremblant-St. Jovite: 5th in practice. Hit on grid at start. Jones; race number 98; DNF.
Can-Am Round 2, Laguna Seca: Jones; race number 98; 1st heat, DNF. 2nd heat, 1st.
Can-Am Round 3, Riverside: Jones; race number 98; DNF.

Sold to Yvan Mahe of France in 1990 who acquired it burnt out to the rear bulkhead. He had a new tub built up by Maurice Gomm and then rebuilt the car.

1993: May 8/9. Silverstone 'Supersports' race: DNF (oil pump failure).
June 27: Thruxton, Supersports race: DNF, (water pump problems).

SL71/25 (Photo on page 31).
Sold to John Mecom. Delivered 26/2/66.
Gearbox number: LG500/45.

1966
16/10: Monterey GP, Laguna Seca: J. Stewart, qualified 22nd; DNS (overheating).
30/10: Riverside: Stewart, race number 43, DNF.
13/11: Las Vegas: Stewart, 5th in practice, RU.

Crashed and stored untill 1980.
Sold to Simon Hadfield in England who had a new tub built by Maurice Gomm/Arnie Johnson at Silverstone. Sold on to France.

SL71/26
Sold to John Mecom on 19/7/66. Ford 427 cu. in. engine.
Gearbox number: LG500-61.

1966
30/10: Can-Am round 5, Times GP, Riverside: Foyt, race number 83; DNF (overheating).
2/12: Governor's Trophy, Nassau: Foyt; DNF.
4/12: Nassau Trophy: Foyt; RU.

Sold to a New York collector who had the car completely rebuilt by Crosthwaite and Gardner, with a Corvette 327 cu. in. engine on carburettors installed. Painted yellow.
1996: Sold to a new owner who took part in the 30th anniversary of the Can-Am at Elkhart lake that year.
1998: Sold through Grand Prix Classics of San Diego to John Schumann of Vero Beach.

SL71/27 (Photo on page 21).
Sold to Charles Bridges. Red Rose Racing Team for Brian Redman.
Engine number: TS51 (Team Surtees).

1966
10/4: Archie Scott-Brown memorial Trophy, Snetterton: Redman; 4th.
30/4: Tourist Trophy, Oulton Park: Redman; 13th. Race number: 28.
15/5: International Trophy Race, Silverstone: Redman. 4th.
30/5: Grovewood Trophy, Mallory Park: Redman; DNF (damaged wheel).
18/6: Rufforth: 1st. Lap record, 1m 12.8, 84.07mph. Redman. Race number: 39.
17/7: Brands Hatch, support race to British GP: 5.9 engine. Redman; 4th.
14/8: Croft: Redman; DNF (accident).
30/8: Guards Trophy, Brands Hatch: Redman; 4th. Race number: 33.
Sold to Robin Darlington.
1/10: Club race, Silverstone GP circuit: Darlington; 1st. Race number: 154.
9/10: BARC Club handicap, Silverstone: Darlington; 1st.
Silverstone Club lap record: 59.4, 97.45mph; Darlington.
27/12: BRSCC meeting, Mallory Park: Formula Libre; Darlington; 1st.

1967
22/1:Racing car show Trophy meeting, Brands Hatch, Guards Trophy: Darlington; DNF after a spin into a ditch (no damage).
12/3: Sports cars 10 laps: DNF, on last lap with broken rocker. Fastest lap 50.0s.
24/3: Oulton Park: Darlington; 1st.
24/3: Formula Libre, Oulton Park: P. Gethin; 1st.
24/3: Sports car 10 laps, Oulton Park: Darlington; 1st.
09/4: Formula Libre, Snetterton: Darlington; 2nd.
16/4: Brands Hatch: Lanfranchi; 2nd after clutch failed.
23/4: Leicester cup, Mallory Park: Richard Kennedy; DNF when anti-roll bar came loose.
23/4: Sports racing over 10 laps, Mallory Park: Darlington; 2nd.
At the end of 1967, the car was sold to David Bridges, then sold to the USA but never paid for. Missing in action.

SL71/28
Sold to John Mecom on 26/2/66. Gearbox number: LG500-55.
Sold to Hall, USA.

1986: In South Africa.
Sold to Trevor Needham.
1991: Sold to J.P. Bertrand of Luxemburg.
This freshly restored car, in yellow, appeared at the Spa historic races carrying this number on May 15/16th 1993. Bertrand was third on the car's first outing at Spa in 1993.
2000: Sold to D. Bohours.

SL71/29
Sold to John Mecom on 3/6/66 for Brown. Chevrolet engine. Gearbox number: LG500-72.

1966
'Ringfree motor oil special'.
18/9: Can-Am round 2, Bridgehampton: Brown, race number 30; 2nd in qualifying heat. Main race: RU.
24/9: Can-Am round 3, Mosport Park, Toronto: Robert Brown, 8th overall.

SL71/30
Sold to Umberto Maglioli of Italy on 29/5/66. Chevrolet 5.9-litre engine. No gearbox.

1969
Sold to Dill Pell, an Englishman, who took the car to New Zealand.
Sold to Jim Boyd.
ACC Sprint meeting, Pukekohe: Standing quarter mile: 12.3 seconds. Boyd; 1st.
Repainted blue and white for the Cambridge Team.
Pukekohe Race: Boyd; 1st.
?/10: Bay Park: Boyd; 2nd.
?/11: Bay Park: Boyd; 1st.
?/12: Parsons Motor Trophy, Bay Park: Boyd; 1st.
?/12: Pukekohe: Boyd; 2nd.

1970
?/1: Timaru: Boyd; 1st.
?/2: Teretonga: Boyd; 3rd.
?/4: Pukekohe: Boyd; 1st.
This car won the 1970 New Zealand Sports car championship.

1971: Crashed at Timaru and was then hit by an errant Corvette.
Sold to Baron Robertson who intended to rebuild it as a road car.
Partially rebuilt by Travis McGregor, sold to Lex Emslie, sold to Norm Masters/Brian Middlemass in Balclutha.
Sold to Rob Boult.
Sold to Ralph Smith.
2000: For sale.

SL71/31 (Photo on page 39).
Sold to Sid Taylor for Denny Hulme. Built up in 1965 by Sid Taylor's Mechanic (Ron Bennett) at the Lola Works. 5.0-litre Chevrolet. Raced in 1966 with 5.9-litre engine. Number: T.S.7. (Team Surtees).

1966
10/4: Scott-Brown Trophy, Snetterton: Hulme; race number 8; 1st overall.
11/4: Formula Libre, Mallory Park: Taylor; 2nd.
30/4: TT Oulton Park: Hulme; race number 4; 1st overall.
15/5: International Trophy Race, Silverstone: Hulme; race number 32; 1st.
21/5: Sports car race, Castle Combe: DNF (Tony Lanfranchi spun when leading). Lap record.
21/5: Formula Libre, Castle Combe: Lanfranchi; 1st. Lap record.
30/5: Grovewood Trophy Mallory Park: Hulme; race number 1; 1st.
09/7: Martini Trophy, Silverstone: Hulme; race number 35; 1st.
17/7: Support race to British GP, Brands Hatch: Attwood; DNF (puncture).
24/7: Formula Libre, Phoenix Park, Ireland: Taylor; race number 1, 1st.
24/7: Gold Flake Handicap, Phoenix Park: Taylor; 4th.
30/8: Brands Hatch: Hulme; DNF (engine).
24/9: Can-Am 3rd round, Mosport Park: Hulme; DNF (drive shaft failure).
16/10: Can-Am, Monterey GP at Laguna Seca: Hulme; 5th in 1st heat, DNF in 2nd.
30/10: Can-Am, Times GP at Riverside: Hulme; DNF.
13/11: Can-Am, Stardust GP at Las Vegas: Hulme; DNF. Gearbox problems on 22nd lap.
4/12: Kyalami 9-hours for Dave Charlton/Roy Pierpoint with 289 Ford. DNF (crown wheel and pinion failure).
Circuit records at: Snetterton (Hulme 1m 33.8, 104.01mph), Silverstone GP (Hulme 1m 28.2, 118.66mph), Oulton Park (Hulme 1m 37.4, 102.5 mph), Mallory Park (Hulme 47.6, 102.1mph), Castle Combe (Lanfranchi 1m 4.8, 102.2mph), and Phoenix Park.

1967
Jan 13. Advertised for sale in *Autosport*. Bought by John Scott-

Davies who took it to Australia when he emigrated there.
21/5: Entered for International 12-hour sports car race, Surfers Paradise Raceway, but DNS due to a dropped valve. Then running a 4.8-litre Chevrolet engine.
Sold to Denis Geary who fitted a GT coupé body for road use.

1973: Sold to Matt Carrol, a film producer from Sydney.
1980-1983: Matt Carrol had the car rebuilt by Kevin Shearer. Carrol did four races in Australasia in support of the Australian Grand Prix. Sold to Nigel Hulme in 1989, since when the car has only been used once in a test session at Silverstone.
1995: Sold to Jean Blaton (Beurlys) of Belgium who has raced it in the Paul Ricard 24 hour event twice.
Sold on since.

SL71/32 (Photo on page 48).
Sold to John Mecom. Delivered to R. Penske Racing in January 1966, (2nd T70).

1966
30/7: USRRC, Kent, Washington: Donohue; 1st overall.
29/8: USRRC, Mid-Ohio: Donohue; DNF.
03/9: USRRC, Riverside tests: Firestone testing accident. Chassis damaged.

1966
11/9: Can-Am, Mont Tremblant-St Jovite: Donohue, race number 6; DNF.
18/9: Can-Am, Bridgehampton: Donohue, race number 6; 5th.
24/9: Can-Am, Mosport. Canadian G.P, race number 6; Donohue; 1st.
16/10: Can-Am, Laguna Seca: Donohue, race number 61; 4th.
30/10: Can-Am, Riverside: Donohue, race number 61; 4th.
13/11: Can-Am, Stardust GP, Las Vegas: Donohue, race number 61; 3rd.
?/12: Nassau: Donohue; 1st.

Car later repaired and sold.
Sold to John Meyer from Connecticut, who raced the car in SCCA and Can-Am races in the late 1960s. Won SCCA 1967/8/9 'A' Championship. 1st at Mount Equinox hillclimb.
1970: Sold to Philip Vanscoy-Smith. Still retained Sunoco blue paintwork.
1971: Sold to Jim Glickenaus of New York.
Re-bodied with coupé bodywork. Used on the road.
1998: Rebodied back to original Spyder configuration.

SL71/33
Sold to John Mecom for Skogmo on 14/6/66.
Gearbox number: LG500-73.

1966
28/8: USRRC, Mid-Ohio: Skogmo; 11th.

SL71/34
Sold to All American Racers for Dan Gurney on 8/6/66. 5.3-litre Ford-Weslake engine. LG500-79. Blue with white flashes.

1966
22/5: USRRC, Bridgehampton: Grant; race number 8; 1st.
11/9: Can-Am Round 1, Mont Tremblant-St. Jovite; Gurney; withdrawn with engine failure.
18/9: Can-Am Round 2, Bridgehampton: Gurney; 1st.
24/9: Can-Am Round 3, Mosport Park: Gurney; DNF after leading with ten laps to go (battery).
16/10: Can-Am Round 4, Monterey GP, Laguna Seca: 1st heat, Gurney; DNF (engine). 2nd heat, Gurney; DNS.
30/10: Can-Am Round 5, Los Angeles GP, Riverside: Gurney; DNF (clutch).
13/11: Can-Am Round 6, Stardust GP, Las Vegas: Gurney; DNF (broken drive shaft).
A car with chassis number SL72/34 has had a Mk III coupé body installed by Charles Bartz.
Sold to Bobbie Thompson of New Orleans but has been sold on since.

SL71/35
Sold to John Mecom on 5/7/66. Gearbox number: LG500-75. This is probably the car that was driven by Foyt at Riverside (DNF) and Nassau. On both occasions bearing race number 83.

SL71/36
Sold to John Mecom on 7/10/66. Chevrolet engine. Gearbox number: LG500-97. Nothing known.

SL71/37
Sold to John Mecom. 'X' prototype. Probably the Mario Andretti Ford 7-litre engined car with automatic transmission. If so:

1966
30/10: Can-Am Round 5, Riverside: DNF (engine).
13/11: Can-Am round 6, Stardust GP, Las Vegas: 21st in qualifying after winning consolation race. DNF (gearbox).
December: Nassau: race number 11; DNF.
A car with chassis number SL72/37 belonged to Dan Hagerty (Grizzly Adams) and has been coupéd with a Mk III body, widened by 8 inches.
Sold to Chuck Haines.
Reportedly sold to Switzerland/Germany.

SL71/38
Sold to Jackie Epstein. Delivered 26/8/66. Alan Smith 6-litre Chevrolet engine. Gearbox number: LG500-82. This car had knock on hubs and front and rear spoilers. Driven by Paul Hawkins.

1966
30/8: Guards Trophy, Brands Hatch: Hawkins; 5th.
11/9: Can-Am, Mont Tremblant-St Jovite practice: Air got underneath the front of car and flipped it upside down onto the rollbar. Hawkins unhurt.
18/9: Can-Am, Bridgehampton: Hawkins. 13th.
24/9: Can-Am, Canadian GP, Mosport: Hawkins; 5th.
16/10: Can-Am, Monterey GP, Laguna Seca: Hawkins; 13th.
30/10: Can-Am, Riverside: Hawkins; 7th.
?/10: North West Pacific GP, Kent: Hawkins; 3rd.
13/11: Can-Am, Stardust GP, Las Vegas: Hawkins; 8th.

Epstein advertised a Mk II in *Autosport*, Jan 6, 1967.
Advertised for sale in March 3 *Autosport* (7 races only).

SL71/39
Sold to John Mecom on 12/8/66. Chevrolet engine. Nothing known.

SL71/40
Sold to John Mecom for Alderman on 18/8/66. Ford engine. Gearbox number: LG500-76.

1966
11/9: Can-Am round 1, Mt. Tremblant-St. Jovite: Alderman; 24th in practice; 11th in race.

SL71/40.

18/9: Can-Am round 2, Bridgehampton: Alderman; disqualified.

1967
Sold to Brett Lunger.
01/9: Can-Am round 1, Elkhart Lake: Lunger; qualified 20th; 12th overall (Lunger then swapped to a Caldwell D7B).
16/10: Can-Am round 4, Monterey GP, Laguna Seca: Lunger; 25th in practice, 19th overall.
24/10: Believed to have been crashed by Brett Lunger at Mosport.

Lunger did Can-Am 1968. If it was with this car, then:
Sold to Matt McLendon.
Sold to Dan Martin, California. Restored with a Mark III GT body. Yellow. 365 cu. in. Chevrolet on Weber carburettors. LG600 gearbox. Took part in historic races.

1998: For sale at Grand Prix Classics, La Jolla, USA. Now converted back to Spyder bodywork in black and silver. Excellent restoration by Phil Reilly.
11/1/98: STPO.

SL71/41
Sold to John Mecom on 22/8/66.
Laguna Seca: Stewart (?); race number 43; DNS.
Nothing else known.

SL71/42.
Sold to John Mecom for George Follmer on 14/9/66. Bartz Chevrolet engine. Gearbox number: LG500-94.

1966
11/9: USRRC, Mont Tremblant: Follmer; 4th.
16/10: Can-Am round 4, Monterey GP, Laguna Seca: Follmer; 16th in practice, 17th in race.
30/10: Can-Am round 5, LA Times GP, Riverside: Follmer; 5th.
13/11: Can-Am round 6. Stardust G.P Las Vegas: Follmer; 7th in practice, DNF.

1967
23/4: USRRC, Stardust Raceway, Las Vegas: Follmer; DNF after a spin which resulted in a damaged radiator.
30/4: USRRC, Riverside: Follmer; 2nd.
21/5: USRRC, Bridgehampton: Follmer; race number 16; DNF.
?: USRRC, Laguna Seca: Pole position. Follmer; DNF.
?: Non-USRRC race at Cotati: Follmer; 1st.
18/7: USRRC, Pacific Raceways: Follmer; DNF (broken oil pump).

1968
The car was crashed and the tub damaged at Riverside tire tests. Tub discarded. Parts kept. Bruce Burness now owns these and is rebuilding the car.

SL71/43
Sold to John Mecom for Team Surtees. Delivered September 22nd, 1966.

16/10: Can-Am, Monterey GP, Laguna Seca: Surtees; 12th.
30/10: Can-Am round 5, Los Angeles Times Grand Prix, Riverside: Surtees; 1st.

SL71/43.

13/11: Can-Am round 6, Las Vegas Stardust Grand Prix, first ever Can-Am series: Surtees; 1st overall.
(Surtees won the Championship and more than $50,000).
Returned to Carl Haas's showroom. Raced by John Surtees in 1967 after problems with his IIIB Spyder.

12/11/67: Can-Am round 6, Stardust GP, Las Vegas: Surtees; 1st.
Returned to Carl Haas in 1971 for a complete rebuild.
1971: Sold to George Ralph who raced it in some Can-Am events. Sold back to Carl Haas. Sold to Michael Hanz who used it on the road.
1977: Sold to David Cowart of Tampa, Florida, who had it restored with Mark IIIb coupé bodywork and air conditioning installed.
2001: Now restored to original specification with very light bodywork. Vintage raced by Cowart. Has 9in front and 12in rear wheels, and has different front and rear suspension geometry (from Surtees' 1967 IIIb Spyder?). Painted in red with white Surtees arrowhead on the nose.

SL71/44 (Photo on page 46).
Sold to John Mecom on 23/9/66 for Parnelli Jones. 5.9 Chevrolet engine. Gearbox number: LG500-95.

1966
16/10: Can-Am round 4, Monterey Grand Prix, Laguna Seca: Jones; qualified 22nd, DNF in first heat, (sump pan detached). Won second heat. 21st overall.
30/10: Can-Am round 5, Riverside: Jones: qualified 37th, DNF (engine).
13/11: Can-Am round 6, Stardust Grand Prix, Las Vegas: Jones; qualified 8th, Stewart; 9th.

Sold to Chuck Haines with a Chevrolet engine, but the owner reports that it had modifications which showed that it had had a Ford 'Indy' engine installed. Sold on since.

SL71/45
Sold to John Mecom on 23/9/66. Spare monocoque.

SL71/46
Sold to John Mecom on 7/10/66. Spare monocoque. All American Racers Bardahl car. Driven by Jerry Grant in Can-Am events. Probably used a new monocoque to replace SL70/10.

1967
30/4: USRRC, Riverside: J. Grant; DNF.
17/9: Can-Am round 2, Bridgehampton: Grant; qualified 12th. DNF, lap 6 (fuel pump).
15/10: Can-Am round 4, Monterey GP, Laguna Seca: Jones; qualified 30th. RU.
29/10: Can-Am round 5, LA Times GP, Riverside: Grant; qualified

23rd. RU.
12/11: Can-Am round 6, Stardust GP, Las Vegas: Grant; qualified 17th. Finished the race.

Now has an Alan Green Chevrolet engine and Mark III coupé bodywork. LG500, 4 speed gearbox. Big brakes.
Sold to Chuck Haines.
Restored by Jerry Weichers of Willows, California.
Sold to Jim Barrington.

SL71/47
Sold to Chris Renwick on 7th April, 1967. No engine or gearbox supplied. However, when consulted, Chris Renwick reported that he had never ordered, taken delivery of, or sold a T70!

SL71/48
Sold to John Surtees on 5/67. Gearbox number: LG500/? Originally Red.
Car used for testing the Aston Martin engine, DP218. It had a detachable rear bulkhead, lightweight body panels and a DG gearbox.
Re-engined with a Chevrolet 6.0-litre, but retained the DG gearbox.
14/5: International Trophy, Silverstone: D. Hobbs; DNF.
30/5: Grovewood Trophy, Mallory Park: David Hobbs; race number 2; DNF.
09/7: Martini International Trophy, Silverstone: Pole position. Hobbs; race number 34; 3rd overall.
Probably the car which Surtees used in the following races:

1966
Lap record at Brands Hatch short circuit in 49.9s: Surtees.
09/7: Martini International Trophy, Silverstone: Hobbs; 3rd.
14/8: Wills Trophy, Croft: Surtees; 1st.
30/8: Guards Trophy, Brands Hatch: Surtees; 1st.
03/9: Road America 200, Elkhart Lake: G. Hill; 3rd overall.
11/9: Can-Am round 1, Mont Tremblant: Surtees; 1st.
18/9: Can-Am round 2, Bridgehampton: Surtees used newer G. Hill car (*Motoring News*)
24/9: Can-Am round 3, Mosport Park: Surtees involved in melee at the start. New start taken. DNF as car "badly wrecked" (*Motoring News*).
Apparently sold in the USA
Other, unidentified Mark II Lola T70s were driven in later Can-Am races by: Tom Dutton, George Drolsom, Leonard Faustina, Tom Terrell, Harry Heuer, Rich Galloway, Ron Grable, Ron Goldleaf, Jeff Stevens, Doug Hooper and Jack Millikan.

MARK III GT Coupé

SL73/101 (Photo on page 52).
First coupé finished on 2/11/66. First Aston Martin engined coupé. Chevrolet-engined when displayed at the January 1967 Racing Car Show. Dark Green with longitudinal white stripe. Tested by Surtees and Hobbs with Aston Martin engine (project 218). Lapped Silverstone in 1min.27secs. Lasted 12 and 14 hour trials at Goodwood. Fitted with Hewland LG600 5-speed gearbox number LG600-1. Gearbox driven alternator. British Racing Green with white arrow on nose edged in red. Third fastest at Le Mans test days at 3 min 31.9 seconds with Aston Martin engine fitted. Fastest in the wet. Car used to homologate the Lola T70 GT coupé into Group 4 on 1st February 1968 (Chevrolet-engined). **Note**: This and 121 have different suspension pick-up points and bulges in the rear pontoons to production Chevrolet-engined cars, to accomodate the Aston Martin V8. This engine gave 380bhp whilst 6-litre Chevrolets gave 420bhp, and were lighter.

1967
28/5: Nürburgring 1000km: Second in practice. Surtees/Hobbs. Aston Martin engine (DP218) now on Lucas fuel injection. Rear wishbone broke on lap 7. DNF.
17/18/6: Le Mans 24-hours: Chris Irwin/Peter de Klerk; DNF due to cracked crankshaft damper.
Re-engined at the factory with a Chevrolet 6-litre unit.
Sold to Max Wilson.
13/8: Wills Trophy, Croft: Wilson; Broke CWP in practice, DNS.
09/9: Holts Trophy, Crystal Palace: Max Wilson; 4th overall.
15/10: Paris 1000km, Montlhéry: Wilson/Hobbs. Race number 2. 2nd in practice, DNF on 15th lap when in second place (sump damaged).

1968
Sold to Jo Bonnier. 6-litre Bartz-tuned Chevrolet fitted. Painted yellow, white and red.
23/3: Sebring 12-hours: Bonnier/Axelsson; 10th fastest in practice with new engine and Goodyear tyres. DNF due to punctures/plug troubles/contaminated fuel. Race number 10.
Sold to David Prophet with Bonnier as driver.
07/4: BoverallC 500, Brands Hatch: 7th in practice, 1m 38.4s, Bonnier/Axelsson. 6th overall, after running 4th (flat battery in last few laps).
27/4: Players Trophy, Silverstone: Bonnier; race number 37; 2nd overall. Set fastest lap of 1:29.2 (118.31mph).
17/5: Martini Trophy, Silverstone: Bonnier; DNF.
03/6: RAC TT, Oulton Park: Bonnier; front row of grid. DNF on lap 17 due to a fuel leak.
16/6: Anderstorp: Race number 33; Bonnier; 1st overall.
30/6: Nuremburg 200, Norisring: Bonnier; 1st heat, DNF, 2nd heat, 1st.
14/7: Watkins Glen 6-hours: Bonnier/Parsons; sixth fastest in practice, 1m 12.4, fourth after 30 minutes, lost gears and 10th overall.
21/7: International Solituderennen, Hockenheim: Bonnier; DNF after leading to within five laps of the finish.
27/7: Martini International Trophy, Silverstone: Bonnier; DNF due to lack of fuel pressure. Car now had fuel injection.
11/8: Karlskoga: Pedro Rodriguez; off track on lap 12, DNF with brake failure.
17/8: Speedworld International Trophy, Oulton Park: Bonnier; 2nd overall.
25/8: Zeltweg 500km: Bonnier; qualified 5th, DNF due to split fuel tank.
31/8: Mantorp Park, Sweden: Prophet; 9th.
15/9: Grosser Preis von Osterreich: Bonnier; DNF when 4th due to split fuel bag. Bartz Chevrolet with injection. Green nose.
??/9: Guards Trophy, Brands Hatch: Bonnier; DNF after running 2nd.
Sold to Jim Beach.

1969
09/3: Mallory Park: Beach; crashed with frontal damage.
Sold to Malcolm Gartlan.
17/5: Martini Trophy, Silverstone: Entered by Malcolm Gartlan. David Hobbs; 18th.
02/8: Nuremburg 200, Norisring: Brian Muir (car reportedly owned by Jim Beach). 14th overall.
16/8: Croft: Piers Forrester; engine blew in practice.
10/8: Thruxton: Forester; DNS.
16/8: Oulton Park: Piers Forrester; 5th.
27/9: Trophy of the Dunes, Zandvoort: Jim Beach; 8th.
19/10: 300 meilen Hockenheim: Jim Beach; RU.
At one time owned by John Woolfe. Sold to John Cooper.

1972
Sold to Nick Cussons. He was told that the original bodywork, complete with aluminium tail, had been sent to the crusher only the week before his purchase! He bought spare boxed Aston Martin engines. Cussons raced the car in the Interseries in 1972/3.
21/5: Silverstone Interseries: N. Cussons; race number 21; DNF.
09/8: Zeltweg Interseries: N. Cussons; race number 21; 8th.
02/8: Norisring Interseries: N. Cussons; race number 21; DNQ.
16/8: Hockenheim. Interseries: N. Cussons; race number 21; 10th.

1973
20/5: Silverstone Interseries: N. Cussons; race number 43; DNF due to fuel starvation.
Cussons then sold the car to his friend, Roger St. John Hart.

1974: June: Sold to Dennis and Nigel Hulme.
1979: May: Sold to Peter Millward.
Developed by Andy Chapman, of Chapman and Spooner, and tested by Jonathan Palmer. Successfully raced in historic events and then sold to Darrell Plumridge in 1990.
1993 Sold in July at Coy's Silverstone Auction to Ean Pugh who races it enthusiastically in Group 4 historic events.

SL73/102 (Photo on page 66).
Coupé. Ryan-Falconer Chevrolet, number RAF 14. Gearbox number: LG600-12. White with a longitudinal green racing stripe. Prepared by Ron Bennett. First Sid Taylor coupé till July 1968 when SL73/134 was built up. Eight wins in fifteen starts. Chevrolet 5.9 fitted. Delivered to Sid Taylor.

1967
24-25/6: Rheims 12-hours: Hulme/Gardner; DNF in 5th hour when centre of crankshaft pulley gouged out. De Udy's car robbed for the part but overheating and misfiring made the car finally retire whilst in the lead.
02/7: Norisring Rennen: Gardner; 1st in both 100-mile heats, 1st overall.
30/7: BoverallC 500, Brands Hatch 6-hours: Hulme/Brabham; race number 4. Fitted with Alan Smith Chevrolet with 48IDA carburettors. Fastest in practice. Led for 40 minutes untill rocker arm broke. DNF in 2nd hour (clutch).
13/8: Wills Trophy, Croft: Hulme; race number 1. 1st heat, 1st. 2nd heat, 2nd. 1st overall. Pouring rain.
26/8: Formula Libre, JDC Silverstone: Sid Taylor; 3rd after a spin.
28/8: Formula Libre, Notts SCC Silverstone: Sid Taylor; 1st.
28/8: Special GT cars, Notts SCC Silverstone: Sid Taylor; 1st.
09/9: Holts Trophy, Crystal Palace: Frank Gardner; race number 111; 1st overall.
Car offered for sale on Oct.6th *Autosport* "after Kyalami".
4/11: Kyalami 9-hours: race number 5. Sideswiped at start by Piper. Frank Gardner/Mike Spence; DNF due to split fuel tank.

1968
07/4: BoverallC 500, Brands Hatch: Charlton/Fisher; race number 1. Practice: 1:39.2. DNF lap 69 (crash).
12/4. Guards Spring Cup, Oulton Park: Brian Redman; race number 73; 1st overall.
27/4: Players Trophy, Silverstone: Hulme; race number 36; 1st overall.
13/5: Special GT and Formula Libre, Mallory Park: Sid Taylor; 1st in both races.
19/5. Glover Trophy and Monte Christo GT races, Silverstone: Sid Taylor; second in both races.
27/5: Special GT race, Mallory Park: Sid Taylor; 1st. Formula Libre: Sid Taylor; 2nd.
03/6. RAC TT, Oulton Park: Hulme; race number 42; 1st overall.
18/6: Anderstorp: Axelsson; 3rd.
23/6. Guards International Trophy (Group 4), Mallory Park: Frank Gardner; race number 61; 1st overall.
Sold to John Woolfe.
07/7: Vila Real, Portugal: John Woolfe; 6th.
21/7: Hockenheim: Wolfe; DNS (car not ready).
27/7: Martini 300, Silverstone: Brian Muir; DNS.
02/9: Guards Trophy, Brands Hatch: John Woolfe; DNF on lap 2 (clutch).
Advertised for sale in *Autosport*.

1969
30/4: Silverstone RAC Group 4 round 1: Hulme; race no 37; 1st overall.
07/4: Snetterton RAC Group 4 round 2: Hulme; DNF with engine tightening up.
April. Advertised for sale in *Autosport*.
26/5: TT at Oulton Park: Race number 34, Woolfe/Martland; 21st.
08/6: Montlhéry: Digby Martland, race number 35; DNF when oil line broke.
16/8: Croft: Digby Martland; DNF when 4th in 1st heat due to overheating. 2nd heat, 3rd, 14th overall.
Sold to Bernd Seidler, Germany.

1970
28/6: Nuremburg 200, Norisring, Interseries: Bernd Seidler; 15th.
24/12: Offered for sale in *Autosport* (£3250) by Malcolm Gartland Racing.

1971
04/7: Hockenheim Interseries: B. Seidler; 12th.
11/7: Norisring Interseries: B. Seidler; 13th.

This may be the T70 Mark III sold to Joe Kretschi, in which case:

1973
15/7: Hockenheim Interseries: J. Kretschi; 10th.
1975: Sold to a Swedish gentleman who drove it from Germany to Sweden.
Sold to Anders Hedborg.

SL73/103
J. Mecom on 10/2/67. Gearbox number: LG500-100.
No history known.
1997: In Switzerland, totally restored.

SL73/104
J. Mecom. Sold to Mike Goth. Sold to Bud Morley.
1967: Riverside: race number 4; 5th.

SL73/105 (Photo on page 71).
Coupé. Delivered April 21st to Michael Grace de Udy, 5.9 Chevrolet, LG600 gearbox. Pipes for cockpit cooling fitted on roof.
1967
01/5: Spa 1000km: De Udy/De Klerk; crashed at La Source on 1st lap of practice and damaged suspension. DNS.
29/5: Crystal Palace 15 laps: De Udy; race number 72; 2nd.
24/25/6: Rheims 12-hours: De Udy/Dibley; 5.4-litres. DNF due to lights not working properly.
30/7: BoverallC 500, Brands Hatch: Traco Chevrolet 5.3-litre engine. Race number 5. DNF (differential) on 179 laps.
13/8: Wills Trophy, Croft: 2nd in qualifying heat, DNF in 2nd heat (battery).
09/9: Crystal Palace: De Udy; 2nd; race number 112.

SL73/108.

4/11: Kyalami 9-hours. De Udy/Dibley; DNF due to lack of oil pressure.
18/11: Cape International 3-hours, Killarney: De Udy; race number 2; 2nd overall. Engine blew with 11 minutes left whilst leading.
16/12: Laurenco Marques 3-hours: De Udy; fastest in practice; race number 2; DNF (core plug blew out).
26/12: Roy Hesketh 3-hours, Pietermaritzburg: De Udy; DNF due to engine damage on lap 9.

1968
06/1: Cape South Easter, Killarney, Capetown: Heat 1, DNF when 3rd after a spin when a water pipe was knocked off. Heat 2, DNF due to scavenge pump failure.
22/23/3: Sebring 12-hours: De Udy/Dibley; 9th on grid; race number 11; DNF due to engine trouble.
23/6: Guards International Trophy, Brands Hatch: De Udy; 3rd overall. Mallory Park, 3rd overall.
07/7: Vila Real, Portugal: De Udy; 1st overall, race number 63.
27/7: Martini International Trophy, Silverstone: De Udy; DNF.
04/8: Crystal Palace: crashed in practice, car badly damaged. De Udy purchased SL73/112.
Car sold to David Prophet and repaired.

1969
07/4: RAC Group 4, 3rd round, Embassy Trophy, Thruxton: Prophet; DNF (broken oil line).
13/4: Brands Hatch: Prophet/Nelson; DNF (oil leak).
17/5: Martini Trophy, Silverstone: Prophet; DNF.
26/5: TT, Oulton Park: Prophet/Nelson; DNF (seized engine).
01/6: Nürburgring 1000km: Prophet/Nelson; DNF (engine).
11/8: Thruxton: Used 11 inch front, 12 inch rear Firestone tyres: Prophet; 11th.
31/8: Mantorp Park, Sweden: Prophet; 9th.
14/9: Crystal Palace: Alastair Cowin; 2nd.

1970
11/1: Buenos Aires 1000km: Prophet/Pascualini; DNF (engine).
Sold to Egmont Dursche, West Germany.
28/6: Nuremburg 200, Norisring: Egmont Dursch; DNF.
05/7: Interseries, Hockenheim: Dursch; DNF.
11/7: Norisring 200 miles: Egmont; RU.
The car was bought by Solar Productions and used in the film "*Le Mans*", carrying Porsche 917 bodywork. Crashed in 1970. Repaired.
11/10: 300 Miles Hockenheim: Dursch; DNF.

1972
01/5: Imola Interseries: Dursch; race number 26; 12th.
21/5: Silverstone Interseries: Dursch; race number 26; 9th.
09/7: Zeltweg Interseries: Dursch; DNS.
16/7: Hockenheim Interseries: Dursch; race number 26; 8th.
02/8: Norisring Interseries: Dursch; race number 26; 7th.

1973
20/5: Silverstone Interseries: Dursch; DNF.

1982: Sold to Peter Gerster of Germany who is restoring the car.

SL73/106
Sold to John Mecom on 17/2/67. Chevrolet engine. Gearbox number: LG500-118. Nothing known.

SL73/107
Sold to John Mecom on 23/2/67. Chevrolet engine. Gearbox number: LG500-119.
1992: Sold to Doug Chandler of Florida, USA and fitted with coupé bodywork.

SL73/108
Sold to John Mecom on 17/3/67. Spyder. Gearbox number: LG500-104.
Donohue's 1967 USRRC winner. 350 cu. in. Chevrolet with aluminium block installed with steel heads and 58mm sidedraught Weber carburettors. LG 600 gearbox. Blue and yellow. George Follmer drove this Mark III in the1967 Can-Am series.

1967
23/4: USRRC, Stardust Raceway, Las Vegas: Donohue; 1st.
30/4: USRRC, Riverside: Donohue; 1st.
07/5. USRRC, Laguna Seca: Donohue; 3rd.
21/5: USRRC, Bridgehampton: Donohue; 1st.
25/6: USRRC, Watkins Glen GP: Donohue; 1st.
18/7: USRRC, Pacific Raceways: Donohue; 1st.
30/7: Road America 500, Elkhart Lake: Donohue; DNS.
03/9: Can-Am Round 1, Elkhart Lake: Follmer; qualified in 2:15.7; 4th on grid. Traco Chevrolet 359 cu. in. motor. 18th overall.
17/9: Can-Am, Bridgehampton: Follmer; 2nd row on grid, 3rd. 327 engine.
23/9: Mosport: Follmer; qualified 7th; crashed in practice; repaired with 'major patch' on tub; 6th overall. LG500 gearbox; 12in rear, 10in front wheels.

Shown at New York Auto Show in 1969.
Sold in March 1969 to John Marr.
1976: Sold to Nick Engles in May.
Sold to Rich Dejaral. Sold to Chuck Haines.
9/6/1986: Sold to Jim Oppenheimer, sold to Clarence Catallo, sold to Rick McLean.
1996: Sold to Pat Ryan.

SL73/109
Sold to John Mecom on 21/3/67. Spyder. Gearbox number: LG500-125.
Sold to Moises Solana of Mexico City on January 11th 1967. Fitted with Traco-Chevrolet 365 engine.

1967
23/4: USRRC Road Racing Championship, Stardust Raceway, Las Vegas: Solana; 5th.
30/4: USRRC, Riverside: Follmer; 8th.
04/12: Mexico City-Puebla Road Race: Solana; 1st overall.
11/12: Cuernavaca Race: Solana; 1st overall.

Sold to Chuck Haines.
1987: sold to Fernando Stirling, sold to Roly Nix in England, and fitted with coupé bodywork after a complete rebuild and new tub (the car fell off its trailer on the motorway!).
1993, September: Sold to Richard Dodkins. The car is blue and has been fitted with very wide rear wheels, (17 inches) and the rear bodywork bulged out to accomodate them. Chevrolet 6-litre on injection. Raced in many International Supersports and Group 4 races.
1997: Driven by Richard Dodkins, it was the fastest small block engined car at the Can-Am reunion at Elkhart Lake.
1999: Sold to Portugal.

SL73/110 (Photo on page 140).
Delivered through Carl Haas to John Mecom on 15/3/67. Gearbox number: LG500-120. Used as a spare car for a few races. Sold to someone in Los Angeles who used it as a road car and then sold it to South Africa where it was used for the same purpose. Bought by Nigel Hulme and Mike Blanchet in 1985. Re-bodied as a IIIb coupé . Fitted with a VDS tuned 5-litre Chevrolet plus injection. Sold to Nick Amey in October 1987. The car races regularly in historic races and is very successful. In 1993, the car was fitted with a 5.7-litre engine and, in 1997, re-engined with its 5-litre unit. It raced in Group 4 events. 1998: Re-bodied back to Mark 3 specification.

SL73/111
Coupé. Ryan Falconer Chevrolet engine no: RAF 11. Originally delivered to Yongue Rosqvist of Sweden on 2/6/67. Won Swedish sports car races and Championship.
Re-purchased by Lola factory.
Sold to Harvey Snow and David Briggs in the USA.

1967
13/10: Can-Am Round 4, Monterey GP, Laguna Seca: Leslie; race number 18; DNF (engine).
27/10: Can-Am Round 5, Los Angeles Times GP, Riverside: Leslie; race number 18; DNF.
10/11: Can-Am Round 6, Stardust GP, Las Vegas: Leslie; DNF.

1971: Sold to San Jose Competition Motors.
1972: Sold to Ron Southern. Several SCCA races.
Sold to Gary Eastern.
1973: Sold to William Otto.
1985: Had Mk IIIB coupé bodywork. Sold to Barry Blackmore.
Sold to Bob Lee in the USA.
1989: Sold to Monte Shallet. Now takes part in historic races in the USA, most notably the GT40 reunion race in 1989 where, driven by Monte Shallett, it won.
1990: Sold to Tony Podell.
1996: Sold to George Stauffer. Restored back to Mark III bodywork.
1999: For Sale:
2000: Sold to Keith Goring/Susan Dixon, Alfas Unlimited.
2001: March: Sebring. Your author enjoyed an excellent dice with this car in the HSR races!

SL73/112 (Photo on page 62).
Coupé. Second customer car finished. (SL73/105 first). Delivered April 21, 1967. LG500 gearbox. 6-litre Chevrolet engine from Sid Taylor fitted. British Racing Green. **Note**: Epstein originated dry-sump engine system (in South Africa with Hawkins) and drive-shaft alternator drive.

1967
01/5: Spa 1000km: Epstein/Hawkins; 4th overall.
17/5: Targa Florio: Epstein/Dibley; DNF on 6th lap with gearbox problems.
29/5: Crystal Palace: Epstein/Hawkins; DNF (clutch).
24/25/6: Rheims 12-hours: Epstein/Hawkins; fitted with extra-high 4th gear giving 6000rpm on straight. DNF, after setting all-time lap record of 142.3mph.
02/7: Norisringrennen, West Germany: Epstein; 4th overall.
Then to Australia for the Spring series.

SL73/109.

08/9: Rothmans 12-hours, Surfers Paradise: Epstein/Hawkins; second with cracked heads and brake problems.
Sold to Paul Hawkins. Hawkins won all Australian club races, car re-painted red.
October: Gallaher GT Trophy race, Warwick Farm, Sydney: Hawkins; 1st overall.
To South Africa for the Springbok series.
4/11: Kyalami nine-hours: Hawkins/John Love; 2nd. Car bothered with oil surge so engine converted to dry sump.
18/11: 3-hour race, Killarney, Capetown: Hawkins; race number 1; 1st.
16/12: Lourenco Marques 3-hours: Hawkins; 1st; race number 1.
26/12: 3-hour race, Roy Hesketh Circuit, Pietermaritzburg: Hawkins; 1st.
1968
06/1: Cape South-Easter meeting, Killarney, Capetown: Hawkins; 1st overall.
08/3: Car advertised by Paul Hawkins for sale in *Autosport*.
26/4: BoverallC 500, Brands Hatch: Epstein/Nelson; 18th overall.
Sold to Mike de Udy.
17/8: Speedworld International Trophy, Oulton Park, Gold Cup: De Udy; race number 49; 1st overall.
25/8: Grosser Preis von Ostereich, Zeltweg: De Udy; DNF due to oil pump failure.
02/9: Guards Trophy, Brands Hatch: De Udy; DNF (sump damage after spin).
15/9: Preis von Nations, Hockenheim: De Udy; DNF.

SL73/110.

9/11: Kyalami 9-hours: De Udy/Gardner; 5th overall.
23/11: 7th Cape International 3-hours, Killarney, South Africa: de Udy, 7th.
01/12: Rhodesian Grand Prix: de Udy; race number 84; 2nd in heat 1, 1st in heat 2; 2nd overall; 5-litre engine.
8/12: Lourenco Marques 3-hours: De Udy; DNF when in lead with 6-litre engine.
26/12: 5th Roy Hesketh 3-hours, Pietermaritzburg: De Udy; DNF after spin (leading till then) and losing a wheel.

1969
04/1: East London 500km: De Udy; DNF, damaged in practice and started without a nose.
January: Took South African land speed record at 191.8mph.
Sold to Tim Stock. Used Vegantune engine.

1970
11/12: Croft Interseries: Stock; race number 14; DNS (engine).
Minor club races in UK. Badly crashed in 197? at Snetterton. Stock kept all parts and sold them to Peter Denty in 1984 to restore.
1989: Sold to Mike Pendlebury. Car for sale.
1992. Re-skinned tub. Has Mathwall 5.0-litre Chevrolet and dry sump. On carbs. 450bhp.

1991
21/7: Donington: Mike Pendlebury; 5th in Lola race. Dark blue.

1992
February: For sale at Coy's Auction. Did not sell.
5.9-litre engine in need of rebuild with car.
May: Supersports race, Brands Hatch: Mike Pendlebury.

1993
27/5: Thruxton: Led David Piper's "Supersports" race until a wheel bearing failed on the last lap.
1994: Sold through Yvan Mahe to France.

SL73/113 (Photo on page 57).
Delivered 28/6/67 as a Spyder to Max Wilson. BRM V-12 engine fitted.
Gearbox number: LG600-13.

1969
01/6: Nürburgring 1000km: Wilson/Walker; race number 22; DNF (crash).
06/7: Vila Real, Portugal: Wilson/Daghorn; RU.

1970
19/4: Zolder 500km: Wilson/Daghorn; 3rd.
03/5: Jarama Group 5 and 6 race: Wilson; 6th.

10/6/1982: Offered for sale in *Autosport* (ex-Hobbs). Now red with Mk IIIb coupé bodywork in the US. I saw it, in very nice condition, on March 11th 1990 at Moroso Park, Florida, where Brian Redman drove it to win a local historic race.
1999: Monterey Historics meeting, with Hillborn injection.

SL73/114
Sold to John Mecom on 9/6/67. Sold to Dana Chevrolet and driven by Lothar Motschenbacher.
Gearbox number: LG500-148. Purchased by Carroll Shelby.

1967
17/9: Can-Am round 2, Bridgehampton: Motschenbacher; qualified 9th; 5th overall; race number 11.
23/9: Can-Am round 3, Player's 200, Mosport Park, Ontario: Motschenbacher; qualified 8th; 9th overall; race number 11.
15/10: Can-Am round 4, Monterey Grand Prix, Laguna Seca: Motschenbacher; qualified 7th; RU; race number 11.
29/10: Can-Am round 5, Los Angeles Grand Prix, Riverside: Motschenbacher; qualified 7th; 15th overall; race number 11.
12/11: Can-Am round 6, Stardust Grand Prix, Las Vegas: Motschenbacher; qualified 10th; DNF; race number 11.

SL73/115
Sold to Carroll Shelby on 9/6/67. Dana-Chevrolet. Can-Am Spyder. Driven by Peter Revson in the 1967 Can-Am season. White/blue.

1967
03/9: Can-Am round 1, Road America 200, Elkhart Lake, Wisconsin: Revson; 8th in practice, DNF on lap 3; race number 52.
17/9: Can-Am round 2, Chevron Grand Prix, Bridgehampton: Revson; 13th in practice. RU.
23/9: Can-Am Round 3, Players 200, Mosport Park, Ontario: Revson; 365 cu.in. Chevrolet. 5th in practice, 4th overall.
13/10: Can-Am round 4, Laguna Seca, Monterey: Revson; DNF accident (brakes).
29/10: Can-Am round 5, Los Angeles Grand Prix, Riverside: Revson; 7th in practice, DNF.
12/11: Can-Am round 6, Stardust Grand Prix, Las Vegas: Revson; 6th in practice, disqualified for push start in pits.
Sold to Robert Gomer in Florida.
This T70 was a basket case before being restored as a coupé by the owner, Jerry Weichers of Willows, California.

SL73/116
Coupé. Shipped to Japan on 26/5/67. Ryan-Falconer Chevrolet engine, number: RAF 15.
Sold in the 70s to the USA.
Sold to Ian Webb in 1980, sold to Bill Hall who had the car restored by John McGuire. Yellow. New 5-litre Chevrolet on Webers with dry sump fitted.
Sold to Jean Guikas.
1998: Sold to ?
2000: For sale in Japan.

SL73/117 (Photo on page 102).
Coupé. Chassis completed August 25, 1967. Fitted with 5.5-litre Chevrolet. (333 cu. in.).
Sold to James Garner's American International Racing Team.

1968
22/3: Sebring 12-hours: Guldstrand/Leslie, race number 34; DNF.
13/10: Can-Am round four, Monterey GP, Laguna Seca: Ed Leslie; qualified 27th, DNF (engine).
27/10: Can-Am round five, Los Angeles Times GP, Riverside: Ed Leslie; qualified 27th; DNF due to overheating.
10/11: Can-Am round six, Stardust GP, Las Vegas: Ed Leslie; qualified 20th, DNF due to engine failure.

1969
4-5/2: Daytona 24-hours: Motschenbacher/Leslie; race number 8; 2nd. Traco-Chevrolet on Weber carburettors and fitted with a wet sump.
18/3: Sebring: Motschenbacher/Leslie; 6th.
Sold to Eddie Hill, USA.

SL73/118
Coupé. Delivered to Schmidlin-Wanger. Standard Corvette engine,

number VG112.

Road driven since new. Probably the most original T70 in existence. Approximately 3400 miles in total. Original gel coat (orange), engine and gearbox. Owned by Bill Lotter, California, USA.

SL73/119 (Photo on page 77).
To USA on 5/7/67. Chevrolet engine. Gearbox number: LG600-17.
Probably the car driven by Peter Revson in the 1968 USRRC season.
1968: Red; 377 cu.in.
Mexico City: Revson; race number 52; RU.
USRRC, Riverside: Revson; race number 52; RU.
Sold to Chuck Haines in 1975. For sale in *Autosport* by Northdown Racing on 11th November 1982.
Driven by John Brindley, Willie Green and Ian Taylor. Coupé bodywork installed 1987 when rebuilt by Rod Butterfield. Raced by Paul Palmer in Supersports. 5-litre Chevrolet on Webers.
Sold to Huismann in Holland.
1997: Sold to Craig Bennet, UK. Rebuilt.

SL73/120
Original invoice dated Sept. 26th, 1967, reference R.H. Greenville.
Sold in USA through Carl Haas. Chevrolet on Webers.

1967
Driven by Ross Greenville of Morrinsville in Can-Am events.
17/9: Bridgehampton. Greenville; crashed in practice in Hurricane Dora.
15/10: Can-Am round 4, Monterey Grand Prix, Laguna Seca: Greenville; qualified 17th; RU.
29/10: Can-Am round 5, Los Angeles Grand Prix, Riverside: Greenville; qualified 36th; RU.
12/11: Can-Am round 6, Stardust Grand Prix, Las Vegas: Greenville; qualified 23rd; 9th overall.
1968: Some Can-Am races with Greenville. Rebuilt as coupé.
Sold to Gary Miller 1976-1989, Monterey Historics race winner, red.
Sold to Ed Wettach, Missisippi, USA.
Sold to Jules Moritz, USA, red.

SL73/121 (Photo on page 63).
Second Lola-Aston Coupé for Team Surtees. LG600 gearbox.

1967
17/18/6: Le Mans 24-hours: Surtees/Hobbs; Aston Martin V8; DNF on lap three when seventh (piston damage).
24/25/6: Rheims 12-hours: Surtees/Hobbs; 5.9 Chevrolet fitted; DNF when engine failed. Still fitted with aluminium tail.
30/7: BoverallC 500, Brands Hatch: Surtees/Hobbs; 5.5-litre Chevrolet with 58DCOE Webers fitted; 2nd fastest in practice; race number 2. Lap record in race. DNF in 5th hour (overheating). Red.
13/8: Wills Trophy, Croft: 1st heat, DNF due to final drive breakage. Hobbs won 2nd heat.

1968
Bought in February 1968 by Jackie Epstein from Eric Broadley. British racing green.
April. BoverallC 500, Brands Hatch: Epstein/Edward Nelson; finished race 18th after a fuel tank split. Race number 3. 5-litre Chevrolet fitted.
26/5: Spa 1000km: Epstein/Liddell; 10th (gasket failure plus piston due to bad fuel).
Norisring: Epstein; 7th (4th in class) after 5-litre roller cam short distance engine (developed by Alan Smith of Derby) fitted.
27/7: Martini Trophy, Silverstone: Hobbs; 5th fastest in practice, eliminated after being T-boned by Ron Fry. Rebuilt at factory. Dark purple bodywork.
02/9. Guards Trophy, Brands Hatch: David Hobbs; 21st. Wrong tyres, seized wheelnut. Flat-tappet long distance engine fitted.
29/9: Le Mans 24-hours: Epstein/Nelson; DNF due to punctures, overheating; diff broken in 17th hour.
09/9: Kyalami 9-hours; Epstein/Charlton; race number 5; 21th overall.
23/11: 7th Cape International 3-hours, Kilarney: J. Epstein/Dave Charlton; race number 37th, 2nd in class.
?/12: Lourenco Marques: J. Epstein; 1st.

1969
06/1: Killarney, Capetown: J. Epstein; (1st in 1st heat, 2nd in 2nd).
Pietermaritzburg: 2nd after engine (5.9 Chevrolet) blew with minutes to go whilst in the lead. Race number 2.
Sold to Brian Bolton who never raced the car. Sold in January 1970 to an Englishman who used it on the road until 1975 when put into storage. Red. I saw this car in its owner's garage in April 1991 and December 1992. The car is original down to the Le Mans lights, still affixed to rear, and the racing number patches. A time machine! Sold to Jean Guikas of GTC in Marseilles in November, 1995. I supplied him with a correct 5-litre Aston Martin V8 from the batch of ten engines which were built for the Lola-Aston project in 1996.
1996: Sold.

Note: Somehow, another T70 chassis was built up as one of the Lola-Astons, (SL73/121). This was then sold to James Freeman in the USA who raced it for some years before the car was then sold on to Japan.

2000: Sold back to the USA.
2001: 17/2: Morose Park: Badly crashed when the suspension broke. Very badly damaged. Only engine, gearbox, uprights (perhaps!), salvageable.

MARK IIIB ROADSTERS 1967

SL75/122
Sold 17/8/67 to Carl Haas. Can-Am Spyder. Gearbox number: LG600-32. Ford engine. Sold to Dan Gurney.

1967
03/9: Road America 200, Elkhart Lake: Gurney; 3rd in practice behind McLaren and Hulme; DNF.
17/9: Bridgehampton: Gurney; 3rd in practice; DNF (injection) lap 4.
23/9: Mosport Park, Ontario: Gurney; 3rd in practice; DNF (engine) 69th lap.
15/10: Monterey: Gurney; 2nd in practice; led initially; DNF on lap 7 (engine).
29/10: Los Angeles Times GP, Riverside: Gurney; fastest in practice (1:39.3); DNF on lap 5 in race.
10/11: Stardust GP, Las Vegas: Gurney; 2nd in practice; DNF (engine vibration) on lap 14.

1968: Sold to Vic Nelli.

1969
October: Can-Am, Riverside: Nelli; qualified 27th; DNF.
Apparently driven by Vic Elford.
Sold to Henry Lassiter, sold to Peter Boyd, sold to John Collins, sold to Gerry Weichers. Rebuilt with Mark IIIb coupé bodywork. Red.

Sold to Bruce Trenery of Fantasy Junction, USA who has raced it enthusiastically for many years. Crashed in 1996 and now restored.
1998: Sold on with new tub.

SL75/123 (Photo on page 73).
To Team Surtees on 22/9/67. Driven by John Surtees in 1967 Can-Am. 5.7 Chevrolet fitted.

1967
03/9: Can-Am round 1, Road America, Elkhart Lake: Surtees; 7th in practice; 3rd after spin.
17/9: Can-Am round 2, Bridgehampton: Surtees; 4th in race.
23/9: Can-Am round 3, Mosport Park, Ontario: Surtees; 5th in practice, DNF 17th lap (misfiring engine).
15/10: Can-Am round 4, Monterey Grand Prix: Surtees; 14th in practice, DNF.
29/10: Can-Am round 5, Los Angeles GP, Riverside: Surtees, race number 7; 9th in practice, DNF.

Car returned to Carl Haas, and SL71/43, Surtees' 1966 Can-Am winning car used for Las Vegas race with the IIIb's wider wheels. Surtees won the race. This is 'probably' the car driven by Tom Dutton in the 1969 Can-Am series, fitted with Chevrolet 427 cu. in. engine. In which case:

1969
01/6: Can-Am round 1, Mosport Park: Dutton; qualified 15th, finished 11th.
15/6: Can-Am round 2, St. Jovite: Dutton; qualified 18th, finished 10th.
13/7: Can-Am round 3, Watkins Glen: Dutton; qualified 22nd, DNF.
27/7: Can-Am round 4, Edmonton: Dutton; qualified 13th, finished 5th.
17/8: Can-Am round 5, Mid-Ohio: Dutton; qualified 15th, finished 14th.
31/8: Can-Am round 6, Elkhart Lake: Dutton; qualified 22nd, DNF.
14/9: Can-Am round 7, Bridgehampton: Dutton; qualified 14th, finished 11th.

The car was seen in 1980, still as a Spyder, and is still in the USA. The original Weslake-headed engine is in Scotland.

SL75/124 (Photo on page 74).
Sold to Penske. Delivered 2/8/67 to Penske Racing for Mark Donohue to drive in that year's Can-Am. Chevrolet engine. Gearbox no LG600-16. Blue and yellow.

1967
20/8: Mid-Ohio: 427 Chevrolet. USRRC 1st.
03/9: Road America 200, Elkhart Lake: 427 Chevrolet; Donohue; 5th in practice. Small block 327 Chevrolet used in race; 2nd overall.
17/9: Bridgehampton: 327 Chevrolet; Donohue; 7th in practice. DNF (engine).
23/9: Mosport: Donohue; 17th in practice after crash; 427 engine, DNF.
15/10: Monterey GP, Laguna Seca: Donohue; 10th in practice; DNF (engine).
29/10: LA Times GP, Riverside: Donohue; race number 16; 10th in practice; 3rd
12/11: Stardust GP, Las Vegas: Donohue; 6th in practice; led race before running out of fuel at end; 2nd.

1968
Sold to Shelby. Tested by Ford.
Sold to the Agapiou Brothers; 427 Ford installed.
15/10: Can-Am, Laguna Seca: Follmer; 8th in practice; race number 16; DNF (crash).
27/10: Can-Am, Riverside: Follmer; race number 16; 22nd in practice, DNF.
10/11: Can-Am, Stardust Raceway, Las Vegas: Follmer; race number 16; 2nd.

1975: Sold to unknown owner(s) in Yucca Flats, San Bernadino, Cal. Car was sent to Randy Berry for conversion to Mark IIIb coupé bodywork.
1976: Sold to Jerry Shoeberries, Oakland, Cal.
1977: Sold to Larry Crossen, Sacramento, Cal.
1978: Installed roll bar and ran Rose Cup SCCA Nationals, Portland Historic and Monterey Historic.
1978: Sold to Tom Black of Portland, Oregon.
1979: Sold to Bill Prout/Collier Museum. Competed in Sebring historic race.
1979: Sold to Miles Collier, Palm Beach, Fla.
1982: Sold to Skip Gunnell, Fort Lauderdale, Fla. He restored the tub in 1984. The car has Mark IIIb coupé bodywork. British Racng Green.
1996: Skip Gunnell has had the car restored back to its original Spyder configuration, complete with all Penske features and paint scheme. It took part in the 30th anniversary of the Can-Am series at Elkhart Lake in 1996.

SL75/125
Sold to Carl Haas on 22/9/67. Sold to Penske Racing. Sold without being used by the team. Spare monocoque to Penske Racing in August 1967. Car built up to replace the car damaged by Follmer at Mosport.

1967
15/10: Monterey GP, Laguna Seca: Follmer; 12th in practice; 3rd overall.
29/10: LA times GP: Follmer; 12th in practice; race number 16; 6th overall.
12/11: Stardust GP, Las Vegas: Follmer; 12th in practice; race number 16; DNF.

Sold to Chuck Haines, sold to John Casado of California in 1987. Sold to Tomi Drisy. Has alternative pick-up points, IIIb roadster type chassis. Has Penske dash. It is Donohue's third Mark III Spyder.
Sold to Stephen Young, Los Angeles. Vintage raced.

All the above were Spyders.

Note: Bryan O'Neil, Ronnie Bucknum, Jeff Stevens and Fred Pipin were listed as driving T70 Mark IIIb Spyders in the 1968 Can-Am series.

End of Mark IIIb Spyder production.

SL73/126
J. Mecom.
Sold to Jerry Hansen in 1967, Daytona speed records at 199mph. Driven to many SCCA victories.
Sold to Dick Kantrud who took the small block engine out and replaced it with a big block. He also installed larger wheels and tyres. Bigger rollcage plus a wing on the back.
Sold to Mark Brown for one year.
Sold to Greg Granum in the early 1970s. Restored to original specification, with Webers, *etc.*

SL75/125.

1973/74
Mid Ohio plus Elkhart Lake Can-Ams.
Granum claims the car has its original bodywork and has Sunoco paint underneath the layers of newer paint.

SL73/127 (Photo on page 76).
Sold to George Bignotti.

1967
11/9: Fitted with Ford Indianapolis four camshaft engine. Gearbox number: LG500-155. Driven by Parnelli Jones. Race number 21.
30/10: Can-Am round 4, Laguna Seca, Monterey: Jones; race number 21; 4th in practice. DNF due to fuel vaporisation.
11/11: Can-Am, Riverside, Los Angeles: Jones; race number 21; 5th in practice, 4th overall.
??/12: Can-Am, Stardust Grand Prix, Las Vegas: Jones; race number 21; led until gear lever broke off on lap 4; DNF.

1968
Ford engine now enlarged to five-litres. Driven by Mario Andretti.
01/9: Can-Am round 1, Road America: Andretti; 8th in practice; DNF in race (engine).
15/9: Can-Am, Bridgehampton: Andretti; 8th in practice; DNF (engine).
27/10: Can-Am, Riverside: Andretti; did not qualify (engine).
10/11: Stardust GP, Las Vegas: Andretti; 6th in practice; DNF in race (puncture).

At one point in the late 1960s, the car was given to a Mr Issy, a local Jaguar dealer, for his 63rd birthday. (Mr Issy attempted to qualify for the Indianapolis 500 when he was 69!)

Sold to Shelton Washburn, California, USA.

SL73/128
Sold to Carl Haas. February 16th, 1968. Chevrolet engine. Gearbox number: LG600-45.
Sold to John Mecom. Simoniz sponsored car.

1968
Raced by either Chuck Parsons or Skip Scott in the USRRC. Race number 10/26.
Raced by Bob Nagel in the 1968 Can-Am with Ford 427 cu. in. engine.
15/9: Can-Am round 2, Bridgehampton: Nagel; qualified 20th, finished 14th.
10/11: Can-Am round 6, Las Vegas: Nagel; qualified 30th, finished 13th.

1969
01/6: Can-Am round 1, Mosport: Nagel; qualified 12th, DNF.
15/6: Can-Am round 2, St. Jovit: Nagel; qualified 12th, DNF.
13/7: Can-Am round 3, Watkins Glen: Nagel; qualified 20th, 13th in race. Race number 24.
17/8: Can-Am round 5, Mid-Ohio: Nagel; qualified 15th, 16th in race.
31/8: Can-Am round 6, Elkhart Lake: Nagel; qualified 17th, DNF.
14/9: Can-Am round 7, Bridgehampton: Nagel; qualified 20th, DNF.
20/9: Can-Am round 8, Michigan: Nagel; DNF.
?/10: Can-Am round 10, Laguna Seca: Nagel; qualified 19th, DNF.
?/10: Can-Am round 11, Riverside: Nagel; qualified 27th, 17th in race.

SL73/128.

Sold to Ian Webb. Sold to Ray Potter.

In 1980 or thereabouts the car was bought by Nigel Hulme with a 7.0-litre Ford V-8 installed and Mark IIIb coupé bodywork. Sold to Peter Kause in Germany and displayed at the Rosso museum in Aschaffenberg.

SL73/129
Sold to Carl Haas, USA, February 16, 1968. Chevrolet engine. Gearbox number: LG600-45. Simoniz sponsored car. Team drivers were Skip Scott/Chuck Parsons.

1968
USRRC; either Scott or Parsons.
01/9: Can-Am round 1, Road America, Elkhart Lake: Scott; qualified 26th; 19th in race.

1969
27/7: Can-Am round 4, Edmonton: qualified 10th; DNF (clutch).
Now belongs to Rob Larogue, USA, has a 5.7-litre engine, and is vintage-raced.
1998: crashed at Sears Point, rebuilt.

SL73/130
Coupé. Delivered to Fuji Company, Japan on 27/2/68. Chevrolet engine. Gearbox number: LG600-63. Painted a dark colour with a white arrowhead, *a la* Team Surtees colours.

1968
03/5: Japan GP: DNF.

SL73/131 (Photo on page 83).
Coupé. Delivered to American International Racers on 9/3/68. Chevrolet engine.
Gearbox number: LG600-73.

1968
23/3: Sebring 12-hours: S. Patrick/D. Jordan; 4th fastest in practice, 2:58.8. Scooter Patrick held the lead (fastest race lap, 2:49), but DNF in the third hour due to steering damage. Race number 9.

1969
01/2: Daytona 24-hours: S. Patrick/D. Jordan; Traco-Chevrolet on carbs and wet sump; 7th.
22/3: Sebring 12-hours: S. Patrick/D. Jordan; DNF (engine trouble).

Sold to Ernest Kensler then Brad Levett who had it turned into a road car. On his death, it passed to Tim and O.G. Levett and was

SL73/132.

then sold to Jerry Weichers.

SL73/132 (Photo on page 84).
Coupé. Ulf Norinder Sportscars Unlimited Team. Ryan Falconer Chevrolet engine (number: RAF 16). Gearbox number: LG600-79. Blue and yellow.

1968
18/6: Anderstorp: Norinder; DNF (fuel leak).
21/7: Hockenheim: Norinder; 4th in first heat, 1st in second heat.
11/8: Karlskoga: Norinder;.DNF.
17/8 Speedworld International Trophy, Oulton Park: Paul Hawkins; 3rd.
02/9: Guards International Trophy, Brands Hatch: Norinder, 2nd, race number 102.
29/9. Le Mans 24-hours: Norinder/Axelsson; disqualified when Axelsson walked further than fifty metres from the car when engine cut out.
13/10: Paris 1000km, Montlhéry: Norinder/Widdows; DNF.

1969
3-4/2: Spare car at Daytona 24-hours (not run).

1970: Used in the Steve McQueen film *Le Mans*. Lola/Ferrari 512? All the T70s were sold to Kilmene La Tours in France after filming. He then sold a Mark III coupé with orange paintwork to Claude Martin, and he, in turn, sold it to another owner who used the car in hillclimbs and crashed it.
Sold to Jacques LePane who showed it in his museum until 1978/80.
Sold to Pierre Brunet, sold to Jean Verchere.
1987: Sold to Rene Giordano of Cannes (now dark blue). Dan Foster of Vichy rebuilt the monocoque.
1999: Sold to Pierre-Alain France.

SL73/133
Coupé. Sold to Robs Lamplough on 9/5/68.
Gearbox number: LG600-88.
Robs Lamplough worked on the Lola stand at the 1967 and '68 Racing Car Shows. This car was sold as a kit of parts to Michel Giorgi in part exchange for an ex-Ford France GT40 (1005). The Lola was assembled in Britain from the parts and driven by H.T. Lamplough to France for Giorgi. Road registered in England. (CLB ---D)

1968
13/10: Paris 1000km: Georgi/Nelso; DNF when the gearbox lost it's oil.

SL73/134 (Photo on page 104 - rear car).
Coupé. Monocoque only to Sid Taylor on 26/7/68. Built up from spares by Sid Taylor's racing team (Ron Bennett). White with a longitudinal green racing stripe. Five wins in seven starts. Driven by Frank Gardner, Denny Hulme, Brian Redman, Sid Taylor.

1968
27/7: (In primer). Martini International 300, Silverstone: Hulme; race number 1; 1st overall.
12/8: Birthday Cup: Croft/Gardner; race number 1; 1st overall.
13/8: Tootal GT Championship, Mallory Park: Sid Taylor; 1st overall.
18/8. Mallory Park: Sid Taylor; 1st overall.
02/9: Guards Trophy, Brands Hatch: F. Gardner, race number 101; 1st.

Sold to Techspeed. Painted orange.
6/10: Aspern, Austria: C. Craft; 1st.
13/10: Preis von Tyrol, Austria: C. Craft; 3rd.

1969
30/3: RAC Gruop 4 Championship, round 1: Chris Craft; 4th.
07/4: Guards International Trophy, RAC Group 4, round 2, Snetterton: Wet sump Bartz Chevrolet on injection; Craft; DNF due to a puncture.
13/4: BoverallC 500, Brands Hatch: Craft/Eric Liddell; race number 7; 8th overall.
25/4: Monza 1000km: Craft/Liddell, 3:3.3 in practice; DNF (CWP failed on the banking).
17/5: Martini Trophy, Silverstone: Craft, race number 2; 1st overall.
26/5: Tourist Trophy, Oulton Park: Jack Oliver, DNF.
14/7: Croft: Craft; race number 3; 1st overall. 1st in 1st heat, 2nd in 2nd.
11/8: Thruxton: Bartz Chevrolet engine. 9in front, 14in rear wheels. Craft; DNF.
Preis von Tyrol, Innsbruck: Craft; 1st overall.

1970
For sale in *Autosport* for £2950.
Sold to David Piper, who then sold it to Solar Productions for use as a camera car in the Steve McQueen film *Le Mans* where it was dressed up as a Ferrari 512 and crashed.
The car with this chassis number was bought from Europe as a 'basket case' in the 1980s by Patrick Smythe in England who is rebuilding it.

SL73/135 (Photo on pages 56 and 57).
Coupé. According to factory records, this car was completed as a road car on 12/10/68 in silver with a standard Chevrolet engine (number VO308MO), and equipped with ZF gearbox number ZF 169G/B.

Sent to Franco Sbarro of Switzerland. Fitted with Morand 7-litre Chevrolet. ZF gearbox number NR180. Shown at 1969 London Racing Car Show. Last Mark III made. £7000 plus tax.

Sold to Valentine Abdi of France. Burnt out when leaving a '*Peage*' in France.

Gebhardt shop.
Restored by Korytko custom design, near Nuremburg.
Partially burnt, but under restoration.

Note: The author has been informed that 'the Franco Sbarro Road car', although damaged, is in a museum in Cannes. Franco Sbarro of Switzerland bought ten Mark III chassis at the end of 1968 from the factory. He built them up as road cars, numbers beginning SL101. SL102 featured the 7.6-litre aluminium Chevrolet from Bonnier's SL102 and was sold to Albert Obrist, then to Colin Clark and tested by *Motor* in 1974. It is presently in America, fitted with a Ferrari 330 GT engine.

MARK IIIB GT COUPÉS

SL76/138 (Photo on pages 96 and 97).
Delivered on 2/1/69. Second IIIb made. Gearbox number LG600/91. White with a longitudinal green racing stripe. Displayed at the Racing Car Show in January.
Sold to Sid Taylor. Bartz Chevrolet 5-litre engine, dry sump, on Weber carburettors.
Driven by Hulme, Attwood, Hailwood, Gardner, De Adamich, Vaccarella and Redman.

1969
30/3: RAC Group 4, round 1, Silverstone: Redman; race number 29; 2nd in practice, 2nd overall.
04/4: RAC Group 4, round 2, Guards International Trophy, Snetterton: Redman; race number 51; DNF due to a blown head gasket.
07/4: RAC Group 4, round 3, Embassy Trophy, Thruxton: Redman; 1st.
13/4: BoverallC 500, Brands Hatch: Peter Revson/Stan Axelsson/Hulme; DNF due to overheating.
25/4: Monza 1000km: Gardner/de Adamich; race number 33; 10th in practice, 2:59.5. Rammed at start. 5th overall after a collision with an Alpine on the last lap.
17/5: Martini International Trophy, Silverstone: Redman; race number 9; 2nd.
26/5: Tourist Trophy, Oulton Park: Redman; 19th.
29/6: Nuremburg 200, Norisring: Redman; race number 3; 1st (fitted with a 6.2-litre Chevrolet engine).
15/7: Croft: Trevor Taylor; race number 2; 8th in 1st heat, 1st in 2nd; 2nd overall.
20/7: Gran Premio Del Mugello: De Adamich/Vacarella; race number 71; 3rd overall.
Using fuel injection for the first time.
10/8: Kodak 8 Trophy, Thruxton: Hulme; race number 3; 1st.
17/8: Karlskoga: Brian Redman; race number 3; 1st overall.
31/8: Mantorp Park, Sweden: Redman; DNF due to rear suspension damage.
14/9: Anderstorp, Sweden: Redman; race number 14; 2nd overall.
5/10: Preis von Tyrol, Innsbruck: Gardner; 1st overall.
8/11: Kyalami Rand Daily Mail 9-hours: John Love/Brian Redman; 6.2 engine; DNF due to differential failure.
23/11: Cape International 3-hours, Killarney: John Love; 6.9-litre engine; 2nd overall.
Sold to John Love (Team Gunston).
1/12: Lourenco Marques 3-hours: John Love; DNF due to a blown head gasket whilst leading.
13/12: Bulawayo 3-hours: John Love; 1st overall.
27/12: Roy Hesketh 3-hours, Pietermaritzburg: John Love; 5.0-litre engine; 1st overall.
2nd in the Springbok series.
Sold to Mike De Udy's Bahamas Racing.

1970
12/4: BoverallC 500, Brands Hatch: De Udy/Gardner; DNF due to a broken camshaft. Fitted with a Bartz tuned Chevrolet.
23/4: Advertised for sale in *Autosport*.
Sold to Paul Vestey who did not race it.

1971
Sold to Mike Coombe.
Car had Mathwall 5-litre engine on carburettors.
09/5: Spa 1000km: Coombe/Vestey; DNF due to a broken rocker arm.
??/7: Vila Real, Portugal: Coombe; RU.
3/10: Hockenheim Interseries: Coombe; 12th.

1972
Sold to Jack La Fort. The car was mauve when he bought it.

1973
19/8: Silverstone: Car crashed and repaired by Classic Motor Works. Converted then for road use, registered MME10L.

SL76/138.

July 1975: Unicognac Trophy, St. John Horsfall Meeting, Silverstone: Qualified on front row of grid. Very wet, DNF at end of first lap (cause unknown).
1977: Sold to John Etheridge who did not race it.
1979: Sold to John Heath. Red with gold stripe.
1979: Sold to Mike Wheatley. Raced continuously by him till 1987. Over the winter, Mike Wheatley re-built the car on a new, Lola-supplied tub. The original tub was sold to Mike Ostroumoff and John Hunt who, in February 1988, commenced building a car on the old chassis. This car first raced in South Africa in 1988 and was bought by the Author in 1989.
Sold to Jonathan Baker in 1994 who raced it in the Group 4 series. Very fast with many victories.
Sold to Spain.

On March 19th, 1988, Mike Wheatley crashed SL76/138 severely, at the East London Circuit, South Africa. The wreck and spares were sold to John Hunt and Mike Ostroumoff who rebuilt the car on it's original chassis and John Hunt used it for several races. (see above). After this, Messrs. Hunt and Ostroumoff built a new T70 with a tub supplied from the factory. They transferred the chassis plate to this car and John Hunt carried on racing this car, thus giving it continuous history as SL76/138.
1997: Sold to Chris O'Neil.

SL76/139 (Photo on page 101).
Finished 30th December 1968. First IIIb completed. Dark blue with gold pinstriping (Sunoco colours). Traco-built 5-litre Chevrolet with fuel injection. Shipped to Penske Racing on 31/12/68.

1969
1-2/2: Daytona 24-hours: Donohue/C. Parsons; race number 6; 2nd fastest in practice, 1:52.7; 1st overall.
21-22/3: Sebring 12-hours: Ran on carburettors after pick-up problems with the injection at Daytona. Donohue/Bucknum; race number 9; DNF after a radius rod pulled out of the monocoque. Stolen from transporter and recovered by Mark Donohue.
The car has now been owned for many years by Jim Landrum in the USA.

2000: Under restoration.

SL76/140
Delivered to Penske Racing on 24th April, 1969. Gearbox number: LG600-97. Penske Racing spare car.

1969
Never raced by the Penske team. Sold to 'Randy's Auto Body Shop'. Red with yellow pin stripes.

1970
31/1: Daytona 24-hours: John Cannon/George Eaton; race number 5; 10th in practice, DNF on first lap ("diabolical handling" ... *Autosport*).

21/3: Sebring 12-hours: Bob Brown/Gregg Young; race number 26; NC.
13-14/6: Le Mans: Robin Orme/David Prophet; race number 17; DNQ.
Rented for three months to appear in Steve McQueen's film *Le Mans*. Race number 4 (red car).

1971
24/7: Watkins Glen 6-hours: Ormes/R. Brown/R/ Bondurant; race number 60; DNF.

1972: Sold through Fred Opert Racing. Sold to William Munstedt who robbed a bank for the purchase money and was arrested.
1973: Bruce Waller purchased the car from a sheriff who was selling it for the bank. The car remained unrestored in his shop, with all original paintwork.
1998: Offered for sale through Symbolic Motor Car Co., San Diego.
1998: Car sent to be restored.
2000: Still under restoration at Bob Akin Motorsport.

SL76/141 (Photo on pages 103 and 105)
Delivered 23rd April 1969 to Ulf Norinder. Traco-Chevrolet on carburettors.

1969
1-2/2: Daytona 24-hours: Norinder/Bonnier; race number 60; qualified 1:54; DNF (accident).
21/22/3: Sebring 12-hours: Norinder/Bonnier; race number 14; qualified 2:44.37; DNF (suspension).
13/4: BOverallC 500, Brands Hatch: Norinder/Widdows; race number 6; DNF (suspension).
25/4: Monza 1000km: Norinder/Widdows; race number 42; qualified 9th, 2:58.9. In at end of lap 1, after a collision with an Alpine. DNF (gearbox).
01/5: Magny Cours: Troberg; 4th.
31/8: Mantorp Park, Sweden: Norinder; 8th.
14/9: Anderstorp, Sweden: Jackie Oliver; race number 8; 6th.

1970
11/1: Buenos Aires 1000km: Oliver/Reutemann; 11th.
18/1: Buenos Aires 200 miles: Oliver; 4th.
Used in the film: *Le Mans*.
Sold to Clive Unsworth of Ashton-in Makefield, Lancs.
Sold in 1994; restored.
1998: Sold to Martin Birrane. Enthusiastically raced in Europe.

SL76/142 (Photo on page 100).
Delivered 5th February 1969 to Nick Cuthbert for Paul Hawkins. Works-assisted. Wet sump Traco Chevrolet 5.0. Gearbox number: LG600-179.

1969
04/4: RAC Group 4, round 2, Guards International Trophy, Snetterton: Hawkins, race number 52; 1st.
07/4: RAC Group 4, round 3, Embassy Trophy, Thruxton: Hawkins, 3rd overall.
13/4: BOverallC 500, Brands Hatch: Hawkins/J. Williams; qualified 9th, 1:34.2; race number 1; 6th after two-hours, DNF (suspension).
29-30/4: Le Mans Test Weekend: 3rd fastest at 3:37.8 (138.33 mph). Note: This MAY have been another works-assisted car.
30/4: RAC Group 4, round 1, Silverstone: Hawkins; 3rd.
01/5: Magny Cours: Paul Hawkins; 2nd.
11/5: Spa 1000km: Hawkins/Prophet; qualified pole position; race number 33; 8th (engine).
17/5: Martini Trophy, Silverstone: Hawkins; 4th; new Traco-Chevrolet.
26/5: Hawkins was killed during the TT in this car at Oulton Park, race number 37. The car is reputed to be buried in a gravel pit at Slough.
The author knows to two other cars that have been constructed since with this chassis number.

SL76/143 (Photo on page 104).
Delivered 17th February 1969 to Jo Bonnier. Yellow, white longitudinal stripe, thin red stripe in centre. Traco-Chevrolet 5-litre (304 cu. in.). Gearbox number: LG600-180.

1969
30/3: RAC Group 4 round 1, Silverstone: Bonnier; 17th.
04/4: RAC Group 4, round 2, Guards International Trophy, Snetterton: Bonnier; 2nd.
07/4: RAC Group4, round 3, Embassy Trophy, Thruxton: Bonnier; race number 1; 2nd.
01/6: Nürburgring 1000km: Fuel injected engine in practice. Carburettor engine in race. Bonnier; race number 55; DNF.
25/4: Monza 1000km: Bonnier/Muller; 8th in practice 2:56.0; race number 40, DNF (overheated).
11/5: Spa 1000km: Bonnier/Muller; Traco-Chevrolet engine; 5th fastest in practice, at 3.57:4; race no 32; 5th overall; 1st in Group 4.
08/6: Montlhéry: Bonnier; 1st overall.
02/7: Nuremburg 200, Norisring: Bonnier; 5.7 engine; race number 2; won 1st heat; DNF in 2nd; 15th overall.
14/7: Magny Cours: Ronnie Peterson; 1st.
17/8: Karlskoga: Peterson, race number 14; 3rd.
31/8: Mantorp Park, Sweden: Bonnier; 6th.
14/9: Anderstorp, Sweden: Bonnier, race number 6; 4th.
19/10: Hockenheim 300: Bonnier; 2nd.
08/11: Kyalami 9-hours: Bonnier/Weisell; 5.8 engine; race number 2; DNF (accident).

1970
11/1: Buenos Aires 1000km: Peterson/Cupiero; 7th.
28/3: Thruxton: Bonnier; 3rd overall.
12/4: BOverallC 500, Brands Hatch: Bonnier/Wisell; 7th overall.
17/4: Spa 1000km: Bonnier; race number 33; DNF.
08/8: Swedish Grand Prix, Karlskoga: Wisell; 5th.
11/8: Watkins Glen 6-hours: Bonnier/Wisell; 8th.
12/8: Watkins Glen Can-Am: Bonnier; 11th.
11/10: Hockenhem 300 miles, Interseries: Bonnier; race number 66; 5-litre engine; 8th.
18/10: Nürburgring south circuit: Muller; 5th.

The author found that this chassis number belongs to a gentleman in Lancashire, England. He says he bought it in exchange for Lister Jaguar 'YOB 1' in 1974. The car is currently in restoration.
David Piper collected this car from Stefan Sklenar in Vienna, Austria and remembers it as belonging to Bonnier and having a 7-litre aluminium Chevrolet engine with special driveshafts to take the power fitted for Interseries races. The owner says that a ventilated small block Chevrolet was installed when he bought the car. Mr S. Sennet of Los Angeles has also owned a car with this number for many years.

SL76/144
Delivered 24th February 1969 to David Preston. Dark blue. Sold to Team Elite (Trevor Taylor). Wet-sump Traco-Chevrolet 305-004. Gearbox number: LG600-181.

1969
30/3: RAC Group 4, round 1, Silverstone: Taylor; crashed whilst

SL76/141.

SL76/143.

SL76/144.

leading.
07/4: RAC Group 4, round 3 Thruxton:Taylor; DNF on lap 1 (clutch).
12/4: BoverallC 500, Brands Hatch: Taylor/Dibley; 8th in practice, 1.36:6. DNF due to cracked rear wishbone.
17/5: Martini Trophy, Silverstone: RU.
26/5: Tourist Trophy, Oulton Park: Taylor; 1st after race stopped due to Hawkin's accident.
02/7: Nuremberg 200, Norisring: Taylor; DNF due to broken tappet.
13/7: W.D. & H.O. Wills Trophy, Croft: Taylor; 2nd.
10/8: Thruxton: Taylor; DNS (cracked heads).
17/8: Karlskoga: Trevor Taylor; 6th.
31/8: Mantorp Park: Trevor Taylor; DNS (engine).
Sold to Ian Webb, Northdown Racing.
Sold to Barrie Smith.
12/10: Salzburgring: Smith; 4th.
19/10: Hockenheim 300: Smith; 6th.

1970
11/1: Buenos Aires 1000km: Taylor/Gethin; DNF (engine).
27/3: Thruxton: Barrie Smith; 4th overall.
12/4: BoverallC 500, Brands Hatch. Howden Ganley/Barrie Smith; very wet conditions, severely crashed, monocoque destroyed.
Remains sold to Mick King of Derby. He used the suspension, steering and engine in a Ford Capri with which he won many saloon car races.

This car was then sold to George Potter of Chapel en le Frith. He sold it to Ian Webb who rebuilt the Lola parts back as a T70 Mark IIIb coupé with a new monocoque made by Brian Angliss, and new bodywork from Specialised Mouldings.
Sold to Nick Mason in England, tested at Goodwood and then sold to Harold Mergard in Germany.
Sold to Rick Weiland.
Sold through D.K. Engineering to Peter Schleifer.

SL76/145
Delivered 28th March 1969 to the Filipinetti Team. Red. Twin fuel filler caps. Traco Chevrolet 305-13. Gearbox number: LG600-154.

1969
13/4: BoverallC 500, Brands Hatch: Bonnier/Muller; race number 3; 3rd fastest in practice at 1.31:6. Crashed in the race by Bonnier. Sent back to the factory.
Laurie Bray, engineer at the factory noted: "Not as bad as it first looked". SL76/151 was supplied by the works "6 weeks later" (*Autosport*). Actually, it was only two weeks later.
SL76/145 was repaired and returned to Garage Filipinetti in early 1970. Resold to Jo Bonnier who used it in the Interseries in 1970, possibly with a big block 7.6-litre engine which later went into Sbarro's SL102, a Mark III coupé built-up from Lola supplied parts.
SL76/145 then passed to Franco Sbarro upon Bonnier's death in June, 1972. At this time, Sbarro had SL76/143, 145, 147, 150 and 151. He cut down three cars into Spyders and raced them in the Interseries. These three cars were SL/147, 151 and 143 according to the oil tanks they now wear.

In 1975, Sbarro removed the Spyder bodywork and sold three cars with spare coupé bodywork to David Piper (Piper says he bought "the old Bongrip car" from Stefan Sklenar in Vienna to re-sell to Tom Fletcher - but it had Spyder bodywork). Piper re-sold them to Peter Norman, (SL76/143), to an American who lived in Germany (SL76/147), and to one other who Piper can't remember. He believes that this car was later re-sold to the USA.
SL76/150 was sold back from Archambaud to David Piper. Peter Norman sold the one with the tag for SL76/143 to Richard Sennett in LA, and SL76/151 was sold to Rene Herzog who re-sold it to Charles Groh (this was rebuilt by Eddie Wysse).
SL76/151 is now with George Stauffer.
SL76/147 is with Raymond Hoeppermans in Germany.
This leaves SL76/145 which is in England, under restoration.

1971
3/10: Hockenheim Interseries: S. Sklenar; DNQ.

SL76/146
Delivered 2nd May 1969 to John Woolfe. Gearbox number: LG600-188.

1969
26/5: Tourist Trophy, Oulton Park: Richard Attwood; race number 33; 20th.
29/6: Nuremburg 200: Attwood; 4th.
14/9. Anderstorp, Sweden: Attwood; 5th. Bartz Chevrolet on injection with cross-over manifolds.
Sold to the VDS Racing Team in Belgium.
12/10: Paris 1000km, Montlhéry: Fuel injection, dry sump. DNS (oil pump).

1970
11/1: Buenos Aires 1000km: Pilette/Garcia Veiga; 4th.
254: Monza 1000km: Pilette/Gosselin; 16th (blown engine changed after practice).
17/5: Spa 1000km: Pilette/Gosselin; race number 34 (35?); DNF (suspension).
21/5: Montlhéry 500km: Pilette; 2nd.
31/5: Nürburgring 1000km: Pilette/Gosselin; DNS (differential).
05/6: Vila Real: Pilette/Gosselin; 1st overall.
13-14/6: Le Mans 24-hours: Pilette/Gosselin; DNF (gearbox/clutch). 492bhp Bonnier/Morand engine on Webers.
21/6: Montlhéry, G5/6: Pilette; 1st.
28/6: Interseries, Nuremburg 200, Norisring: Pilette; race number 16; fitted with Bonnier's old 6.2-litre engine. Qualified pole position; DNF (engine).
05/7: Vila Real 500km: Pilette/Gosselin; 1st.
11/7: Interseries, Croft: Pilette, race number 8; 6th.
08/8. Swedish Grand Prix, Karlskoga: Pilette, 12th.
23/8: Interseries, Keimola: Pilette; race number 6; 5th.
20/9: Interseries, Thruxton: Pilette; race number 20; 7th.
11/10: Interseries, Hockenheim 300 miles: Pilette; DNF.
18/10: Montlhéry 1000km: Pilette/Gosselin; Morand engine, DNF (clutch).

1971
09/5: Spa 1000km: Pilette/Gosselin; 6th overall.
12-13/6: Le Mans 24-hours: Pilette/Gosselin; DNF after one hour (piston).

Sold to James Landrum in America.
2000: In restoration.

SL76/147
Delivered 20th May 1969 to Jo Bonnier as Lola agent. Sold to Louis Morand, brother of the well-known engine builder. Gearbox number: LG600-169. To Switzerland. Dark green.

1969
13/7: Hockenhem, Solituderennen: Morand; DNF (engine).
10/8: Austrian 1000km, Osterreichring: Louis Morand/Gerard Pillon; RU.
19/10: Hockenheim, 300 Meilen: DNF.

1970
11/1: Buenos Aires 1000km; Morand/Pillon; DNS (accident in practice).
25/4: Monza 1000km: Morand/Pillon; DNQ.
17/5: Spa 1000km: Morand/Pillon; DNF. Chevrolet on Webers.
11/10: Interseries, Hockenheim 300 miles: Pillon; DNF.
18/11: Montlhéry 1000km. Pillon/Claude Cochet; DNF (gearbox).

Sold to the Argentine, where crashed.
Rebuilt by Franco Sbarro as a Spyder.

Possibly the car sold to Denis Veyrat, in which case:

1972: Took part in the Interseries.
21/5: Silverstone Interseries: D. Veyrat; race number 24; 6th.
09/7: Zeltweg Interseries: D. Veyrat; race number 24; DNS.
16/7: Hockenheim Interseries: D. Veyrat; race number 24; RU.
Sold then to Gregor Fischer.

1973:
15/9: Hockenheim Interseries: Gregor Fischer; DNF.
30/9: Hockenheim Interseries: G. Fischer; 9th.

Rebuilt to original specification, and sold to an American collector who lived in Germany. Since then it's been sold to Raimund Hoeppermans of Germany, with thick, road-going bodywork. Raced by Hoeppermans at the Spa-Francorchamps 6-hours in September 1996.

SL76/148 (Photo on page 130).
Completed 12th March 1969. Gearbox number: LG600-184. Engine number: 304-011 Traco-Chevrolet. Sold to Picko Troberg via Jo Bonnier.

1969
11/5: Spa 1000km: Troberg/Rothstein; slight damage to left front; race number 34; 11th overall.
01/6: Nürburgring 1000km: Badly crashed by Bjorn Rothstein. Sent to the factory for a rebuild in August, which took 6 weeks (re-chassised).
Sold to Barrie Smith.
14/9: Anderstorp, Sweden: Barrie Smith; 7th.
27/9: Trophy of the Dunes, Zandvoort: Barrie Smith; DNF (spin).
19/10: Hockenheim 300 Meilen: Barrie Smith; 6th.

1970
11/1: Buenos Aires 1000km: Barrie Smith/Ed Swart; DNF.
28/3: Thruxton G4/6 race: Smith; 4th overall.
21/6: Montlhéry G5/6: Team 'Avalon', Smith; 4th.
28/6: Interseries, Nuremburg 200 miles, Norisring: Smith; 9th.
05/7: Interseries, Hockenheim: Smith; 14th.
11/7: Interseries, Croft: Smith; DNA.
19/7: Magny Cours, G5/6/7: Smith; 5th.
08/8: Swedish Grand Prix, Karlskoga: Smith; 11th.
27/8. Car for sale in *Autosport*.
7/11: Rand Dail Mail Nine-hours, Kyalami: Smith/Pretorious; 7th. 5-litre engine.
Sold to Farley who converted it for road use. Registered UKY ---H. Blue.
To Mike Weatherill in 1974, who did not use it.
Sold to Richard Bond in October 1974.
Rebuilt by Lorenzini.

1975
July: Unicognas Trophy, St. John Horsfall AMOC Meeting, Silverstone: Bond; 2nd overall.
In five races in 1975 Bond came 1st twice, 2nd once, plus 5th and 7th (overheating problems).

Sold to Geoffrey Marsh (Marsh Plant Hire) in 1976, raced by Gerry

Marshall.
Sold to David Piper/Richard Attwood in 1985.
Raced up to the present in David Piper's 'Supersports' series.

1993
27/6: Thruxton: Jonathan Baker; 2nd overall.
25/7: Silverstone: Baker; 2nd in class.
08/8: Nürburgring: Mauro Borella; 4th in class.

SL76/149
Delivered 7th March 1969 to Michael Grace D'Udy (Bahamas Racing). Wet sump Bartz Chevrolet 5-litre engine. Gearbox number: LG600-182. Light green.

1969
04/4: Guards International Trophy, RAC Group 4, round 2, Snetterton: Frank Gardner; DNS (suspension).
07/4: RAC Group 4, round 3, Thruxton: Gardner; DNF (clutch).
06/6: Vila Real, Portugal: Frank Gardner; 2nd (lap record of 104mph).
13/7: W.D. & H.O. Wills Trophy, Croft: Frank Gardner; 2nd in 1st heat, DNF in 2nd heat (fuel starvation).
10/8: Thruxton: Gardner; race number 1; 2nd.
18/8: Oulton Park: Gardner; 1st.
8/11: Rand Daily Mail 9-hours, Kyalami: Gardner/De Udy; 2nd.
23/11: Cape International 3-hours, Killarney: De Udy/Gardner; 1st.
1/12: Lourenco Marques 3-hours: De Udy/Gardner; race number 7; 1st.
13/12: Roy Hesketh 3-hours, Pietermaritzburg: De Udy; DNF (differential).

1970
21/3: Sebring 12-hours: De Udy/Hailwood; DNF after one hour.
Sold to Rod Leach of 'Nostalgia'.

1986: Sold to Terry Jones of Cerritos, California. Totally restored, with a new tub made by Jim Chapman. 5.7-litre engine built by Dennis Fischer.
Sold to Reginald Howell, USA.
For sale in December 1993.
Sold to Bob Akin, raced extensively in historic events.
2000: Sold to John Littlechild.

SL76/150 (Photo on page 114).
Delivered 7th March 1969 to David Piper (Autoracing Modena). Bartz Chevrolet 5-litre engine. Gearbox number: LG600-183. British Petroleum Green (colour impregnated bodywork).

1969
30/3: RAC Group 4, round 1, Silverstone: Piper; 5th.
04/4: RAC Group 4, round 2, Guards International Trophy, Snetterton: Piper; DNF (blown head gasket).
07/4: RAC Group 4, round 3, Embassy Trophy, Thruxton: Piper; 4th.
13/4: BoverallC 500, Brands Hatch: Piper/Pierpoint; DNF.
20/4: Montlhéry, Group 3/4/5/6 race: Piper; 1st.
25/4. Monza 1000km: Hawkins/Prophet; race number 41; DNF (seized front wheel bearing).
01/5. Magny Cours: Piper; 3rd.
17/5: Martini International Trophy, Silverstone: Piper; 3rd.
26/5: Tourist Trophy, Oulton Park: Piper; 2nd (revised overhead exhaust system).
02/7: Nuremburg 200, Norisring: Piper; race number 1; 18th in 1st heat, 4th in 2nd; 8th overall.

SL76/149.

16/7: Solituderennen, Hockenheim: Hans Hermann, race number 20; 1st.
31/8: Mantorp Park, Sweden: Piper; 4th.
14/9: Anderstorp, Sweden: Piper; 9th.
21/9: Prix de Salzburg: Piper; 2nd.
27/9: Trophy of the Dunes, Zandvoort: Piper; 2nd.
12/10: Paris 1000km, Montlhéry: Attwood/Parkes; race number 1; 10th.
19/10: Hockenheim 300 Meilen: Hans Hermann; race number 8; 4th.
Sold to Switzerland.

1970
11/1: Buenos Aires 1000km, Argentina: Chris Craft/Richard Attwood; DNF (overheating engine).
27/4: Thruxton: 3rd on grid for Group 5/6 race; 15th.
24/5: Group 5/6, Montlhéry: Richard Attwood; 1st.
07/6: Dijon: Attwood; 1st.
21/6: Group 5/6, Montlhéry: Attwood; 3rd.
28/6: Interseries, Nuremburg 200 miles, Norisring: Attwood; 21st. 5.7-litre engine.
05/7: Interseries, Hockenheim: Piper; 4th.
11/7: Interseries, Croft: Attwood; DNA.
Took part in Steve McQueen's *Le Mans* film with Richard Attwood (green spinning Lola).
19/7. Group 5/6/7, Magny Cours: Jean-Pierre Beltoise; 1st.
Sold to Archambaud, Paris. Archambaud raced the car in French National events; driven by Gerard Larousse who won some races.

1972
19/3: Coupés ACIF, Montlhéry: P.H. Archambaud; 5th overall.
03/4: Nogaro: P.H. Archambaud; 5th in Group 5/7.
01/5: Magny Cours: P.H. Archambaud; 4th in Group 5/7 national race.
07/5: Paul Ricard: P.H. Archambaud; 6th in Group 5/7.
Sold to Franco Sbarro.
Sold back to David Piper.
Sold to Mike Knight and completely rebuilt. Raced in historic events

SL76/150.

in 1980/81.
Won Donington round in June 1981, and Phoenix Park (Ireland). 3rd at Montlhéry. Sold to Graham Cook who repainted it in Bonnier colours.
Sold to Mike Taradash, Connecticut, USA.
Sold to Brian Redman who tested it at Savannah raceway, September 1984.
1984: October 25, Sold to Time Machine Racing, Sun Valley, California.
1986: January 20, Sold to Sam Dunn of Auburndale, Florida.
March: Sebring Vintage Race: Dunn; 1st overall. 186mph on straight.
1987: September 5th. Sold to Lief Nielson of Sweden, sold to Per Arwidsson, Stockholm. Car in storage. Still in Bonnier colours (yellow overall, broad longitudinal white stripe, thin red stripe in centre). Still retains original monocoque. Fitted with Fisher 5.7-litre engine.
1994: Sold to Simon de Latour in France.

SL76/151
Delivered 16th April 1969 to Filipinetti Team in Switzerland. Red. No engine or gearbox supplied (probably used the units from SL76/145).

1969
Replaced SL76/145 which was crashed at the 13th April BoverallC 500.
4-5/5: Targa Florio: Bonnier/Muller; race number 190; third after passing 60 cars on first lap! DNF due to puncture.
26/5: Tourist Trophy, Oulton Park: Bonnier/Muller; DNF (crash).
01/6: Nürburgring 1000km: Bonnier/Muller; pole position, DNF (sriveshaft failure).
14-15/6: Le Mans 24-hours: Bonnier/Gregory; race number 2; practiced in 3.36:2; DNF due to engine failure after mechanics changed both cylinder heads in 2hours 49 minutes.
14/7: Watkins Glen 6-hours: Bonnier/Muller; DNF (blown head gasket).
15/7: Watkins Glen, Can-Am: Bonnier; 7th (earned $3100). 5.9-litre engine.
11/7: Osterreichring 1000km: Bonnier/Muller; race number 33; 2nd in practice, 1.48:2; 2nd overall.
18/8: Gold Cup, Oulton Park: Bonnier; qualified pole; DNS.
31/8: Mantorp Park, Sweden: Muller; 3rd.
14/9: Anderstorp, Sweden: Muller; race number 3; 3rd.
12/10: Paris 1000km, Montlhéry: Bonnier/Muller; race number 18; 8th.
19/10: Hockenheim 300 Meilen: Bonnier; 2nd.

1970
11/1: Buenos Aires 1000km, Argentina: Bonnier/Wisell; DNF (engine).
18/1: Buenos Aires 200 Miles: Bonnier; 5th.
17/5: Spa 1000km: Bonnier/Wisell; 10th.
28/6: Nuremburg 200 miles. Interseries: Bonnier; DNF. Brand new alloy 7-litre Chevrolet, built by Swiss mechanic Michel Clement, with Kinsler fuel injection. Exhaust system, gear linkage, rear cockpit wall and oil pump were all changed. 50lb lighter than 5-litre smallblock, gave 580bhp.
05/7: Hockenheim, Interseries: Bonnier; race number 4; 3rd.
08/8: Keimola, Interseries: Peterson; race number 1; 3rd.
09/8: Swedish Grand Prix, Karlskoga: Wisell; 5th.

Sold to Franco Sbarro.
Sold to Rene Herzog.
Sold to Charles Grohs. Accident in hillclimb, restored by Eddie Wysse in 198?
1982: Sold to Koni Leutziger.
1995: Sold to Marcel Schaub.
1998: November, sold to George Stauffer in the USA.
2001: Restoration completed.
14/2/2001: Sebring HSR races; Stauffer.

SL76/152
Autumn 1969, delivered to Jo Bonnier (agent) who sold it to Jacques Ray, France, in October, 1969. Blue and white. Engine: 5.7 Chevrolet on Webers. LG600 gearbox.

1970
11/1: Buenos Aires 1000km: Ray/Bernay; withdrew when black flagged.
18/1: Buenos Aires 200 miles: Rey/Bernay; RU.
28/4: Montlhéry Group 5/6 race: Rey; 3rd.
24/5: Montlhéry 500km: Rey/Bernay; 5th.
07/6: Dijon 3-hours: Wollek; 3rd.

SL76/151.

??/6: Turckheim-Trois Epis Hillclimb: Rey; 1st in class.
21/6: Montlhéry: Rey/Wollek; DNF (engine problems).
19/7: Magny Cours: Rey; 4th.
??/8: Bellegrade Hillclimb: Rey; 1st in class.

1971
06/6: Interseries, Zolder: Wollek; race number 41; 11th overall.

Sold to Phil Hinnery, USA, who then sold it to Randy Berry of Marauder Cars Inc.; Potomac, Illinos., USA, without the engine. Berry disassembled the car to copy the body.

1986
October 3. Sold to present owner, 'in boxes', who had it restored by Autotrans Competition A.B., Sweden, using only original parts.

1987
14-15/8: Nürburgring, AVD Historic Race: Nilsson; 18th overall, 4th in class.
21/9: Knutstorp Ring, MGCC club race, Sweden: DNS (rain).
11-14/8: Nürburgring, AVD Historic Race: Nilsson; 14th overall, 3rd in class.
18/8: Falkenberg MK Swedish Land Speed Record, Flying Kilometre, Class 5000-8000cc.

Reputedly never crashed. 5.7-litre Chevrolet with Weber carburettors built by Autotrans Comp. A.B. Sweden. Car in storage.
1994: Sold to Geoff Harris in England who had the car completely rebuilt by Clive Robinson Cars, with a 5.0-litre engine on injection. Medium blue with a white stripe. Raced in Group 4 events in 1996, 1997 and 1998.
1998: December. Sold to Jean Guikas, GTC.
1999: STP0.

SL76/153
Sold to Jo Bonnier on 3/12/69. Gearbox number: LG600-332. Sold to A.J. Motors, Terry Crocker. To South Africa.

1970
12/4: Entered as a reserve in BoverallC 500 race, Brands Hatch: Crocker; DNS.
28/6: Interseries, Nuremburg 200 miles: Vegantunte 5-litre. Croker did not start, however, as the engine would not scavenge in practice.
05/7: Interseries, Hockenheim: Crocker; DNF.
27/11: Sold to Carlos Avallone, driven by Wilson Fittipaldi.

1971
07/9: Interlagos 500km: C.A. Avallone; 5th overall.

Car sold to Africa and crashed. Remains, including the tub, bought by Mauro Borella in 1994.
1996: Sold to Nigel Hulme.
Car rebuilt by Clive Robinson Cars.
1998: Raced by Hulme.

In the 1970s/80s, several cars were built up after production ceased, and shipped to the USA.

SL76/154
Continuation car. Built up as post-production car. Originally owned by David Augar.
Sold to Australia, then sold to Nigel Hulme, who sold it to Paul Palmer (raced).
Crashed. Rebuilt at the factory. Re-numbered as SL76/137. Sold to Chris O'Neil. Yellow with blue wheels.

SL76/154.

1990
20/5: Spa-Francorchamps. Competed in 4th Trophy D'Auvergne.
03/6: Brands Hatch: Finished in wet race.
10-11/7: Nürburgring "Old timer" Grand Prix: 13th.

Raced in International Supersports from 1991 to 1996.
1997: Sold to Ian Duncan in January.
1998: 6.8-litre engine fitted.

SL76/155
Sold to Theodore Gildred, USA. Red. 335 cu. in. Chevrolet on Weber carburettors. Driven by George Follmer in American historic racing.
2000: Still with Gildred; front full-lengh spoiler fitted.

SL76/156
To Designer Associates in Switzerland, and bodied by Michelotti. Big Block 427 Chevrolet installed and then sold to the USA. Red.
1997: Sold to Simon de Latour in France. Re-bodied as Mark IIIb coupé .

SL76/157
Yellow. Chevrolet 5.6-litre engine. LG600 gearbox. Delivered to Paul Vestey.
Sold to the USA in 1981 by Adrian Hamilton.
Sold to Paul Bernhard, sold to Charles Gnaedinger in Switzerland.
Sold to Sweden. Re-numbered as SL76/142.

SL76/158
Sold to Carl Haas. Sunoco Blue.
Sold to John Hugenholtz at Geneva Auction.
Sold to Marty Yacobian. Has a 350 Chevrolet with injection, LG600 gearbox Mark 2, and is indigo blue with gold striping.
1996: Sold via US Customs auction.

SL76/155.

SL76/161.

SL76/136
Chassis number not issued originally.

1984, reputedly: Built up from parts from Bonnier's car (SL76/145) which crashed at the 1969 Brands Hatch BOverallC 500. Re-chassised and sold to Nigel Hulme. Blue. Then yellow (sponsored by Red Star - 12/89).

1986
08/4: Silverstone: 2nd in class E.

HU220/68.

SL160/8.

11/5: Oulton Park: 1st in class E.
8-9/6: Brands Hatch: 3rd in class E.
22/6: Silverstone: DNF.
07/7: Thruxton: 1st in class E.
20/7: Silverstone: 1st in class E.
26/8: Thruxton: 1st in class E.
02/9: Silverstone: 1st in class E.
29/9: Snetterton: 1st in class E.
15/10: Silverstone: 2nd in class E.
HSCC: 2nd overall and class champion.

1990: Steigenberger International Supersports Cup: 2nd overall

and class B champion.
1996: Sold to Carlos Babot in Portugal.
1997: Coy's Group 4 race, Silverstone: Babot; RU.

SL76/160
Sold as spares to Perth in Western Australia.
Sold to Don Sullivan and then Toby Bean in the USA. Raced by Toby with success in many historic races, including the 30th anniversary of the Can-Am in 1996 at Elkhart Lake. Red. 350 Chevrolet with one Holley carburettor.

SL76/161
Sold as spares to the USA. Built up and raced in vintage events.

T160s

SL160/8
Sold to John Littlechild, USA.
2000: Sold to Bob Akin.

SL160/12
Sold to Dan Martin, USA.

HU163-15
1969
Sold to Haas. Simoniz car. Race number 5. Parsons' car.
1st race: Parsons spun; tweaked tub. Stiffeners fitted.
2nd race: Rebuilt around new tub. No tag (number 16?). 27/28 thou. skin thickness. Original tub was shelved as Haas' place.
Riverside: Used cut-off tail; 494 cu inch Chevrolet fitted.
Texas.
Japan-Fuji.
11/69: Sold to D Durant.

1970
06/70: St Jovite: Crashed.
28/6: Haas approached, sold original tub (number 15) to Durant, who kept everything. 'Laboratory tub no. 5' was on the side of this tub.
23/8: Mid Ohio: D Durant; race number 81; 6th.
30/8: Elkhart Lake: D Durant; race number 81; 9th.
13/9: Road Atlanta: D Durant; race number 81; 8th.
18/10: Laguna Seca: D Durant; race number 81; 15th.

1971
13/6 Mosport: D Durant; race number 81; DNF.
27/6: St Jovite: D Durant; race number 81; 10th.
11/7: Road Atlanta: D Durant; race number 81; 6th.
22/8: Mid Ohio: D Durant; race number 81; 12th.
08/71: Elkhart Lake: Crashed again, original factory lightweight tub removed (number 15). Repaired with a replacement tub (number 16?). Tube framed from rear of bulkhead.

1972
11/6: Mosport: D Durant; race number 81; 14th.
09/7: Road Atlanta: D Durant; race number 81; DNS.
06/8: Mid Ohio: D Durant; race number 81; DNF.
27/8: Elkhart Lake: D Durant; race number 81; DNF.

1973
10/6: Mosport: D Durant; race number 81; DNF (oil leak).
08/73: Sold to Dick Zingre.

1976: Won SCCA S. Cal Championship.
Raced till 1977.
Sold to Chuck Haines.
1982: Sold to Jim Bartel.
Spares and tub sold to Bill Kasmer.
Original tub built up again with spares by K&K Racing Design (number 15).
This car sold to Larry Teaberry.
1987: Sold to R. McLean.
2002: Sold to Don Bell. He has two tubs, both with 'Laboratory car no. 5' on them.

HU163-16
Nothing known. Almost certainly a spare tub used to re-build HU163-15.

HU/T165/25
Sold to Bobby Thompson.

HU220-02
Sold to Bobby Thompson.

T220: HU220-08
Sold to John Hunt in the 1980s, re-engined with a small-block Chevrolet.
Sold to Geoff Hobbs. Re-engined with a big-block Chevrolet.

APPENDIX 2

OWNER'S COMMENT

I owned and raced a Lola T70 Mark IIIb for four years in the early 1990s. I first saw the car in 1969 when Denny Hulme was driving her in a Mallory Park race. Of course, he won, but even before that I'd fallen in love with the sight and sound of this glorious coupé.

I've had my share of rapid motor cars to race. I've owned a Ferrari 250 GT, 'Tour de France' Berlinetta which had won the 1958 Mille Miglia, and I did three of the 'retrospective' events in 1982, '84 and '86. That gave me a thirst for real racing (I had hill climbed for years) and I then spent three very enjoyable years in a 1974 Porsche RSR. I discovered that the man I bought the RSR from was selling a T70: I had seen him briefly in it at Silverstone and envied him mightily for being able to drive such a wonderful car. I had to re-mortgage my house to buy the Lola but, what the hell, you only live once and I have a VERY understanding wife!

When I went to see the car I discovered its history. The car's chassis is ex-Sid Taylor and was the very same one I had seen carry Denny Hulme to that victory at Mallory Park some twenty years earlier. Since then it had become (briefly) a road car(!) before being bought by an Englishman who raced it for fourteen years until it was involved in a very bad accident in 1988. After the accident the car was sold to the man I bought it from. He had undertaken a ground-up restoration.

Every time I climbed into the cockpit of the Lola, I still felt privileged to be able to drive this wonderful beast. Belted, with a six-point harness, into the tight-fitting bucket seat, the view forward was of large swoopy wings diving out of sight on either side. Designed for endurance racing, the dashboard featured an impressive array of instruments, including a water temperature gauge, electronic tachometer, oil pressure gauge with, on another panel to the right, oil temperature and fuel pressure gauges and an ammeter. Switches below controlled the injection lift pumps, windscreen wiper and washer.

The view to the rear through a small window was of impressive injection trumpets. The wing mirrors gave the only other rearward vision. The windscreen was so well shaped that rain simply poured off, and the large wiper was actually unnecessary at speed.

When I first drove the Lola she had a carburetted 5-litre Chevrolet. Then we installed a 6.4-litre engine on injection. The acceleration was amazing: the dyno showed that the engine put out some 630bhp and the car's weight was down to less than 800 kilogrammes. We worked out that 0 to 162kph took only 4.9 seconds with 0 to 320kph in around 18 seconds. But above that was the handling. If you took your foot off when you entered a corner the Lola wanted to go straight on. It asked - no, demanded - that you apply the power to help you through a bend. If you adopted this approach the car would go just where you wanted it to and, even though the slicks at the time gripped mightily, you could still 'hang the tail out' with complete confidence that the Lola wouldn't bite.

The stubby gearlever controlled a change which was not particularly fast. You could almost feel the weight of those big gears revolving in the massive, magnesium-cased box, whilst the steering, with more castor and camber added to cope with the slicks of the day, was heavy, although it did lighten up with speed. Denny Hulme once told me that at Druids Bend at Brands Hatch: "You could just flick it around with one finger on the wheel." Not anymore, Denny!

A particular memory I have of life with a Lola was when I was testing in November at Silverstone for the first time. I came into the pits and got the car on the frost in front of the pit garages. It slid straight on and slewed to a stop just inside a garage, where two very startled mechanics stopped working on their formula three car to stare at my embarrassed face! Another is of watching the cars in front in the international sportscar races in which I ran the Lola seemingly coming backwards at me as I accelerated on any decent straight (although the Can-Am cars, such as Charlie Agg's McLaren M8F, were brutally faster still).

Recently, I raced a 1984 March 84G in HSR events in America. This is a full ground effects device, with a 6.4 litre Chevrolet engine on injection, with adjustable wings, suspension and anti-roll bars. Recently, during a race at Sebring, I found myself in a dice with a 1968 T70 coupé Mark III, (chassis number SL73/111). It had had a NASCAR Busche series engine installed, giving some 650 horsepower. Even in a car sixteen years its junior, I couldn't catch the Lola in the first race we were involved in. Oh sure, I had better brakes and ground effects and could both out-corner and out-brake the Lola. But its clean shape helped it to just run away from me on the straights and I couldn't get close enough to it to out-brake it into a corner. It should be said, though, that we took off some wing and beat the T70 in the next race, but I still found myself

The author in his Lola T70 Mark IIIb.

sitting back on the straight in the March during that first race, marvelling at just how quickly the T70 was pulling away and thinking: "Perhaps I should get another Lola!" One month later I had another Lola T70 coupé which I am racing and enjoying at present. I have no intention of selling it.

Once, outside our hotel at Stavelot, whilst attending the Spa historic race, two small boys came running up crying "Monsieur, Monsieur! is that a Ferrari?" When I told them proudly that, no, this was a Lola, their faces fell and they walked off muttering to one another. When, and if, they get the chance to drive a T70, I think their opinions might change!

INDEX

Note: Entries in **bold** type refer to captions and/or pictures.

Index of individual Lola cars